WINTER
OF
FIRE

WINTER
OF
FIRE

The Abduction of General Dozier
and the Downfall of the Red Brigades

RICHARD OLIVER COLLIN
and
GORDON L. FREEDMAN

DUTTON   NEW YORK

DUTTON
Published by the Penguin Group
Penguin Books USA Inc., 375 Hudson Street,
New York, New York 10014, U.S.A.
Penguin Books Ltd, 27 Wrights Lane,
London W8 5TZ, England
Penguin Books Australia Ltd, Ringwood,
Victoria, Australia
Penguin Books Canada Ltd, 2801 John Street,
Markham, Ontario, Canada L3R 1B4
Penguin Books (N.Z.) Ltd, 182–190 Wairau Road,
Auckland 10, New Zealand

Penguin Books Ltd, Registered Offices:
Harmondsworth, Middlesex, England

First published by Dutton, an imprint of
New American Library,
a division of Penguin Books USA Inc.

First Printing, August, 1990
10 9 8 7 6 5 4 3 2 1

Library of Congress Cataloging-in-Publication Data

Collin, Richard.
    Winter of fire : the abduction of General Dozier and the downfall
of the Red Brigades / Richard Oliver Collin and Gordon L. Freedman.
—1st ed.
        p. cm.
    ISBN 0-525-24880-3
    1. Dozier, James Lee—Kidnapping, 1981–1982. 2. Brigate rosse.
3. Radicalism—Italy—History—20th century. I. Freedman, Gordon
L. II. Title.
E840.5.D69C65   1990
364.1'54'0945—dc20   89-71448
                                                                 CIP

Printed in the United States of America
Set in Trump Medieval
Designed by Earl Tidwell

for Thea and Amanda

Revolt and terror pay a price
Order and law have a cost.
What is this double use of fire and water?
Where are the rulers who know this riddle?
—CARL SANDBURG,
Harvest Poems

CONTENTS

Preface   xi

Prologue   1

BOOK I
The Stalking   13

BOOK II
The Kidnap   61

BOOK III
The Hostage   103

BOOK IV
The Rescue   165

Epilogue   221

Who's Who of the Dozier Kidnapping   231
Sources and Acknowledgments   237

Eight pages of photographs follow page 144.

PREFACE

During the turbulent winter of 1981/82, the world's press dedicated passionate attention to the terrorist abduction of General James Lee Dozier. A great deal of what they reported turned out to be wrong; as is so often the case, most of what really happened was never revealed. Hence our interest in writing this book.

We want to take the reader behind the shroud of secrecy and examine how one of Europe's most formidable terrorist organizations functioned and how—ultimately—it failed. In the process, we want to introduce the three extraordinary men around whom this story revolves: a young revolutionary, an American general, and an unusual Italian policeman who shared with the terrorists he hunted a passion for social justice.

For a variety of reasons, our story could not be written until now. We needed to wait until General Dozier's retirement from active duty gave him the leisure and the freedom to talk extensively about his experiences. In addition, the Italian government did not permit us to interview Antonio Savasta or his colleagues until these former revolutionaries had finished the last of their many trials and received definitive prison sentences. Police Commissioner Salvatore Genova was serving as a deputy in the Italian Parliament between 1982 and 1987 and wanted to complete his career as a politician and return to private life before discussing some aspects of the Dozier affair.

Furthermore, the "Iran-Contra" scandal brought some previously unknown information to light, and the end of the Reagan administration made several key government figures feel easier about speaking candidly about the Dozier kidnapping. In the Sources and Acknowledgments section at the end of the book, we have provided a full listing of our source material.

The resulting book represents the combined best efforts of a political historian and a journalist. We decided at the outset to write for the general reader, avoiding the encumbrance of footnotes and scholarly marginalia, but we also resolved to ensure that the narrative would be as accurate as possible. We have reported conversations as accurately as witnesses could remember them, and we have only "dramatized" scenes when we were sure of the substance of a given conversation but lacked the specific dialogue. In some cases, we were fortunate enough to have access to tapes or transcripts of recorded conversations and/or testimony; for example, the negotiations between the late General Carlo Dalla Chiesa and imprisoned terrorist Michael Galati come almost word for word from a secret recording done by the Carabinieri and made available to the authors.

In a very small number of cases, and for reasons that will be obvious, we have disguised or withheld the identities of certain individuals and/or sources. We were given valuable insights by serving members of the Italian police, some of whom continue to work in undercover counterterrorist units and need to protect their identities. In other cases, we were fortunate enough to interview former members of the Red Brigades who are now living under the Italian witness protection program and spoke to us only after we provided guarantees of anonymity. Furthermore, we received some important information from U.S. government officials on the condition that they not be identified.

A complete listing of the "players" in the Dozier affair is given in the Who's Who at the end of this book as a guide for the reader who becomes lost among the revolutionaries, policemen, and American officials in this story. Red Brigade militants often disguised their identities behind a series of "battle names" and their faces behind ski masks. In the text, we have used their real legal names in order to prevent confusion, even in some cases where authentic names were not known at the time. Many of his fellow *brigatisti* knew Antonio Savasta only under his code name "Emilio," and General Dozier—who did not learn Savasta's real name until much later—called him "the little guy." We have simplified matters by using his actual name throughout.

For the most part, we have told the story from the perspective of its principal actors: General and Mrs. Dozier; Red Brigade leader Antonio Savasta and his companion, Emilia Libera; Commissioner Salvatore Genova of the Italian State Police; and Colonel William Reed of the U.S. Army, and to all of these people we are grateful.

We send affectionate thanks to Albert Zuckerman of Writers House, Incorporated, for his wise counsel and encouragement during the composition of this book. Our gratitude also goes to Mr. Richard Marek of Dutton, for his meticulous editing of the manuscript. Our thanks also to our wives, Thea Collin and Amanda Freedman, who put up with many late-night and early-morning telephone calls. Finally, we want to acknowledge the indomitable assistance of Dr. James P. Walston, who was there, as always, when he was needed.

We also received help from a few anonymous sources who assisted us without precisely wishing to do so. For example, thanks are due to those vigilant policemen in Verona who treated Gordon Freedman to a free but uncomfortable lesson in Italian criminal procedure by arresting him for taking pictures of the Dozier apartment building during a fact-finding trip. For his part, Richard Oliver Collin wishes to acknowledge the contribution of those university students in Padua who—mistaking him for a nefarious CIA agent—beat him up while he was trying to interview a source. The incident served as a reminder that political passions still burn brightly in the back streets of Padua.

RICHARD OLIVER COLLIN
GORDON L. FREEDMAN

WINTER
OF
FIRE

PROLOGUE

The Years of Lead

Fact or fiction, any story set in the Verona of Romeo and Juliet is likely to be at least partly about love, and the present narrative is no exception. The reader who is sensibly more interested in romance than politics, therefore, should turn immediately to the beginning of Book 1 and think no further about the ideological aspects of this story.

On the other hand, there will certainly be readers who want to go beyond the drama of a brave American general and a tormented Italian terrorist. How, in fact, did the "Winter of Fire" relate to the history of contemporary terrorism?

When they think back upon the fifteen years between the great student uprising of 1968 and the Dozier kidnapping of 1981/82, Italians will always remember them as the *anni di piombo*, their "years of lead." It was a time when the fragile Italian economy seemed to go to pieces under the impact of inflation and exorbitant oil prices. Italy's political elite was rocked by one appalling corruption scandal after another. Drug abuse among young people soared, while the Mafia seemed to enjoy magic immunity from prosecution.

But the real hallmark of this time was an unprecedented wave of terrorist violence; for fifteen years, the lead literally flew, day after day, as Italian society fought a long and lethal battle with an invisible enemy.

The statistics are horrifying: between the enormous student riots of 1968 and the Dozier kidnapping in December 1981, Italian terrorists murdered 370 people. Although extreme right-wing, neofascist bombers accounted for many of the killings, the majority were carried out by Marxist urban guerrillas from the extreme Left of the political spectrum. Furthermore, Italy's revolutionaries also took responsibility for 172 deliberate woundings,

1

during this period, and committed thirteen thousand separate terrorist crimes and acts of industrial sabotage.

Italy's left-wing guerrillas nearly all traced their intellectual origins to the watershed year of 1968, when university students in many countries experienced feelings of violent resentment and anger. Like restless young people in America and France and China, Italian undergraduates mounted noisy but mostly non-violent protests against the hypocrisy of the educational system, the chronic housing shortage, America's war in Vietnam, and especially the inefficiency and dishonesty of their own government. Nineteen sixty-eight was a year of mass meetings, speeches, protest marches, housing "squats," and brutal encounters with the police. When the shouting was over, however, the generation of '68 knew that the experience had been a failure. The government had outmaneuvered them; the great inert mass of the public had ignored them; and the Italian police had pounded them into the ground.

As a result, a small, radicalized group of young people began to think in terms of serious violence. A few were disillusioned Roman Catholic intellectuals; some were hard, bitter men from the factories of the industrialized north; others were deserting a staid and middle-class Communist party. A significant few were discontented university professors.

Since the end of World War II, political leadership in Italy had been monopolized by the Christian Democrats, a conservative and clientelistic party plagued by corruption and inefficiency. The permanent opposition was the giant Italian Communist party (or PCI), which had grown bureaucratic in the years since the war. Italy's "official" Communists had long since surrendered any notion of revolution, although they seemed incapable of winning power through electoral means. For the Red Brigades, the pseudo-Marxists of the Communist party had become traitors to the working class.

By the beginning of the 1970s, some of these lefter-than-left militants had decided that the overthrow of the Italian government was both desirable and possible. Had Marx not taught that capitalism contained the seeds of its own inevitable self-destruction? The progressive decline of the inflation-torn Italian economy and the hardship being suffered by much of the working class seemed to suggest that Marx's moment had come.

The Red Brigades

The *Brigate rosse* (or Red Brigades) launched their campaign against the Italian state in 1970, although for the first few years they limited themselves to violence against property and generally avoided bloodshed. In time, other revolutionary organizations began operations as well, forming loose partnerships with the Red Brigades: *Prima linea* (Front Line) and the *Nuclei armati proletari* (Armed Proletarian Nucleus) were prominent examples.

By 1975 and 1976, however, the Italian police began to strike back. One by one, the "historic leadership" of the Red Brigades vanished, a few into exile, some into maximum-security prisons, and—as they seldom allowed themselves to be arrested without a fight—others into cemeteries. The highest-ranking survivor from the original group was a talented revolutionary named Mario Moretti, an orphan and a former factory worker with an infallible sense of street smartness. During his years of dominion over the Brigate rosse, Moretti shared his life with a woman named Barbara Balzarani, whose beauty attracted attention, but for a long time the two of them seemed immune to arrest.

By 1977, Moretti was counterattacking with a whole second generation of *brigatisti*, many of them working-class Romans like Antonio Savasta and his companion, Emilia Libera. Under Moretti's leadership, the Brigate rosse became more violent, killing dozens of business executives, judges, senior policemen, prison officials, and journalists. In 1978, they carried out their most sensational operation: the kidnapping and murder of Aldo Moro, Italy's best known and most respected statesman.

By the end of the decade, the battle between the Italian state and its enemies was beginning to resemble a civil war. Under Moretti's leadership, the Red Brigades fought with amazing tenacity as determined revolutionaries recruited even more urban guerrillas and organized one deadly operation after another.

Much of the resiliency of this revolutionary movement came from the way it was structured. Red Brigade militants (or *brigatisti*) were organized into "columns," and further subdivided into rigorously compartmentalized "brigades" of five to seven people apiece. There were well-established columns for the cities of Turin, Genoa, Milan, and Naples, with an extended regional column covering the Veneto, the rich farming territory around Venice in northeastern Italy. The largest single community of *brigatisti* could be found in Rome, where two separate columns were active.

The *Organizzazione* (as its members called it) distinguished between two kinds of revolutionaries. Senior figures (perhaps numbering about one hundred by 1980), were called "regulars," full-time, salaried members of the group, always armed and living clandestine lives with false identity papers. "Irregulars," on the other hand, were those who continued to maintain a legal existence under their own real names, but who participated secretly in revolutionary activities, killings, kidnappings, and sabotage. The number of "irregulars" was perhaps close to a thousand by the end of the decade.

How was this large, clandestine organization administered? At the national level, long-range policy was set by an elected parliamentary body of twenty-five to thirty members called the Strategic Directorate (*Direzione strategica*). To run the Red Brigades operationally on a day-to-day basis, the Strategic Directorate in turn selected a small Executive Committee (*Comitato esecutivo* or sometimes just *Esecutivo*) of four or five experienced guerrillas who supervised all major operations. In governmental terms, the Strategic Directorate functioned as a kind of legislature, while the Executive Committee acted as a sort of cabinet.

Antonio Savasta and the 1981/82 "Winter of Fire"

Suspected of involvement in more than a dozen homicides, Antonio Savasta built his reputation as a gunman for the Roman column, but as he rose in rank, the young Roman turned out to have one of the group's best brains for organization and logistics. A policeman's son who had grown up in Prenestina-Centocelle, a bleak slum on the eastern periphery of Italy's capital city, Savasta became a master at surviving in a clandestine environment.

For a professional revolutionary, Savasta was a cautious man. He routinely forged all of his own identity papers himself, creating several sets of false documents that allowed him to change names as the situation demanded. To create a new identity, Savasta would locate an unsuspecting person of the same age and physical characteristics. Pretending to be an irritable government bureaucrat, he would then telephone his bewildered victim with an inquiry about an unpaid parking ticket or a missing tax form, extracting all the personal data that would normally turn up in a government record or computer file.

With a supply of stolen but authentic blank documents (driver's licenses, identity cards, and passports), he would then create fresh identification papers. In their effort to combat terrorism, the police were conducting millions of identity checks a year, demanding documents at random from the public and then cross-checking this information by radio against data stored on a police computer. When Savasta's people were stopped and interrogated, they knew that their documents could withstand expert scrutiny and that the personal information they provided would match the data stored on the government's own computers.

Although Antonio Savasta never enjoyed a comfortable relationship with his father, a patrolman who had served with the Polizia di Stato until his retirement, the younger Savasta did grow up with an instinctive feeling for police operations. When moving into a new operational setting, he made a practice of keeping a radio switched on and tuned to a police frequency in order to develop a sense of the ebb and flow of police activities, learning when shifts changed and in what parts of the city the authorities were concentrating their energies.

Savasta's methodical mind had also focused on the mundane business of transportation, because *brigatisti* were at their most vulnerable when moving from city to city. For mobility, he seldom relied on stolen cars, wishing to avoid the common but ironic fate of being sent to prison for car theft while trying to overthrow international capitalism. When preparing for an operation, Savasta used forged identification papers to rent vehicles legally from normal rental agencies. He would then avoid the risk of having his cars identified by exchanging their original license plates with high-quality forgeries created by a Red Brigade metalworker in Rome.

His competence in mundane matters notwithstanding, Savasta's rise within the Red Brigades was due in large measure to his charismatic personality. In a powerful book of memoirs, *Arms and Baggage* (*Armi e bagagli*, Genoa: Costa & Nolan, 1987), a Red Brigade intellectual named Enrico Fenzi remembered Antonio Savasta with great affection. According to Fenzi, Savasta was "loved by everyone. This was partly because of his warm personality and partly because there was nothing he would not do for the Organization. Without exactly trying and certainly without striking any poses, Savasta exercised a certain natural authority ... he communicated a sense of unshakable and reassuring mental health. . . ."

In December 1980, the chief of the Veneto column, Michele Galati, was unexpectedly arrested. With the entire column in danger of dissolving, the Organizzazione dispatched Savasta to northeastern Italy as the new Veneto *capocolonna*, or column chief. After reorganizing the faltering group, Savasta was elected in January 1981 to a seat on the Executive Committee, becoming one of the top revolutionaries in Italy.

A few months later, Mario Moretti walked into a police trap and disappeared into prison. Savasta and his colleagues on the Executive Committee rallied their troops, responding to the loss of their leader by carrying out a bold series of kidnappings and political assassinations.

One of these operations was the kidnapping of Giuseppe Taliercio, chief executive officer (CEO) of Italy's giant Montedison petrochemical firm. The Red Brigades had long alleged that Montedison abused its work force and polluted the Adriatic Sea; in fact, they had punctuated their criticisms of the company's policies by shooting one previous Montedison CEO. Savasta's kidnapping of Taliercio was intended to force the company into an admission of guilt for its practices, but the company balked, bringing in antiterrorism experts from around the world in an attempt to find Savasta and rescue Dr. Taliercio.

In the end, the police and the experts were unsuccessful. Faced with Montedison's refusal to deal, the Executive Committee of the Red Brigades passed sentence on the unfortunate engineer. He was executed by Antonio Savasta, and his body was dumped at Montedison's front gate.

Thanks to Savasta's successes, the Red Brigades appeared to the public to be as strong as ever, but the Organizzazione was stricken by several internal feuds and disputes over both policies and personalities. The leader of one of the two columns in Rome was Giovanni Senzani, a former student at the University of California at Berkeley and a professor of criminology. At the time of the "Winter of Fire," Senzani was becoming less and less willing to obey the Executive Committee's orders; later he broke away from the main body of the Red Brigades altogether.

In June 1981, the Italian political system reacted to the terrorist crisis by selecting a new prime minister. All of Italy's chief executives since World War II had been chosen from a field of often mediocre Christian Democrat politicians, but this time the country turned in desperation to a man named Giovanni Spadolini, leader of the tiny but influential Republican party. Spadolini was one of Italy's best-known intellectuals, having successively achieved fame as a historian, a newspaper editor, and then a dynamic political leader. He was also known to be a man of total, inflexible determination as far as terrorism was concerned.

The Brigate rosse had always feared a strong, competent government in Rome. With morale within the Organization sagging, Savasta and his colleagues were united in the belief that their survival depended on driving the brilliant Spadolini from office as quickly as possible.

The result in 1981/82 was a carefully articulated campaign that was code-named "Winter of Fire." At a series of meetings in the summer and early autumn of 1981, the Executive Committee contemplated four major operations, designed to demonstrate that Prime Minister Giovanni Spadolini was no more competent than his hapless predecessors. The four original Winter of Fire operations planned were the following:

1. *The Rovigo Penitentiary breakout:* this was intended to be a daring attack on the maximum-security prison in Rovigo, a medium-size city southeast of Verona. The jailbreak would utilize resources and safe houses provided by the Red Brigades but would actually be carried out by men from the allied Prima linea (or Front Line) organization, who were anxious to rescue four Prima linea women from custody in Rovigo.

2. *The Romiti kidnap:* to be carried out by the Rome column, this operation involved the kidnapping of Italy's most powerful business leader, Cesare Romiti, the CEO of the giant Fiat Corporation. By holding Romiti for a princely ransom, the Red Brigades could show that not even mighty Fiat could defend its executives from terrorism.

3. *The Simone operation:* the deputy chief of the State Police *Divisione per le investigazioni generali e per le operazioni speciali* or *DIGOS* (General Investigations and Special Operations Division) office in Rome was a expert investigator named Nicola Simone who had been systematically pounding the two Rome-

based columns. Having located a secret apartment used by Simone, the Red Brigades planned to kidnap him and interrogate their prisoner for information about State Police antiterrorist operations and the possible existence of police informants within the Red Brigades. Simone would be held long enough to demoralize the entire DIGOS organization and then executed, because he was far too implacable an adversary to be allowed to survive.

4. *The raid on the Christian Democratic party:* the next operation was the most violent exploit ever devised by an Italian revolutionary group. Planned by Professor Giovanni Senzani in Rome, the operation called for a military-style assault on a meeting of the Christian Democratic party leadership scheduled for January 1982. Senzani's group intended to attack with rocket launchers, military explosives, and heavy machine guns in an effort to provoke as many casualties as possible. Savasta and his colleagues on the Executive Committee were concerned about the bloodthirsty character of this operation but feared that Senzani would break openly with the Red Brigades if they attempted to disapprove his plans.

As the Executive Committee prepared its Winter of Fire, they faced two separate and competing police departments, both with serious organizational difficulties and a systemic inability to cooperate with one another. The Carabinieri are a militarized corps resembling the Canadian Mounties. At the time of the Dozier abduction, the best-known Carabiniere officer was Major General Carlo Alberto Dalla Chiesa, a subtle, energetic man who was later murdered by the Mafia.

The so-called civilian police in Italy are the State Police or *Polizia di Stato.* Within the State Police headquarters in Rome, the central antiterrorist office is called *Ufficio centrale per le investigazioni generali e per le operazioni speciali,* or *UCIGOS,* which stands for Central Office for General Investigations and Special Operations. The regional branch offices of UCIGOS were simply called DIGOS.

Dazzled by all these acronyms, the Italian public tended to use the term *DIGOS* for the whole antiterrorist apparatus of the State Police, a usage followed in this book. Although less glamorous than General Dalla Chiesa's Carabinieri, the DIGOS had produced several skilled investigators, among them Commissioner Nicola Simone in Rome and Commissioner Salvatore Genova, confusingly assigned to the northern Italian city of Genoa, which is called *Genova* in Italian.

Like most of the terrorists he hunted, Salvatore Genova was himself a product of the 1960s student movement. An idealist and a political liberal, he had taken part in demonstrations during his university days before going on to serve as a university lecturer and a labor lawyer. His move to the Polizia di Stato came as a result of his growing conviction that terrorism was delaying the social reforms he ardently sought.

The Winter of Fire: The Americans and Europe in 1981

In autumn 1981, the Red Brigades Executive Committee was preparing these four operations but wondering whether this offensive would be sufficient to destroy the Spadolini government and regain revolutionary momentum. Barbara Balzarani, one of Savasta's colleagues on the Esecutivo, had been calling for the mounting of a fifth, even more dramatic operation, specifically targeted against the American presence in Italy.

From an ideological point of view, there was a great deal to recommend what the Esecutivo came to call the "Yankee option." The Red Brigades had always resented what they regarded as covert American control over political, military, and economic life in Europe. Since the end of World War II, the Italian peninsula had been filled with American military bases, located in such major Italian cities as Livorno, Naples, and Vicenza. Furthermore, many American nuclear weapons were based in Italy, making the peninsula an obvious target for Soviet missiles in the event of an all-out nuclear exchange.

Within the European "hard Left" it was believed that the omnipotent Yankees ran Italy from behind the scenes. As Antonio Savasta expressed it in a recent letter to the authors:

> The massive American interference in postwar Italian affairs is one of the factors that caused the growth of an anti-American political culture in Italy . . . in fact, the debate among traditional leftists like the Italian Communist party and New Leftists and Extraparliamentary Leftists always focused upon the attitude that a revolutionary force ought to adopt in the face of American foreign policy.

There had been American nuclear forces all over Europe for decades, but by the end of the 1970s, the U.S. government was proposing the deployment of both the Cruise and the Pershing 2 missiles in various NATO countries. As a result, many sectors of European public opinion became inflamed with the most virulent outburst of anti-American feelings since the end of the Vietnam War. From the Greenham Common Air Force Base in Britain to Comiso's USAF installation in Sicily, dramatic protests erupted and peace camps were created with marches becoming repetitive, massive, and sometimes violent.

In the past, serious anti-Americanism had been a passion reserved mostly for left-wing political parties. Thanks to the missile crisis, however, dislike of the United States was threatening to spread into the educated middle classes of Great Britain, West Germany, Holland, and Italy, normally moderate people who feared the angry cold war rhetoric of the new Reagan administration and worried that the Americans might be preparing to fight World War III in Europe.

The American community in Italy was largely unaware of this shift in public opinion. Although there had been actual violence against U.S. commanders serving in Germany, the Americans in Italy seemed immune from terrorism. Nor had the American intelligence community ever picked up a specific threat; for most American service personnel Italy was a dream post.

To the Red Brigades, the events of the recent past suggested that the once-powerful Americans were now a spent force who could be antagonized with impunity. In 1975, the Viet Cong had marched into Saigon. In spring 1979, the American-sponsored Shah of Iran had been driven from his country. In the summer of that same year, the U.S.-backed dictator of Nicaragua, Anastasio Somoza, had been chased into exile as victorious Sandinista forces poured into Managua. And by the end of 1979, revolutionary students had taken diplomatic hostages in Tehran, while the Russian army had marched into Afghanistan with no fear of a paralyzed America. As Antonio Savasta later remarked, "From all over the world, news was coming in that nations were rebelling against the omnipotent Americans and American puppet regimes . . . why not in Italy? Why should the chain of imperialism not snap in Italy, its weakest link?"

Complicating the situation, 1981 was a time of unusual political tension all across Europe. Pope John Paul II had been wounded by a Turkish terrorist earlier in the year. Russian troops were poised on the borders of Poland, ready to intervene should the Warsaw government be unable to manage the Solidarity crisis. With a dying Leonid Brezhnev in the Kremlin and the vigorously anti-Communist Ronald Reagan installed in the White House, the cold war seemed to grow frostier by the day.

How would the United States respond to a terrorist attack against an American? The new Reagan administration had come to office proclaiming its ability to deal with political violence. The combative new secretary of state, Alexander Haig, had even announced that antiterrorism would be a principal focus of the Reagan years, issuing what seemed to be a challenge to revolutionary movements all over the world.

Despite the presence of a large U.S. community in Italy, the Red Brigades had never in the past paid any attention to the Americans, who had responded by thinking of Italian terrorism as a purely domestic problem. The notion of targeting a senior American military man was therefore risky. The Yankees would not be expecting an attack from this quarter, but they would surely respond with fury to this insult.

Despite the encouragement of his colleagues on the Executive Committee, Antonio Savasta privately questioned the wisdom of an attack on American forces. For the revolutionaries of northeastern Italy, 1980 and 1981 had been hard years. Several column chiefs in a row had been arrested, and Savasta had only been able to carry out a series of impressive operations in the Veneto area by using a hard core of experienced *brigatisti* borrowed from other columns. Some of his people were exhausted; other members of the Veneto column resented Savasta as an outsider. And there were even those who were looking for a way to abandon the revolution altogether.

As he debated the Winter of Fire with his colleagues on the Esecutivo in September 1981, Antonio Savasta realized that if they decided upon a direct attack against an American target, the Red Brigades would be taking what he had always called a *scommessa con la storia*, a "wager with history."

BOOK I

THE
STALKING

1

4:15 P.M., 11 SEPTEMBER 1981
CENTRAL QUESTURA (POLICE HEADQUARTERS)
VIA AURELIO SAFFI, GENOA, REGION OF LIGURIA

"When did it all begin for you?" asked the commissioner with studied nonchalance as he sorted through the papers on his desk. The woman was looking past him out the window at the Mediterranean, where something on the waves had caught her attention. She did not respond.

"Do you know where the others are?" he went on, leaning forward in his chair with a ballpoint pen in his hand and signing a routine authorization form. "Francesco Lo Bianco, for example?"

The woman focused her brown eyes on him for so long it was almost painful. There was a sympathetic smile on her lips, amused, full of complicity, as if they shared a secret. It would have been a chaste secret; there was no sex in her now and the men had already begun to treat her as a sort of homicidal nun.

She shook her head and looked away, returning her gaze to the water. There were yachts coming into the harbor, dropping their sails as they passed the breakwater.

Genova pulled the woman's dossier toward him and then pushed it impatiently away because he had long since memorized every word. The woman's baptismal name was Fulvia Miglietta, although she was "Nora" to her colleagues in the Red Brigades. She was forty and very slender, with short brunette hair that never seemed to get brushed. For a long time, she had been a schoolmistress, a *professoressa* of Italian literature. For years after that she had been a terrorist and a fugitive, one of the most wanted women in Italy. If she would talk, if she could evolve past this self-imposed autism, she could tell them everything. Fulvia went all the way back to the beginning, a decade or more, and she knew everyone in the revolutionary movement, the thinkers and the shooters, those who could be captured in their sleep and those who never seemed to sleep. . . .

15

Now Fulvia Miglietta was a prisoner, although—like most aspects of this wretched business—it had been mostly an accident. Arriving at the Genoa station on a slow train from Naples, Fulvia had taken an illicit shortcut across the tracks toward the terminal. Passengers were supposed to exit through a tunnel, and this minor transgression had caught the attention of a Polizia di Stato officer who was there looking for faces like hers. When the detectives found the automatic pistol in her handbag, they took her to Commissioner Genova like a Christmas present.

Since her arrest, she had hardly spoken. At the very beginning, on her first visit to this office, she had given him a sympathetic look and commented simply, "I will never talk!" Once, when she had become ill down in the cells below, he had brought her medicine, and she had said, "Grazie." Since then, nothing, although whenever the commissioner's schedule permitted, he had her brought to his office. Hours would pass and she would stare out the window at the harbor or sit on the chair near his desk while he worked. But she never said anything.

"Did you know that this was once Antonio Esposito's office?" he asked. Esposito had been the DIGOS officer before him in this Questura, an older man who worked hard during the day and went home every night to his wife. Fulvia's colleagues had caught him alone on the street one evening, three years ago, and—because he posed a distinct threat to them—they had riddled his body with machine-gun bullets.

"When he was killed, they sent me here to take his place, so I never knew him," Genova continued. "Although the people here all loved him. Were you . . . ?"

Were you there, he wondered, when they killed him? Francesco Lo Bianco was there with his machine gun, but who else? I need to know.

There was the usual silence, and Genova turned away, feeling desperate. At times, he was tempted to explain his dilemma to her in purely human terms. He was a DIGOS commissioner, an antiterrorist cop and a successful one. The Red Brigades would assassinate him if they could, just as they had shot Antonio Esposito. On one level, he had always accepted the logic of his profession.

But there was a woman he wanted to marry, another *professoressa* of Italian literature. For many years it had been understood that they would have a family and a house and a future together, all things that could not happen as long as the Red Brigades compelled him to live like a criminal.

Thanks to the men and women Fulvia was protecting with her silence, the commissioner was forced to slip anonymously through life, unknown to his neighbors, a man who lived in rented rooms, coming and going at night in fast cars, bringing danger to the woman he loved every time he came to her door. . . .

"Ti voglio bene," she said suddenly. "I love you." Salvatore Genova turned in surprise, realizing that he had long since forgotten the sound of her voice.

"Life is complicated enough," he shook his head, feeling angry. "Tell me what I need to know!"

For a long time, she gave him one of her enciphered gazes. He bit his tongue, waiting to see whether this would be the moment for names, addresses, and descriptions.

Instead, she turned toward the window and gazed again at the sea. The last of the sailboats had docked now, and the only craft still on the water was a scow dredging mud from the bottom of the harbor. Commissioner Genova watched it for a while with a certain collegial affection and then rang for a man to take Fulvia back to her cell.

"I'll see you tomorrow then," he said. She nodded, confirming their appointment, and followed the detective down the hall.

2

6:50 A.M., 16 SEPTEMBER 1981
VIA PORTO, VILLAGE OF SAN GIOVANNI LUPATOTO
SUBURB OF VERONA, VENETO REGION

"Antonio! Are you all right?"

"*Cristo!*" he mumbled, breathing hard as he tried to make a controlled entrance into the reality of another day and realizing that he had just cried aloud in his sleep. Savasta was a hard, dedicated revolutionary. Awake and in control of his mental facilities, he knew who he was and why it was occasionally necessary to shoot the enemies of the working class. These nightmares are a normal psychological reaction to the experience of violence, he instructed himself. We do not cease to be human when we take up arms in defense of the proletariat.

"Antonio, wake up!" Emilia was saying, her hand soft on his shoulder. "You've been dreaming again!"

"It's all right." He sat up. His undershirt was soaked with perspiration and he was embarrassed that she should have seen him yet again suffering from a bad dream. Instinctively, he rested his head against her full breasts, looking for comfort. The woman wrapped her arms around his neck and administered a perfunctory hug, then pushed him away and stood up.

"Do you want coffee?" she asked. At twenty-four, Emilia Libera was a shy young woman with short brunette hair, high cheekbones, and dark eyes that could sometimes be bright and sometimes melancholy. She was the first and only woman in Savasta's life, and he loved her with a great passion.

"Yes . . . I'll exercise and then have coffee." He rolled out of bed and stretched. There was an autumn sun shining in the window, and the room was warm. Before dressing he began a set of punishing deep knee bends, the first in his rigorous daily regimen of exercises.

Antonio Savasta was twenty-five, a lithe, well-muscled young man five feet ten inches tall. With his thin moustache and heavy frame glasses, he presented an unremarkable appearance. During the six years of his clandestine existence, that nondescript quality had been invaluable; policemen somehow never looked at him too closely.

He and Emilia had grown up together in an awful Roman slum where no one needed to read *Das Kapital* to know that capitalism wasn't working. They had both become radical Communists in their early teens, joining political action committees, battling the police, and marching against American aggression in Southeast Asia. In their very first year at the University of Rome, they were recruited for the revolution by a Red Brigades operative; while Emilia studied chemistry and served as a talent scout for the Organizzazione, Antonio neglected his formal studies and moved into leadership positions, beginning his rapid climb up the Red Brigades chain of command.

"The coffee is ready!" Emilia called from the kitchen, breaking his concentration, and Savasta completed his round of pushups and climbed into his jeans and sneakers, hearing the sputter of the *caffettiera* as it created the inky black espresso he loved in the morning.

"How are you?" he asked as he entered the kitchen.

"I'm all right." She was sewing a button on one of his jackets. It was not something they ever managed to talk about, but Savasta knew that she was beginning to doubt that their imagined revolution would ever become a reality. For the men and women of the Italian Red Brigades, the police were a manageable problem; the real enemy was despair.

And she missed their native Rome, feeling isolated and exposed in the north. There had been no choice about the move to the Veneto, he reminded himself, remembering how the police had almost exterminated the Veneto column in a series of devastating raids. Even Michele Galati, the *capocolonna* for this corner of Italy, had been arrested, and the whole Red Brigades edifice in the Veneto had needed immediate reorganization. The Executive Committee had ordered their transfer from Rome to the Veneto and Savasta had dashed north to take command.

And he had been successful. By December 1980, he had stabilized the badly traumatized Venetian group, stopped the hemorrhage of arrests, and launched the column into a bold kidnapping and several assassinations. Gratefully, the Organizzazione had rewarded him with a seat on the Executive Committee, making him one of the top revolutionaries in Italy.

Obedient but unenthusiastic, Emilia had followed, setting up a home for them here in this safe house on the outskirts of Verona while she kept the books and worried about logistics for Antonio's operations. Every Red Brigades establishment was maintained by a *vivandiere,* or "housekeeper," a citizen above suspicion who maintained a legal existence as a cover for services to the Red Brigades. Here on the Via Porto, their host was a radical schoolteacher named Armando Lanza, who liked to sleep late in the mornings despite his commitment to the revolution.

"Well, the Executive Committee meets at ten," Savasta volunteered with strained cheerfulness as he sat down to drink his coffee. "I'll stay over in Milan tonight and come back tomorrow."

"How . . . how are things going? Have the four of you reached any decisions yet?" Emilia was already dressed for the day, wearing one of the sensible plaid skirts she liked and a simple white cotton blouse. With her short brown hair neatly brushed and her face lightly made up, she looked like the kind of well-bred, soft-spoken girl every young policeman would like to take home to meet his family. No one had ever stopped Emilia for a document check.

"No, but we've talked about a whole range of possible operations," he muttered, annoyed that she should press him for more information than the Esecutivo's rules of compartmentalization permitted him to give.

"We're not ready for another operation here," she said. "These Veneto people are all middle-class schoolteachers! We don't know any of them well enough yet to decide who we can trust. We need to be cautious!"

"Emilia, it's going to be okay!" Savasta seized her hand, trying to turn on the magic that had worked for so long. "We're getting the momentum back . . . this year has been one successful operation after another!"

"Because you're bringing in people from Rome!" She pulled her hand away. "But we can't carry out a major operation with a bunch of schoolteachers! Make sure they understand that!"

"Look, we'll talk about it," he promised. Finishing his coffee, he rose from the table and poked his arms into the sleeves of his tan corduroy jacket. He checked the safety on his Browning automatic and put it carefully into an inside pocket. "Will . . . listen, will you be okay?"

"I made you a sandwich." She ignored the question as she turned up the collar on his jacket. She put the *panino* into his pocket, some prosciutto and cheese on a soft white roll. "Do you have enough clothes? It's supposed to rain."

"I'll be okay," he assured her as they fumbled into each other's arms for an unhappy good-bye kiss. He paused at the door, but there did not seem to be anything more to say, and so he picked up his bag and left. Outside, it was bright and sunny, although there were dark clouds off to the west in the direction of Milan.

He caught the bus at the corner, paid the five hundred lire fare, and put the ticket into his wallet so that he could claim it later against expenses. Twenty minutes later, he got off at the Verona *centrale*, finding the place thronged with travelers. There was a line at the *biglietteria*, but Savasta waited patiently because he felt safe in a crowded train station. After purchasing a round-trip ticket to Milan, he walked onto platform 1 and found a westbound express waiting on the track. He got into a smoking car because there were more people there and located an empty seat by the window.

Savasta slouched down in his seat, put a newspaper over his face, and pretended to be asleep. This tactic avoided the unnecessary risk of being identified by a DIGOS detective patrolling the aisles and allowed him to think without distractions. Because the previous night's sleep had been flawed by nightmares and he was anxious to be fresh for the meeting, he even allowed himself a long, authentic doze. He awakened when the express began to lose speed entering the bleak industrial periphery of Milan.

He pulled down the newspaper and saw that the sky had become overcast. There were gloomy gray apartment buildings on either side of the tracks, reminding Savasta of the slum in east Rome where he and Emilia had lived as children. The buildings were all crudely mass-produced from prestressed concrete, nine or ten stories high. Outside, the paint had long since been covered with soot from nearby factory chimneys or ash from passing trains.

On every roof, there was a forest of television antennas bringing soul-destroying messages of capitalist advertising to thousands of wretched, flickering, black-and-white television sets. Tonight, after a day's dehumanizing labor in some awful factory, the workers who lived in these cages would stagger home; drink too much cheap, adulterated wine at dinner; and then watch a badly dubbed version of "Dallas," that obscene hymn to America's wealth.

The houses of the rich are all different, he thought, but poor people's houses are always the same. Inside, he knew that every apartment would be a warren of tiny, airless rooms, leading to a narrow balcony from which the leaseholder could gaze down on narrow, dingy streets with burned-out cars, and shattered bottles, and discarded hypodermic needles, and broken windows covered with cardboard, and crippled people hobbling around on canes, and crazy old women screaming obscenities, and sad junkies and rapists, and drunken men. . . .

Savasta took a deep breath to master his fury. He ran on rage like cars run on gasoline, but too much of it made you stupid.

Caution, he reminded himself, as the express pulled into Milan's Stazione centrale. Emilia was fond of observing that the revolution would not be accomplished if all the revolutionaries were in jail. And caution was advisable in train stations because the DIGOS routinely posted a man with a good memory for faces at the intercity exits.

The platform was to the left and as the other passengers lined up at the exit, Savasta slipped to the door on the right of the carriage. There was another train already there, a local, and its passengers were now disembarking onto a different platform.

A local was less likely to attract attention and Savasta pushed open the door and swung into the adjacent train. There were four nuns ahead of him, struggling with luggage. With a smile, he selected the sister with the biggest suitcase and offered to carry it for her, insinuating himself into the party of reverend nuns as they walked down the platform toward the central hall of the *stazione*.

He stayed with the sisters through the lobby, down the escalator, and past the ticket booths on the ground floor. At the taxi stand, he returned the suitcase to its owner and left the nuns with a cheerful wave. Outside in the Piazzale Duca d'Aosta, he spent a thousand lire for a Metropolitana ticket and let the underground train carry him to a residential district in the southwest portion of the city.

On the subway, Savasta picked up a discarded *Corriere della sera* and used the newspaper as camouflage while he thought about the coming Executive Committee meeting. The past twelve months had been dramatic, but the momentum had gone out of the Red Brigades and there were those who were talking about a strategic withdrawal, a hunkering down, a pause in which to reconsider and rebuild. Even Emilia . . .

When the underground train pulled into the Piazza Baracca station, Savasta moved to the door, still apparently engrossed in his *Corriere della sera*. The doors opened, and he stepped aside to allow other passengers to get off but did not join them until the last possible moment, just as the pneumatic doors began to close, when he jumped out onto the platform, moving too abruptly for anyone to follow him.

There was a crucial motive for these precautions. The Executive Committee had gone to great expense to create a secret headquarters in an upper-class Milan residential district. The address was known only to the members of the Executive Committee and to the headquarters housekeeper. If the police ever managed to follow just one member of the Esecutivo to this secret apartment, they would find enough information there to smash the Red Brigades.

Climbing to the street, Savasta stopped at a newspaper kiosk and scanned the magazines for a few minutes while he ensured that all the other disembarking passengers were dispersing normally. Then he walked a short distance to the Via Andrea Verga, a quiet, leafy avenue with expensive apartment buildings and boutiques.

At the far end of the street was the Piazza Po, a broad green park with slides and swings and monkeybars. Savasta saw a crowd of boys playing a furious game of soccer. They were big kids, fed on steaks and vitamin pills, and they all seemed to be wearing designer jeans and Adidas sneakers.

Savasta crossed the street toward his destination. In front of him there was a four-story white stucco palazzo that overlooked the Piazza Po. On the ground floor was a deliberately old-fashioned *farmacia* with antique bottles of Korean ginseng and herbal medicines in the window. Next to the drugstore was a dry cleaners, with a sign in the window promising to deal gently with one's more delicate linens and silks. Between the two shops was an anonymous doorway, 22 Via Andrea Verga.

Savasta rang the bell and heard footsteps descending the stairs. Like every other Red Brigade safe house, the headquarters apartment had been legally rented by a trusted irregular who qualified as an "unsuspectable," a person who had no police record or detectable affiliation with the radical Left. The housekeeper or *vivandiere* for 22 Via Verga was a certain Signorina Giovanna Esposito, a twenty-six-year-old Italian-born Swiss citizen studying literature at the University of Milan.

The door opened. Giovanna was a tall, dramatically good-looking young woman with a sumptuous figure and a dark Mediterranean complexion.

"Ciao, Emilio!" she greeted him simply, using Savasta's current nom de guerre within the Organization. She did not know his real name and would not have used it in any case. "The others are already here."

"Ciao," he said with a smile. She hugged him with enthusiasm and Savasta hugged her back. He had noticed that this *vivandiere* always showed him a special warmth whenever he came to the Via Verga. He was scheduled to stay overnight and it occurred to him that if he were to gaze meaningfully into her eyes over dinner, she would perhaps come later into his bed.

Climbing the stairs behind her, he tried to put the notion out of his head, albeit a little regretfully. The Organizzazione had come to believe that a mutually faithful heterosexual couple made the most stable team. It was ironic that a group of subversive atheists should reach the same conclusion as the Roman Catholic church, but clandestine life was complicated enough without the added distraction of infidelity. Besides, there were enough problems in his relationship with Emilia without adding a love affair to the equation.

In the living room on the second floor, the other three members of the Esecutivo were waiting for him. Savasta kissed Barbara Balzarani on both cheeks and then shook hands with Francesco Lo Bianco, the Genoa *capocolonna*, and Luigi Novelli, an old friend who had become commander of the Rome column.

"Where do we stand?" As the three men took their seats, Barbara Balzarani spoke, asserting her right to chair the meeting. Balzarani had a slender, willowy figure and a quick, nervous intellectuality about her that suggested a schoolteacher or a poetess rather than an urban guerrilla. At thirty-two, she was the oldest person in the room, and she had been near the top of the movement since nearly the beginning. Like Savasta and Novelli, she was a Roman, and for years now she had been the *Pasionaria* of the Red Brigades.

"I don't think we can mount anything major in Genoa," Francesco Lo Bianco murmured, his eyes on the floor. The Genoa *capocolonna* was originally from Calabria, that poverty-stricken region at the toe of Italy's boot. His great passion had once been painting, and for years he had worked in a steel mill by day and labored in an artist's studio by night, cranking out paintings of starving, gaunt, exploited Calabrian peasants. In the early seventies, Francesco had decided that the machine gun was mightier than the paintbrush, trading art for revolution.

"I think we're better off with you here on the Via Verga helping us manage the rest of the Winter of Fire campaign," Savasta said, because they all appreciated how limited Lo Bianco's resources had become. Three years previously, as if to confuse an already complicated situation, the State Police had assigned to the city of Genoa ("Genova" in Italian) a DIGOS commissioner named Salvatore Genova. The eponymously resourceful Commissioner Genova and his colleagues had almost eliminated the Red Brigade presence in the city. Even Francesco's wife, Fernanda, was behind bars.

"In Rome?" Barbara turned to Luigi Novelli. The chieftain of the Rome column was a tall, unassertive man with a genius for logistics. There was something gray and neutral and passive about Novelli and it was said that he survived violent firefights with the police simply because he never looked important enough to shoot. Luigi and his wife, Marina, were two of Antonio Savasta's oldest friends in the Organization.

"We're going ahead with the planning of our end of the campaign," Novelli said, looking up from the task of hand-rolling one of the dozens of cigarettes he would consume in the course of the day. "But Winter of Fire would have a better chance of success in central Italy if the police could be distracted by some high-profile incident here in the north."

"There will be that jailbreak in Rovigo," Balzarani reminded him.

"I want something big," insisted Novelli calmly. "You're asking us down in Rome to kidnap two of the best-protected targets in Italy, and Senzani still wants to conduct his military assault on the Christian Democratic party headquarters. If you could think of a way of enticing some policemen up here, it would give us some breathing space."

There was a moment of silence. Savasta felt three pairs of eyes turning on him. Caution, Emilia had urged. With a gang of middle-class schoolteachers, we cannot carry out a major operation. . . .

"Over the years, we've talked about targeting a senior American figure," Savasta began. "Barbara, this is something you've always advocated, but we shouldn't think of it as just a diversion. It would be a major operation with a high risk potential. . . ."

"The payoff would be equally high," said Balzarani, her eyes bright and hard. "With a top American in our hands, we could force the government to open the prison doors and turn loose some of our colleagues. The Americans would force them into a trade!"

"The Yanks have been running Italy from behind the scenes since World War II," Novelli commented. "If we got their top man, we could force him to reveal how they secretly control this country."

"The major NATO headquarters for Italy is located in Verona," Savasta told them, getting out some notes he had prepared. His investigations had revealed that there were three American generals in northern Italy, but only one of them belonged to NATO. "There have been newspaper stories about a senior American general, a war criminal from Vietnam, assigned to a NATO command called LANDSOUTH."

"I like it," Balzarani smiled. "A war criminal from Vietnam! Look, do you remember how the Israelis kidnapped Adolf Eichmann from Argentina? By making an example out of him, they put the whole Nazi generation on trial. We could put an American war criminal on trial and remind the whole world how the U.S. Army committed genocide in Vietnam!"

"But can we capture him?" Lo Bianco questioned. "A man like that will have protection. . . ."

"I'd need some help from Rome," Savasta said, remembering Emilia's demand for caution. But caution can freeze you, he was thinking. At this stage in the revolution, would Nicaragua's Sandino have been cautious? Or Che Guevara? Or Fidel Castro? Or Ho Chi Minh?

"You can have anybody you want," Novelli told him.

"Then we can do it." Savasta shrugged. Oh Emilia, stay with me a little longer, he thought, and we will take our little band of schoolteachers and steal an American for Barbara. Che Guevara said it a long time ago, before the pigs of the CIA murdered him in the mountains of Bolivia. The business of revolutionaries is to make revolutions.

And caution is for accountants.

3

5:30 P.M., 16 SEPTEMBER 1981
CENTRAL VERONA
VENETO REGION

There had been a light rain over Verona in the morning but now the cobblestone streets were dry. The sun was sinking behind the red-tile rooftops of the old town, but the late September afternoon was still friendly and warm.

This is first-rate weather, thought General James Lee Dozier, reflecting that northern Italy seemed to jolt you with a nasty patch of cold and rain in late August to warn that beach weather was ending, only to relent in September and serve up a few more weeks of summer. In fact, today was almost Florida weather. In Jim Dozier's considered opinion, that was about as good as weather got.

In his fiftieth year, Dozier was a lean, muscular man of medium height, a physical-fitness fanatic who ran several miles every morning. Relaxing now after a hard day at his headquarters, he gazed affectionately at Verona as his driver whisked the NATO staff car through the late afternoon traffic.

To their left was the broad brown expanse of the Adige, a powerful river that splashed down from the Alps and then meandered through the city center of Verona. To the right, there was an intricate tapestry of narrow, winding streets and tiny piazzas; the general wondered whether he would ever grow tired of this gentle, ancient city.

Jim Dozier had reported here for duty in June 1980, with his wife, Judy. Over the past year, the two of them had come to love the visual unpredictability of Verona, the twisting cobblestone passageways, the little shops, the pink marble palazzi with bronze gateways opening into secret courtyards with fountains and gardens. From the balcony of their penthouse apartment, they could look down on the Adige, moving past them toward the Adriatic Sea.

Born and raised in Arcadia, Florida, where the Peace River ambles down to the Gulf of Mexico, Jim Dozier had always liked living near the water. He had grown up during the Depression. With his mother a schoolteacher and his father an employee in a department store, there had never been much money in the Dozier home. And no one would have predicted that the hellraising Dozier kid would someday become a general in the United States Army.

In fact, the army had been an accident. In 1950, as a not-very-studious engineering student at the University of Florida, Jim Dozier had followed a crowd of his friends into the Florida National Guard. The North Korean Army marched south across the thirty-eighth parallel that same year, and by 1951, Dozier became a private first class on active duty in a federalized National Guard unit.

After the usual battery of aptitude tests, the army decided that the schoolteacher's kid was West Point material, sending him first to a preparatory school, and then up to the military academy itself. In his senior year at the Point, he met Judy during a trip to Washington; they were married just after Jim received his second lieutenant's commission in 1956—

Sergeant Di Nardo spun the wheel hard and Dozier snapped back quickly to the reality around him as the Fiat swung sharply to the left across the Vittoria Bridge. On the other side of the river, there was a cluster of *alimentari*, little food shops with prosciutto and sausages in the windows, but the streets were wider here and Di Nardo began to put on speed.

Sitting stiffly behind the steering wheel of the navy blue Fiat 131, the normally chatty Carabiniere sergeant was silent today, concentrating on his driving as he maneuvered the unmarked staff car through the chaotic traffic. Dozier was sitting in the backseat, where generals are supposed to sit, although he had never been comfortable with the arrangement. Like most combat veterans, he was impatient with protocol and as a former enlisted man, he found it difficult to regard sergeants as a separate species.

He found himself wishing that he could find some polite way to tell his driver that he would prefer not to be driven quite so fast. He was not a nervous man, but after surviving a number of firefights in South Vietnam, he did not much relish the anticlimax of perishing in a car wreck in Verona.

Di Nardo was a compact, muscular man in his forties, an experienced, watchful policeman. He had served as the chauffeur-bodyguard to several previous American generals because he could drive and shoot and because—at least according to NATO Security—that lightness of touch might someday be needed to whisk an important passenger away from menace. As a normal precaution, Di Nardo frequently altered their route home from the office and these sudden turns and high speeds were all calculated to make life difficult for anyone who might be following them with evil intent.

But he's taking it more seriously today than usual, Dozier realized. He's heard that the Red Army Faction attacked Fritz Kroesen, and he wants to make sure the same thing doesn't happen to us—

Dozier winced as he recalled the morning cable traffic on the Kroesen incident. The attempted assassination had taken place in

Heidelberg, Germany, where a terrorist had fired a Russian-made rocket-propelled grenade at General Frederick Kroesen, the commander of all U.S. Army units in Europe. Fritz and Mrs. Kroesen had been riding in a specially designed armored vehicle, but all that extra steel would not have saved them from a Soviet-made RPG-7 had the terrorist managed to score a direct hit. The grenade had detonated against the rear of the vehicle, however, and the two Americans had escaped unhurt.

Instinctively, Dozier ran his fingers over his left forearm as an uninvited memory came to him. While serving with the Eleventh Armored Cavalry Regiment, he had been ambushed one day near the Cambodian border. The regiment was responding well when some anonymous Viet Cong gunner fired an RPG-7 in their direction and a metal fragment had sliced into Dozier's arm, inflicting a painful wound and sending Dozier to a field medical facility where he spent an uncomfortable night.

The general shrugged, dismissing the incident and reflecting with a chuckle that no one would try to kill him in sleepy old Verona because in this assignment he wasn't important enough to bother assassinating.

It was hardly the sort of thing he could say to his driver, but as far as Dozier was concerned, it was the regrettable truth. Coming back from Vietnam with a Silver Star on his chest, he had done another stint in Germany with the First Armored Division and then served as a staff officer in the Pentagon before heading south to Fort Hood to drive tanks with the Second Armored Division. When he received his first star, somebody in the Pentagon had decided that all brigadier generals needed to do at least one tour of duty on a multinational staff. Obediently, Jim and Judy Dozier had packed their bags in June 1980 and come to the Verona headquarters of LANDSOUTH, NATO-talk for Allied Land Forces in Southern Europe.

Living in Verona was turning out to be wonderful, but as LANDSOUTH's deputy chief of staff for logistics and administration, Jim Dozier realized that the job itself would only be important if the Russians invaded. In the meantime, most of the routine work was done for him by a competent multinational staff while he was supposed to perform what were essentially protocol functions: go to receptions, make speeches, conduct inspections, and award medals. Granted, this was alliance-building, and cocktail parties were fun, and Judy had enough charm for both of them when it came to the diplomatic side of things, but there were quite a few moments when the general sorely missed being in the field with troops.

"Here we are, sir," said Di Nardo, breaking into the general's private thoughts. The staff car turned onto the Via Lungadige Catena, and pulled up on the sidewalk in front of the apartment building at number 5. Beneath his sports coat, Di Nardo carried a nine-millimeter service automatic; Dozier watched him touch the pistol with his fingertips, as if to reassure himself that it was still there. Then Di Nardo stepped gingerly onto the sidewalk, quickly scanning their environment for danger. Finding none, he opened the rear door to permit his passenger to emerge.

"Buona sera, Di Nardo."

"Signor Si!" snapped the sergeant, straightening to a position of attention, his eyes still sweeping the street. "Buona sera, Signor Generale!"

Dozier walked directly into the apartment building, knowing that Di Nardo would not move until his *generale* was safely inside. He closed the glass front door of the apartment building behind him and turned to wave good-bye as the sergeant climbed back into the staff car and shot off down the Via Lungadige Catena. For a moment, he stood at the door, gazing out at the river and still thinking about terrorists.

It's Cheryl I worry about, he decided. His son, Scott, was enjoying the comparative safety of a community college in Florida while he studied art, but the Doziers had a daughter who was now a lieutenant in the U.S. Air Force, stationed at Rhein Main Air Force Base in Germany, not far from the attack on General Kroesen.

Jim Dozier knew West Germany well and liked the country and its people, but nobody in the American military underestimated the seriousness of the terrorist situation in Germany. Bombings and murderous assaults on U.S. personnel had been going on since the early seventies and would probably continue indefinitely.

But do I need to worry down here? There had been terrorism in Italy for a decade now, and Italian terrorists had even kidnapped and murdered a former prime minister, Aldo Moro, but there had never been an incident involving an American.

Theoretically, of course, Sergeant Di Nardo and his colleagues were always available should Dozier feel the need for protection when he and Judy went out in the evening, but they had never summoned a bodyguard-driver after the end of the normal working day. What was the point? He and Judy had dozens of friends in Verona, both Italians and Americans. They went out very frequently in the evenings, sometimes to official functions and sometimes to the Arena opera house in the Piazza Brà. Because their apartment was close to the center of town, they wandered home on foot, strolling hand in hand over the cobblestones of the dark streets.

And at five-thirty every morning, Dozier went out alone, jogging a few miles down the west bank of the Adige River. Do I want escorts dogging my heels day and night, he thought, just because some screwball up in Germany took a potshot at Fritz Kroesen? And what good would it do? Fritz knew he was a target and they almost nailed him!

I don't sense a problem here, he decided, turning away from the glass doors and heading for the creaky elevator that would carry him up to the apartment. I survived Vietnam. I ought to be able to survive Verona.

4

2:50 A.M., 19 SEPTEMBER 1981
GALLIATE CARABINIERE BARRACKS
VILLAGE OF GALLIATE, PROVINCE OF NOVARA

The bullet-resistant glass of the armored car was too thick to see through easily, but Michele Galati tried anyway, straining his eyes to read the signs along the darkened shoulder of the *auto-strada*.

We're going east, he realized, an involuntary shiver running through his heavy body as he glimpsed a familiar highway marker. A foolish dream took possession of him. The Swiss border isn't far from here. If I could get out of this damn car!

"Sit back, Galati!" growled the Carabiniere captain sitting opposite him, reading his thoughts. "You're not going anywhere!"

Michele Galati nodded bitterly. He was chained hand and

foot and enclosed in a steel-plated truck with an officer and six armed guards. There were two Carabiniere squad cars, one ahead of them riding shotgun and one behind. It would take a miracle to get him out of this, and good Marxists did not believe in miracles.

Feeling a sullen, irresistible sadness, the former leader of the Veneto column slumped back against the seat, realizing that escape was always going to be impossible. Galati was facing trial for two murders, and a life sentence was inevitable. At the Novara Maximum Security Penitentiary, he lived with many of the other former leaders of the Red Brigades and most of them seemed to be thriving on jail, exercising endlessly and writing long revolutionary documents to be smuggled out of prison and disseminated among the faithful. The revolution, they all still believed, was inevitable.

But increasingly, Michele Galati found himself unable to share their optimism; a remorseless depression swept over him whenever he contemplated the prospect of spending the rest of his life in prison.

Was there an alternative?

Galati could turn State's evidence, collaborate with the police, send all his friends and former colleagues to prison, and get his sentence reduced to a few years in a minimum-security prison. Apart from the emotional problems involved in betrayal of the Organizzazione, however, an open sellout was dangerous. Once his prison companions realized that there was information in the hands of the police that could only have come from Michele Galati, the Red Brigades would do to him what they had already done to other traitors, strangle him in a corridor or cut his throat in a prison courtyard.

Hence the dilemma: life imprisonment was unthinkable and betrayal was impossible.

Two weeks ago, unexpectedly, a nebulous, fragmentary compromise had presented itself. Galati had fallen ill with a stomach infection and spent a few days in the Novara prison hospital. Alone one night in his room, he was approached by a Carabiniere undercover agent posing as a nurse who offered to arrange a "conversation" with Carabiniere general Carlo Dalla Chiesa, the famous terrorist hunter.

It would be just a conversation, Galati had been assured. He would be asked to reveal nothing that could jeopardize his personal safety and the police would continue to treat him outwardly as a defiant, unrepentant terrorist. But if Signor Galati could provide some information that the Carabinieri found helpful, then at some point in the future General Dalla Chiesa would find a way of expressing his gratitude. The arrangement would be open-ended. The Carabinieri were merely asking for a quiet nocturnal conversation.

The armored car stopped. A flashlight's beam slapped into Galati's face, reflecting off his thick spectacles. Stumbling, he followed his escort through an open door and down a corridor. His eyes drifted to a clock on the wall, and he saw that it was nearly three in the morning.

"In here, Galati," came a deep voice from over his shoulder, and as he turned into an office, he felt the chains being removed from his wrists.

"Signor Generale?" There was a bulky figure behind the desk, a big man with a bristly moustache and glasses.

"Sit down, Galati." Dalla Chiesa was wearing a rumpled, unstylish civilian suit that made him seem unthreatening and middle-aged. "Are you going to give me something I can put in my pocket and take away?"

"The problem is . . . I'm going to tell you what the problem is," Michele Galati began, looking around to ensure that they were alone and then settling gingerly onto a folding chair in the corner of the room. The office belonged to the Carabiniere warrant officer who commanded this remote rural police station. On the wall was a picture of a homely dark-haired woman and some children. On the desk was an old manual typewriter.

"I know what the problem is," Dalla Chiesa said. "Listen, we're talking about credibility here, yours and mine. Let's start slowly, with you doing a little something for me, and then I'll see what I can do for you. Something easy like . . . let's say, tell me who took your place as leader of the Veneto column, eh?"

"I don't know. If I . . ." Michele Galati stalled. There would be no great personal danger in telling Dalla Chiesa things that everyone in the Red Brigades would know, but he resolved to identify none of the *brigatisti* he himself had recruited, not Lisa Arcangeli nor Armando Lanza nor Ruggiero Volinia nor little Emanuela Frascella.

"If what?"

"If I name names, who do you have to tell?"

"Nobody. There are things I do not even tell the prime minister. Do you know who took charge of the Veneto column after you were arrested?"

"It's a Roman named Antonio Savasta," said Galati, letting the treason slip from his lips before he could change his mind. It would make no difference, he tried to reassure himself. They were never going to catch Antonio. "There's Savasta and his woman, Emilia Libera."

"Antonio Savasta," Dalla Chiesa repeated the name slowly, remembering that an informant had testified that Savasta was responsible for seventeen homicides. "All right, since Moretti was captured, who has been serving on the Executive Committee? There would still be Moretti's girlfriend, Barbara Balzarani, right? Is Lo Bianco still a member?"

"Balzarani is on the Esecutivo, and Francesco Lo Bianco too, but he has less influence now that most of the Genoa column is gone. And Luigi Novelli represents the Rome column. And Savasta is the fourth."

"Savasta again? Who is taking Moretti's place as the real leader? Balzarani?"

"At first maybe," Galati said. "But from what I hear, Savasta has become more and more important, really. . . ."

"And what are they planning?"

"I don't know exactly, but I hear that there's another winter campaign being put together. They're calling it 'Winter of Fire,' and before I was captured, Barbara had been talking about the Americans, wanting to do something about their military in Italy, maybe . . . I don't know, shoot a general or something. . . ."

"Shoot an American general?" asked Dalla Chiesa, as if he had just been told the results of a local soccer match. He reached into his jacket for a leather-covered notebook and balanced it on one knee. Then he extracted a fountain pen, took off the cap, and made a few random marks on the paper to test that the ink was flowing.

"We have very little time and a great many things to discuss," the general said, speaking with a sudden intensity that made Galati feel afraid. "Tell me about Savasta."

5

It was a hodgepodge of shadow and whisper, like all raw intelligence data, suspicions that might be true mingling incestuously with suggestions that could not be valid, unless eventualities now regarded as remote were somehow verified from sources thought in the past to be unreliable.

Colonel William Reed spread the papers out on his desk, using coffee cups and cigarette lighters to hold everything in place while he structured his thoughts. There had to be something coherent in all of this.

Some of the reports before him were highly classified U.S. Defense Department cables; others were documents from SISMI, Italy's foreign intelligence agency, each page stamped in red RISERVATISSIMO, or "Top Secret." A few were in-house studies generated by his own staff, the cautionary words WARNING: SENSITIVE SOURCES AND METHODS printed across the top of each sheet. There was a scattering of recent press clippings from English, Italian, German, and French newspapers.

In the middle was a concise memorandum that had just arrived by urgent, enciphered cable from the Rome station of the Central Intelligence Agency. Reed scanned it for the tenth time, then picked up the telephone on his desk and dialed a four-digit number. A moment later, the call was answered in a nearby building by a secretary in the office of Major General George McFadden, the commanding officer of Vicenza's Southern European Task Force.

"You need to make me an appointment with the boss before he leaves tonight," Reed told her.

"Colonel, he's pretty busy this afternoon. What did you need to see him about?"

"I don't need to see him. He needs to see me."

"Better come over right now," the secretary said.

Putting the phone down, Bill Reed assembled his papers for

the briefing. As commander of the Vicenza detachment of the Army's Sixty-sixth Military Intelligence Group, the stocky, muscular colonel was the highest-ranking American intelligence officer in northern Italy, with responsibility for an assortment of clandestine affairs. His unit ran routine background investigations, coordinated with Italy's intelligence agencies, and worried about the security of the Southern European Task Force, the American unit based at Vicenza's Camp Ederle.

For the past year, however, Reed had been spending a lot of his time worrying about political violence, sometimes reading half the night in an effort to master the tactics and strategies of European terrorist movements. Two tours in Vietnam as a combat intelligence officer had taught him the dangers of underestimating revolutionary movements, even in wonderful places like Italy.

Methodically, the colonel dropped his documents into his briefcase, wondering how difficult it would be to convince George McFadden that the situation was serious. For more than a decade, U.S. military personnel based in Germany had been targeted by a murderous revolutionary group calling itself the *Rote Armee Fraktion*, the Red Army Faction, or what journalists called the Baader-Meinhof Gang. In Italy, everybody had heard of the famous Red Brigades, but it was conventional wisdom that Italian terrorists were not particularly anti-American. For the past several months, Reed had been trying to convince his superiors that a shift in Red Brigade thinking was taking place.

You could see it in their propaganda statements, the mimeographed communiqués the Red Brigades released after every operation. There were anti-American and anti-NATO statements creeping into the rhetoric, extravagant praise for the German Rote Armee Fraktion whenever they hit a Yankee target, complaints about American-owned multinational corporations exploiting the Italian worker, and attacks on the Reagan administration's plan to site Cruise missiles in Sicily. It was all there, and yet—well, the intelligence community had always demanded a specific threat, and the Red Brigades had never before provided one.

With his briefcase under his arm, Reed marched out of his office into the brightness of a crisp October afternoon. It was a normal day at Camp Ederle, and there were families driving past him in big American station wagons, Fords and Buicks, with bumper stickers saying nice things about Jesus. The wives were heading for the commissary to buy their groceries while the teenagers ducked into the PX to check out the latest records from across the "big pond." Afterward, folks would congregate at the Stars and Stripes Bookstore to buy English-language newspapers, and Superman comics, and *Playboy* and *Cosmopolitan*. Then a pizza or a submarine sandwich at the bowling alley, or perhaps a Reuben at the Club—in every definable, observable way, Camp Ederle functioned as a small midwestern American town.

Except for one crucial detail.

When their station wagons were loaded with Skippy peanut butter and Special K cereal and cartons of Marlboro cigarettes and cases of Budweiser beer, these families would drive out Camp Ederle's casually guarded front gates into a foreign country called Italy. Few of the Americans stationed here spoke Italian or knew anything about Italian politics. Most people found their Italian neighbors to be friendly and helpful. Everybody felt safe here.

And nobody is going to love me, Reed thought as he reached the door to the commanding officer's suite, for saying that we are no longer safe here.

"Come in!" came McFadden's deep voice. The base commander was a brainy, mild-mannered two-star general who had seen combat in both Korea and Vietnam. Having served as the number-two man in the Defense Department's code-making and -breaking National Security Agency, McFadden also knew a lot about intelligence operations.

"Good morning, sir."

"Hello, Bill," said McFadden, looking up from a stack of papers. "What do you have for me?"

"General, I think we've got trouble. There is an army of Red Brigade terrorists here in the Veneto region, and since the first of the year, they've shot several senior policemen, a judge, and a corporation executive and kidnapped a couple of industrialists."

"We've been over this before," said McFadden. "I know the Red Brigades are a headache to the Italians, but have they ever threatened an American?"

"Well, you, I think," Reed told him.

McFadden gazed thoughtfully out of his window for a long moment and then turned back to the room with an apologetic smile.

"You have my undivided attention."

"Do you remember my briefing you some time ago that the Carabinieri had raided a deserted Red Brigades hideout in Mestre and turned up a kind of terrorist clipping service? In the file, there was a nice big photograph of you, with a couple of news stories about Camp Ederle."

"I remember," McFadden muttered. "But I'm not sure..."

"It gets worse. This morning we received a cable from the Agency saying that the Carabinieri have got a Red Brigade prisoner talking. It's a man named Michele Galati who was arrested about ten months ago and he says that the Veneto column may be planning to kill an American general."

"There are only three U.S. general officers in northern Italy," McFadden said with a frown. "There's me, Cooney from the Air Force, and Jim Dozier over at NATO. Which one of us is it likely to be?"

"The Agency thinks it's you, and I agree," Reed told him. "You outrank the other two and you've got more visibility. The hard Left sees the U.S. military as the vanguard of American imperialism and you're the imperialist in charge!"

"Damn! Okay, Bill, what do we do?"

"We take it seriously. Bodyguards for you, around the clock, an armored car, and beefed-up security here and at your home. Plus, we need to tell General Cooney and warn General Dozier, just in case."

"Okay," McFadden said. "It won't be easy. We don't want to stir folks up unnecessarily. Cooney and I can move into base housing where we'll be easier to protect. But Jim Dozier is going to be difficult to shield. There's no base in Verona and he's got to move around downtown Verona to do his job."

"At a minimum, we need to run a check on General Dozier's apartment," suggested Reed, grateful that Dozier's security was NATO's responsibility and not his. "Look at the windows, brief his bodyguard, that kind of thing. Will you talk to him, sir?"

"Yeah," agreed McFadden, turning again to look out the window. "Darn! It was so peaceful here...."

"Yes, sir," said Colonel Reed, "but it's not going to be peaceful anymore."

6

5:45 A.M., 18 NOVEMBER 1981
VIA LUNGADIGE CATENA, VERONA

At number 5, Via Lungadige Catena, the American general let the door swing closed behind him and trotted down the front steps to the street. It was still dark. Like medieval sentries guarding a sleeping town, there were streetlamps shrouded in mist and glowing at intervals along the river's edge. The Adige itself was invisible, a dark, sullen presence beneath him, felt and smelled but not yet seen. There had been a frost during the night, and the air was still cold.

There was no traffic, and he jogged across the sidewalk and down into the center of the empty Via Lungadige Catena. A row of oak trees stood along the bank. The actual acorns had long since been expropriated by the squirrels but Dozier's feet crunched over the empty husks.

This is ankle-breaking country, he thought, getting his knees up high, and watching for potholes in the street. There was a layer of frost on the cars parked along the curb, and Dozier began checking to see whether each one had the same white snowy sparkle. A vehicle without frost would be a new arrival, but what would that mean? A teenager on a late date or a night-shift worker? Or a surveillance team sent by the Red Brigades?

Let's face it, he thought, they can take me out any time they want to. And if somebody were going to shoot me, they would have done it long ago.

He was moving too fast now to check on each car, and he tried to forget terrorism and concentrate on jogging. There were a lot of fifty-year-old men who let themselves go, but Dozier was determined not to allow his body to deteriorate. The exercises were imperceptibly harder every year, but he lashed himself into a daily regimen of boot-camp physical conditioning, a long run to start the day, and then a tough round of calisthenics to keep his body supple and strong.

Damn the terrorists, he was thinking as he jogged, recognizing that the whole business was becoming an irritant in his well-ordered existence. The intelligence boys had come up with a prediction that the Red Brigades would try to assassinate one of the American general officers serving in Italy. Because Dozier's NATO assignment freed him from ties to any controversial U.S. base and his position was low-profile and administrative in character, the security people had taken the view that the Red Brigades were unaware of his existence.

George McFadden was deemed to be the most likely target. He was the senior American army officer in Italy with atomic weapons under his operational control. George's duties brought him into daily contact with prominent Italian personalities, some of them politicians opposed to the U.S. presence in Italy, and there had already been antinuclear protest demonstrations in front of SETAF's front gate.

McFadden was no sissy, but he was worried enough to wear a bulletproof vest whenever he appeared in public. The Department of Defense had even produced a specially designed Mercedes armored limousine to carry SETAF's commander back and forth to work, and the major general was under strict orders from NATO Security to alter his schedule daily.

I'm glad the folks over in Vicenza are taking it seriously, he thought, but I like living with a schedule. And how can I go to work at a different time every day? If we get crazy about this, it could get in the way of the important things. Maybe our suspicions are running away with our common sense. Anyway, everybody seems pretty sure that this is a Vicenza problem and not a Verona problem.

Furthermore, it was the wrong season to catch a case of paranoia, not with Thanksgiving a week away and major LANDSOUTH festivities to organize. In fact, in the middle of one of those weeks where every hour has a name tag, a young man from George McFadden's security shop over at SETAF had turned up, requesting permission to tear the Dozier apartment into tiny pieces while he looked for security problems.

You look for security problems, you find 'em! The window leading from the roof terrace into the penthouse bathroom didn't close properly, which meant that the Red Brigades could stroll into their upstairs john any time they wanted to. And nobody had ever thought to install a safety chain for the front door or drill a peephole in it, oversights that breached some obscure regulation somewhere.

Oh, it will all have to be taken care of eventually, Dozier

decided, feeling his body loosen up as he neared the end of the Via Lungadige Catena. And then there was Christmas, only six weeks away! Both of the kids, Cheryl and Scott, were coming for the holidays, and Dozier warmed at the notion of having his family together. Where do we stand on the presents? Gifts for the kids had been ordered, and some serious thought had gone into this year's principal present for Judy, a gold necklace with the Lion of Saint Mark, the symbol of NATO's Southern Command, engraved on a pendant with a gold chain.

Dozier swung away from the river and cut left down a short street to the Via Magellano, a nondescript residential avenue running behind the more stylish Via Lungadige Catena. It was still dark, but the homes here belonged to working-class people, factory foremen, police sergeants, and shopkeepers, most of whom needed to get up early in the morning. Already, there were a few dark shapes on the street, men in leather jackets, their shoulders hunched against the cold, hurrying toward the bar at the corner for a cup of espresso.

Politely, Dozier circled around the pedestrians he met, conscious that dour laborers whose pay packets depended on getting up this early would think him an idiot for being out here voluntarily. Working-class Italians, he had observed, did not jog, hoarding their energies for activities like work and love and—these days—revolution.

At the foot of the Via Magellano, Dozier crossed over into a park and then cut back again onto the main shopping street in their part of Verona, the Via Cristoforo Colombo. Settling into a steady rhythm, he sprinted past food stores and bakeries and bars, some of them already open for early morning customers. There was the scent of freshly baked *cornetti* in the air, and his body was starting to feel good, lithe and healthy.

A short dash up the Via Cristoforo Colombo brought him back to the river, and as he approached the Catena bridge, he caught a hint of the sunrise, a touch of light in the east peeking over the buff-colored rooftops in the Piazza Vittorio Veneto.

A moment later, Dozier could see the door to his residence, and he galloped the last few hundred yards home, feeling like an old war-horse racing for the stable. Judy would still be asleep, and he would turn on the English-language morning news from the American Armed Forces Radio station and hear what was happening in the world while he showered and shaved.

It's Thanksgiving next week, he was thinking, already beginning to plan his schedule for the day and the week to come. And
Christmas will be here before we know it! I hope Judy likes that
pendant.

7

5:45 P.M., 26 NOVEMBER 1981
CENTRAL VERONA

Shivering with the cold, Savasta followed the Via Mazzini as it
meandered into the Piazza Brà, circling north of the giant old
Roman amphitheater. On the edge of the piazza, there were sidewalk cafés but the tables were almost all empty now except for a
few hardy Germans drinking beer.

At the end of the Via Roma, he spotted Cesare Di Lenardo,
sitting outside a sidewalk café opposite the front entrance to
NATO headquarters. Cesare was parked at a corner table, his back
against the wall, his old army duffel coat buttoned up against the
wind. He was heavily bearded, well over six feet, and built like a
prizefighter. Two years earlier, Michele Galati had found him
working for slave wages in a shipyard and recruited him as a Red
Brigades "irregular."

Ever since, the tough, taciturn northerner had proved to be a
good man. A tour with the Italian army had given him a useful
familiarity with heavy weapons and explosives. He was only
twenty-one years old and had no police record. When Savasta took
command of the Veneto column, he put Cesare on the payroll and
made him a full-time clandestine operative. Except for a slight
tendency to take everything too seriously, Di Lenardo had been a
first-rate assistant ever since.

"You're just in time!" he murmured as Savasta slid into a
chair beside him. "That should be our general!"

Savasta looked across the street at the entrance to the NATO
headquarters, a huge, ancient building known as Palazzo Carli.
On either side of the main gate, there were bronze plaques. One
read HEADQUARTERS, ALLIED LAND FORCES SOUTHERN EUROPE in
English and the other repeated this information in Italian, FORZE

TERRESTRI ALLEATI SUD EUROPA. At the moment, the gate was open, and a number of official-looking cars were entering the Palazzo Carli's large inner courtyard.

In the courtyard, there was an American wearing a dark, well-tailored civilian suit, and Savasta recognized him from his photograph in the newspapers. Italian dignitaries were getting out of their limousines, some of them wearing military uniforms, and General Dozier was shaking hands with each of them, smiling and chatting as his guests filed into NATO headquarters.

"Isn't that the *prefetto* standing next to him?" Savasta's interest rose as he spotted the prefect of Verona, the Italian governmental official who functioned as the governor of the entire province. "What do you suppose is going on?"

"It could be . . . maybe the Solidarity crisis is blowing up in Poland," said Di Lenardo. "If there's a war, our general would be in command of NATO's southern front!"

"No, it looks like a party of some kind," Savasta decided. "Our masters are diverting themselves. Look, they're going in!"

The American turned, his arms outstretched as he invited the others to follow him. He strode toward an inner door and disappeared into the depths of LANDSOUTH with all of the important men in Verona trailing behind him. A moment later, the courtyard was empty, except for some limousines. Savasta rose, his mind turning to operational procedures.

"You say he's got a Carabiniere escort who brings him downtown every day?"

"Yeah. This is the third day I've spotted him," said Di Lenardo, throwing some coins on the table to pay for his orange juice and then following Savasta down the Via Roma. "He arrives every morning by eight-thirty and works until five-fifteen and then the Carabiniere takes him home. You could set your watch by the guy."

"Let's see if we can find out where he lives," said Savasta. "But remember that Carabiniere will be looking in his rearview mirror for a tail. Be careful. This could be a trap."

"How could it be a trap? It'll be easy!"

Savasta fell silent. The general did not appear to be well guarded and perhaps it would be easy. On the other hand, there was something about the way the American moved, a kind of body language visible when he led his guests into the NATO building.

I used to be a street fighter, Savasta thought. And that guy was also a street fighter once. I'm going to remember that when we go for him.

8

6:20 P.M., 26 NOVEMBER 1981
LANDSOUTH HEADQUARTERS
PALAZZO CARLI, VIA ROMA, VERONA

The company fell silent. In Palazzo Carli's great medieval hall, most of Verona's dignitaries were assembled to join the American community in the celebration of Thanksgiving, *la festa del ringraziamento*. There were turkey and sweet potatoes and pumpkin pie and a dozen other American recipes that the Italians had never before seen or tasted.

General Dozier glanced at a three-by-five card on which he had written out the blessing in Italian, as he was anxious to avoid a linguistic fumble in his communication with the Almighty. In his private life, Dozier was an itinerant prayer who consulted with his maker whenever the spirit moved him; it was an awkward, unnatural feeling, therefore, this formality of praying publicly and in a foreign language.

"Signore," he said. "We ask you to bless this company and the friendship that unites our peoples and our two nations. Let us always live in peace. Bless this beautiful city where we have found such happiness. Thank you, Lord, for this feast, and for the food we are about to receive. Amen."

"Amen!" responded his guests and the crowd surged toward the turkeys.

9

3:35 A.M., 28 NOVEMBER 1981
PORTO VECCHIO DISTRICT
CENTRAL GENOA

Let at least one of them be here, the commissioner prayed as Blondie spun the Alfa into a dark street near the harbor. Let it be Lo Bianco or let it be Savasta, I don't care! Or let them both be here and we will finish it tonight, one way or the other.

The car slowed as they scanned the shadows for the address provided by their informant. The old harbor district, the Porto Vecchio, was the roughest neighborhood in Genoa, precisely the sort of slum where Lo Bianco preferred to hide, a jungle of cheap hotels and all-night restaurants catering to prostitutes and sailors and undercover DIGOS agents. There were no pedestrians. At this hour, no one in his right mind walked the streets of Genoa.

"Second floor!" Blondie snapped, pointing to an old brick building that might have been a flophouse in better days. "First door on the right."

Blondie was an affable, good-looking undercover officer. They called him *il biondo* because of his great mane of golden hair, and he functioned as Genova's assistant, bodyguard, and driver. In moments of danger, there was no one the commissioner trusted more than Blondie.

Together they raced into the open front doorway of the three-story palazzo and up two flights of stairs. Right behind them came the "boys," the five other members of Commissioner Genova's undercover investigative team, the best in the business.

"Take it down!" Genova roared, and his men threw their shoulders against the doorway. Splintering, the door fell inward, dangling by the bottom hinge, and the commissioner jumped over it into the darkness.

A second later, someone hit the lights, and the team fanned out into a dingy, three-room flat. In the living room, there were two threadbare easy chairs, an old couch, and a badly stained coffee table. Genova kicked open the bedroom door and found only a mattress lying on a wooden floor. The mattress was soiled and smelled of mold. There were no sheets or blankets anywhere.

In the kitchen were stained linoleum on the floor and the remains of dinner still on the table. Genova sniffed, gingerly, learning that two people had consumed plates of linguini garnished with pesto and Parmesan cheese not long before. There was a chipped, dirty beaker on the table with a few drops of cheap red wine still moist at the bottom. The smell was fresh; this was tonight's dinner.

One of the boys kicked a wall in frustration, but they were too well trained to waste time complaining about the disappointment. While someone called a report into the Corso Aurelio Saffei headquarters of the Genoa police, the rest of the team began a methodical search of the deserted flat. Genova's men were occasionally criticized by straight-laced senior Polizia di Stato officials for their unconventional investigative techniques and extraordinary sloppiness of attire, but the boys usually got results, even if they routinely ignored the rule book in the process.

Salvatore Genova wandered over to a window and gazed out at the darkened city while his heartbeat slowly returned to normal. In his thirty-fourth year, Genova was a big man, over six feet in height, with the chest and biceps of a boxer. His rugged appearance notwithstanding, he was an intellectual who had come to police work after first working as a professor of jurisprudence at the University of Bari and then practicing labor law for a few years. In the restlessness of his early thirties, he had taken a competitive Interior Ministry examination for senior civil service positions. To his surprise, the State Police had offered him an appointment as a *commissario* of police.

He had reported for duty in 1978, a few months before the Red Brigades murdered Aldo Moro. After his training, the Ministry assigned him to antiterrorist work with the DIGOS. When Antonio Esposito of the Genoa Questura was assassinated by Francesco Lo Bianco, DIGOS headquarters had shipped in Genova as Esposito's replacement.

And I've been hunting Lo Bianco ever since, he thought, Lo Bianco and Barbara Balzarani and Antonio Savasta, the untouchables. And who among them had been here tonight, eating linguini? This is the sort of dump Lo Bianco might use for a crash meeting of some kind; would Savasta have come over from the Veneto region to give his old companion in arms a helping hand?

Genova shuddered at the thought. Savasta was the son of a policeman who had grown up to become a cop killer. In the summer of 1979, a Carabiniere colonel named Antonio Varisco had been making a series of important arrests, hurting the Rome column badly. Anxious to destroy a dangerous adversary, the Red Brigades assigned Savasta the task of eliminating him.

Somehow, Savasta managed to locate Varisco's private apartment. On the appointed day, Savasta followed the colonel across town in a stolen car. To force him to stop, Savasta fired a smoke grenade through the window of the speeding BMW. When the stunned Varisco slammed on the brakes, Savasta methodically shot him dead with two blasts from a shotgun.

It had all happened in broad daylight, in the city center with dozens of witnesses. And Savasta had promptly vanished. A few months later, the Rome DIGOS cornered Savasta in a fifth-story apartment, but as they broke down the door, Savasta jumped out the window, swinging from balcony to balcony like an acrobat until he had descended a hundred feet to the street level and disappeared, as usual, without trace.

"Whoever it was, they won't be back for breakfast, *capo*," said one of his men, handing Genova three crumpled mimeographed sheets of paper. "But we found this by the bed."

Genova studied the document with a trained eye. At the top of the first page, there was the classic five-pointed Red Brigades star. Below this in capital letters were the words RISOLUZIONE STRATEGICA GENERALE.

"The crisis of capitalism creates imperialist war!" proclaimed the General Strategic Resolution.

> Only anti-imperialist civil war can bring an end to war! In this era of imperialism by multinational corporations, the urban proletariat has constituted itself as the vanguard of proletarian revolution across the world. War against the dominion of American imperialism! Attack the imperialism of the multinational corporations and NATO. . . .

Since when do the Red Brigades worry about NATO? Genova shrugged, puzzled at this new ingredient. Red Brigade propaganda statements were poorly written and made tedious reading, but they often contained crucial insights into subtle shifts in revolutionary thinking. He tucked the document into his pocket for further study.

"Coming, *capo?*" asked Blondie.

"Be right down," muttered the commissioner, wandering back into the bedroom for one last look. There was nothing there. It was pointless to expect that Lo Bianco would forget his address book or that Savasta would leave an autographed photograph of himself. Had there been something to find, the boys would have found it.

It's got to be over soon, guys, he thought, trying to ward off dispair as he addressed himself mentally to Lo Bianco and Savasta. One of these days, I'm going to kick a door down and you will be there and I will either arrest you or kill you. You've had a run for your money, but someday soon you're going to make a mistake. And when you do, I'm going to be standing right behind you.

10

5:15 P.M., 3 DECEMBER 1981
ADIGE RIVER, VERONA

He should be there any minute now, Di Lenardo assured himself as he chained the Lambretta to a fence.

In the fast-fading light, the former soldier edged through the empty cars in the parking lot toward the Adige River. It was already after five. At the riverbank, Di Lenardo dropped to one knee and trained his binoculars on an apartment building six hundred feet away on the opposite shore.

The address was 5, Via Lungadige Catena, a suitable one for a senior officer in the American army of occupation. The neighborhood was low-key but eminently respectable and upper middle class. The general's residence was in an eight-story building with a balcony extending out from each apartment.

Di Lenardo glanced at his wristwatch. The familiar navy blue Fiat was crossing the Catena bridge and it was precisely twenty minutes after five. Dozier might be a militarist pig, he thought wryly, but you really could set your watch by the guy.

The staff car came to a halt on the pavement in front of number 5, and the American jumped out, waving over his shoulder at the Carabiniere driver before heading into the building. A few minutes later, Di Lenardo spotted a light on the seventh floor, followed a moment later by a second light on the top floor as the general moved through his split-level penthouse apartment.

Di Lenardo walked out of the parking lot and crossed over the Catena bridge. Along the river side of the street, there were a row of oak trees and a few park benches where a surveillance team could plausibly sit and read when the time came to bring the apartment under continuous observation. In fact, bus stop number 5—a few steps from the general's front door—would also be convenient, because a couple of *brigatisti* could stand there and pretend to wait for the downtown bus without arousing suspicions.

Would there be a guard? How could he get inside the apartment building for a reconnaissance without arousing suspicions?

In a ground-floor window at number 5, Via Lungadige Catena, there was a sign announcing the presence of a company called Sports Systems. Without breaking his stride, Di Lenardo crossed the avenue and pushed the Sports Systems doorbell. It was a *citofono*, a standard European double-buzzer system with separate outside and inside door locks, both electronically controlled, as well as an intercom over which visitors could identify themselves.

"Chi è?" A woman's voice from the Sports Systems office issued from the loudspeaker.

"Municipio!" said Di Lenardo, identifying himself as a municipal council employee. A second later, there was a buzzing sound; the front door was being unlocked from within and he stepped into the foyer. There were some potted plants, the entrance to an elevator, and a hallway leading to a backdoor. Di Lenardo gave the lobby a careful glance before knocking at the inner door to the Sports System office. When a second buzz told him that this door was also unlocked, he put his head into the office.

"Is this number 5, Via Porta Catena?" he asked, mentioning a nearby street with a similar name.

"No, this is number 5, Via Lungadige Catena," said the typist. "Go back out, turn right, and keep going after you pass the bridge."

"Grazie!" Di Lenardo sang out, shutting the door behind him. He then walked through the empty foyer and took the elevator up to General Dozier's floor. When he looked out, he found the hallway empty. On three of the four doors, there were Italian family names identifying the residents. On the fourth door there was no name, an apparent attempt by the general to be discreet. But there was no spyhole or any evidence of a security system.

He let the elevator door close and pushed the button for the ground floor. A moment later, he was back on the street, walking toward the Catena bridge. He paused at the top of the bridge and looked back up at the lights from the penthouse apartment, feeling the anger within. Cesare had spent his army days learning to shoot guns and hate officers. The higher their rank, the more he hated them.

Good night, Generale Dozier, he thought. Sleep tight, pig.

11

8:15 P.M., 5 DECEMBER 1981
VIA MONTE ORTIGARA, VERONA

"What do you suppose Savasta wants?" Alessandro Arcangeli was saying as he spooned the last of the *ragù* over the few remaining strands of fettucini on his plate. "You know, I preferred Michele Galati as leader. He had a sense of style."

"It's wonderful how Michele manages to stay in contact," Lisa Arcangeli agreed. "Even though he's in prison and it must be dangerous for his brother to bring us messages. Brave little Paolo!"

"Oh, Savasta's not bad," Ruggiero Volinia said. As a comparative newcomer to the Verona brigade, he was beginning to find this treasonous conversation uncomfortable.

"Well, he's technically proficient and awfully lucky," conceded Alessandro. "What do you suppose he'll want with us?"

"I don't know," said Ruggiero, hoping that whatever Savasta wanted would not involve him.

"I think Savasta has a rich physical presence, a kind of inner intensity," Lisa Arcangeli said. "Don't you think so, Ruggiero?"

Volinia shrugged, preferring to dodge the question. He looked into his woman's eyes wondering what it was that had brought them together. Lisa was an intellectual, and, like her brother, she was a schoolteacher with a university degree. Ruggiero was merely an unemployed factory worker without academic credentials.

"You're jealous," she giggled at him, and he felt her fingers reaching amorously for his hand beneath the table. She was a short woman, only twenty-four, but already becoming a little thick in the waist. Her carelessly cut brown hair, wire-rimmed glasses, and bib jeans gave her an unglamorous, bohemian appearance, and yet. . . . He looked at his watch. The sooner Savasta came, stated his business, and went, the sooner the two of them could snuggle into Lisa's big bed.

There was a knock at the door.

"I'll go," Ruggiero offered, because no one else seemed inclined to move. He walked through the book-lined salon to the front door of the comfortable middle-class apartment Alessandro Arcangeli shared with his younger sister.

He opened the door and saw a figure standing in the shadows of the garden.

"Emilio?" he inquired, using Savasta's code name. "Come in! We'll give you some wine, and the others are still—"

"No, we'll talk here," Savasta told him. "Listen, we have something in the works, and I'm going to need your help."

"What do we have to do?"

"I need a driver, somebody who knows Verona," Savasta said. "Get your things and tell Lisa you won't be seeing her for a while."

Volinia reentered the apartment, his emotions boiling, wondering what would happen if he refused. He and Lisa could go away, find jobs, and start a family. If there were only a little money—

"What . . . where is he?" asked Lisa.

"He wants me to go with him," Ruggiero explained, hoping that she would tell him not to go, that she needed him here by her side. "He says I could be gone for a while."

"Oh, *carissimo!*" She hugged him. "Oh, I'll miss you so much. . . . I'll be right here, waiting for you . . . when you come back."

"It's an honor for you!" Alessandro Arcangeli called out.

Ruggiero kissed Lisa again, feeling her body trembling. He wanted to talk but she put a finger against his lips and said that they mustn't keep "Emilio" waiting. He stopped in her bedroom for the suitcase of extra clothes and toiletries he kept there and then went out into the garden.

In silence, Savasta led him to a waiting Fiat Ritmo. There was a woman sitting in the passenger seat; Ruggiero guessed that this might be "Martina," the famous Emilia Libera. But Savasta did not offer to introduce her, and Ruggiero did not dare to ask.

"Would you lie down on the backseat on your stomach?" Savasta demanded as he started the Ritmo's engine.

"Why?" Ruggiero asked.

"We try to keep information compartmentalized," the woman explained, her voice a soft, pleasant purr. "We're taking you to a house where we'll spend the night but—"

"But there's no need at this time for you to know where it is," said Savasta. "Get your head down, okay?"

"Okay." Ruggiero was glad that Lisa was not there to see this humiliation. Lying down on the seat, he watched the stars and the streetlamps as Savasta drove him through the night. When they stopped, he knew that they had taken him to a suburb called San Giovanni Lupatoto, because he had been able to feel from the motion of the Ritmo when they turned and where. But he kept silent. Savasta was supposed to have killed a large number of people in his career.

It was better to say nothing.

12

2:45 P.M., 6 DECEMBER 1981
THE ENVIRONS OF PADUA

"I think it's a bad idea," Emilia Libera said as Savasta turned off an obscure country road and took their elderly Fiat into the southern suburbs of Padua. "Do you seriously want to use an apartment registered under the real name of an untrained irregular, a pot-smoking rich girl with boyfriends coming and going?"

"Emanuela isn't going to have any pot or boyfriends for a

while," Cesare Di Lenardo commented gruffly from the Ritmo's backseat. "And we'll feel more comfortable in Padua."

"I'd feel more comfortable in Rome," Emilia retorted and lapsed into irritated silence. The landscape began to change as they turned onto the Via Guizza in the far south of Padua. It was a strange, jumbled neighborhood where century-old stone farmhouses coexisted with inexpensive high-rise apartment buildings that had been built ten years ago and would be torn down in another decade. There were empty bottles in the gutter and rusted bicycles and abandoned cars and garbage that looked as if it were never going to be collected.

"There's Emanuela's building over there," Cesare pointed at a large apartment building over a supermarket. "That's the Via Pindemonte."

Antonio maneuvered the car into the parking lot on the corner of Via Guizza and Via Pindemonte, and they all got out to inspect the building. The entire ground floor was occupied by the Dea Supermarket, so they would not have to go far for provisions. Emilia calculated that the nine-story building would have sixty-four smallish apartments; the *portiere* would be unable to remember all the unfamiliar faces he saw in a day. The outside needed a coat of paint, and there was the usual disorderly forest of television antennas on the roof. Each apartment had the inevitable tiny balcony; some were overflowing with plants, and others looked seedy with washing lines and piles of rusty garden furniture. There were ten thousand palazzi just like it between Sicily and the Alps, and Emilia guessed that nobody would ever look at this one twice.

Following the two men through the supermarket's crowded parking lot, Emilia grappled with anger and fear. Antonio was doing his best to reassure her, bringing in trusted Romans to play all the key roles in the actual kidnap operation, but he planned to use the inexperienced Ruggiero Volinia as a driver for the escape vehicle, because Ruggiero knew the streets and avenues of his native Verona more intimately than any of the Romans.

Savasta had also insisted on having a male nurse from the Veneto column standing by not far from the scene of their operation with enough medical equipment to deal with possible gunshot wounds. The nurse would not need access to any information about the operation. He would be instructed to stand by in a specified and convenient bar near a public phone. If he were needed, he would be called. Otherwise, he could go home and forget what had happened.

After the abduction, Savasta planned to move their captive out of Verona and they needed an absolutely secure safe house in a nearby city to serve as a "proletarian prison." To provide the apartment, Di Lenardo had proposed that they use as their *vivandiere* in Padua a young woman named Emanuela Frascella, another "native" from the Veneto column.

Nothing that Emilia Libera knew about Emanuela Frascella struck her as reassuring. The girl was untrained and inexperienced in clandestine operations. She had never fired a gun. And worst of all, Emanuela came from a wealthy family. Emilia found it difficult to accept that the rich could ever make an authentic commitment to the overthrow of the economic system that kept them rich. Emanuela's father was a physician who specialized in lung diseases; the mother was a psychologist; the family owned a yacht.

"How long has she been with us?" Emilia asked as they reached the entrance to the apartment building. There was a porter's station on the right, but no *portiere* was on duty at the moment.

"Michele Galati brought her aboard a couple of years ago, but he never used her for an operation," Cesare Di Lenardo explained. "She's rich but Emanuela intends to exploit her family's wealth for the benefit of the proletariat—and she rejects her parent's bourgeois values, which is why she lives down here on the Via Guizza."

"Who owns the apartment?" Emilia demanded.

"She does. Her father gave it to her."

"Always easier to reject bourgeois values when you own your own apartment." She followed the two men up the stairs to the second floor. The door to apartment number 2 opened promptly in response to Cesare's knock, and the physician's daughter stood before them. She was a slender young woman with hair teased into tight little ringlets, wearing designer jeans and a sweatshirt with HARVARD UNIVERSITY written across the front of it. Her body was slim and attractive and her face was gamine.

"Ciao," she whispered, her eyes darting from face to face. "I'm Emanuela. Come in, please."

The apartment was not large. In a glance, Emilia could see that it consisted of four smallish rectangular rooms with a corridor at one end connecting them all and leading into a minuscule bathroom with a shower stall and a toilet and a bidet. The kitchen was clean but cluttered, with a television sitting on the breakfast table and bottles of olive oil and wine crowded on top of the refrigerator. At the far end of the kitchen, there was a set of French doors leading out onto the balcony, which was piled with junk. There was no work space; Emilia tried to imagine creating dinners for a gang of hungry urban guerrillas and one captive American general without a decent place to cook.

The next room was the *soggiorno*, or living room, with a couch and a music center. Along one wall there was a sideboard with a marble top, and in the middle of the room there was a large desk. There were two smaller rooms, one with a single bed and one with a double. Emanuela obviously liked teddy bears, because there was at least one in every room. Teddy bears, thought Emilia wearily. She wants to overthrow the government without quite managing to outgrow teddy bears?

Do I want to live in another woman's home, she wondered, for weeks or maybe months? The place was too small and too disorderly and—no, it was out of the question. Antonio and Cesare had disappeared into the back bedroom and were deep in a technical discussion about cameras and darkroom supplies and machine guns and mimeographs and chains and a tent, and how it all had to fit somewhere with enough room left over for five *brigatisti* and a prisoner.

Without warning, Emanuela Frascella entered the *soggiorno*, carrying a cup of tea.

"I . . . do you like tea?"

"Oh, well, thank you." Emilia was startled at this sudden thoughtfulness. It was a real teacup, not a mug, and Emanuela had remembered to put it on a saucer. Feeling awkward, Emilia sank onto the living room couch and sipped. It was terrible. God help the general, she thought bleakly, if he wants a cup of tea.

"Listen . . . ah, I wanted to say, ah . . ." Emanuela began as she sat down on a wicker chair, twisting her hands between her knees. "I know I'm silly sometimes, but I believe what the rest of you believe, and I want to be part of what you're doing."

"Well, Emilio is the chief of the Veneto column," Emilia said stiffly. "It will be his decision. . . ."

"No, don't put me off like that!" Suddenly, there were tears brimming in Emanuela's eyes, and she reached out and seized one of Emilia's hands. "I know I'm not supposed to know who you are but I've heard how brave you are and I could learn so much from you, and I need, I mean, my life is so empty without something to believe in, and people, some people to share it with and . . . everything."

There did not seem much to say. Savasta and Di Lenardo came into the *soggiorno*, still talking. "We could put the tent in there," Antonio was saying, pointing into the first of the two bedrooms. Then he glanced in Emilia's direction and raised his eyebrows questioningly.

"This will do, won't it?" he demanded. "I think this should be fine."

"Where will everyone sleep?" Emilia asked. What madness it has all become, she was thinking. We're going to infuriate the most powerful country in the world and place our fate in the hands of a rich doctor's daughter and a collection of teddy bears.

"We'll need some more mattresses, but the two of you can take the double bed in the back bedroom," Cesare decreed. "And I'll sleep in the living room."

"And I . . ." Emanuela stammered nervously, her eyes focused on Cesare's face. "I—"

"You'll sleep in the living room with me," Di Lenardo added, as if this were the merest of details. Emilia watched as the young girl blushed.

"All right then?" Antonio asked, his eyes on Emilia's face. "Shall we get the stuff in from the car?"

I don't want to do this, she thought. Is this the time to quit? I could go to Paris and study medicine at the Sorbonne. Others have left before me, but it would mean looking Antonio in the face and saying what we always swore we would never say, that the passion is gone, that the revolution is never going to happen, that nobody really believes in it anymore.

Either you go away now or you stay a little longer, she told herself as she nodded her consent and rose to help with the unpacking. So you stay a little longer. You move in with the teddy bears and see what happens to people who kidnap American generals.

13

4:45 P.M., 17 DECEMBER 1981
VIA PORTO, SAN GIOVANNI LUPATOTO
SUBURB OF VERONA

"When is your general going to come home so we can kidnap him?" Pietro Vanzi asked, putting his feet on the sofa and yawning. One of Savasta's oldest friends, Vanzi was a big man, over six feet tall and well muscled, and he was one of the quickest thinkers in the Organizzazione. A few months earlier, the big Roman had found himself trapped inside a building and surrounded by police. With incredible coolness, Vanzi had rushed out, waving a pistol and shouting, "I'm a policeman! Let me pass!" By the time the Polizia di Stato officers realized that he was not one of them, Vanzi had vanished.

"I don't know," Savasta confessed. It was Thursday. The operation had been planned for Monday, but General Dozier had disappeared, leaving his apartment early one morning with a light valise and failing to return, although his wife had been observed coming and going normally.

Could he have been warned? Impossible. Even if he had fled, the general would hardly leave the Signora Dozier behind.

Ever since Monday, the group had been ready to move, and every day Di Lenardo's watch team had reported that the target was still missing. Savasta was beginning to wonder how much longer he could keep his people cooped up before the neighbors noticed the presence of a small army in Armando Lanza's front room.

"When are the rented cars due back?" Vanzi asked, his mind also working on the implications of the delay. The previous week, Savasta and Cesare Di Lenardo had gone to an obscure rental agency in Milan and hired two Fiat sedans, a 127 and a 128, for general passenger use, and a Fiat 238 van for the actual transport of their target.

"Tomorrow," Savasta told him. On Tuesday, they had called to extend the rental until the end of the week, but the car-hire firm would not revise the rental contract a second time without the payment of an additional deposit. Because they had rented the cars using false identity papers, it would not be safe to visit the agency again. Unless the operation could be carried out within twenty-four hours, therefore, the three rented vehicles would have to be driven out of Verona and dumped, delaying the operation until fresh "wheels" could be secured.

"Are the Sterlings in good shape?" Vanzi was working his way down his own checklist.

"Di Lenardo has test-fired all five Sterlings, and we've got those American hand grenades," Savasta assured him, mentally thanking the tangled world of Palestinian politics for his arsenal of heavy weapons. Two years earlier, the PLO chairman Yasir Arafat had secretly promised to keep Middle Eastern terrorism out of Italy in return for a more pro-Palestinian Italian foreign policy. The Italian government had consented, but Palestinian extremists had supplied a hoard of weapons to the Red Brigades as a way of demonstrating that Arafat's guarantees were worthless. The bulk of the weapons were stored in a secret Red Brigades arsenal in Mestre, near Venice.

"With this crowd, we should be able to fight our way past anything smaller than an army platoon," mused Vanzi gesturing at the team of *brigatisti* sprawled in Armando's front room.

It was a good group. Giovanni Ciucci was the veteran leader of a Red Brigades unit in Tuscany, a would-be scholar who carried an enormous pile of books on Marxism around with him. Opposite him was Marcello Capuano, an experienced, intensely committed Red Brigades professional on loan from the Rome column, flicking cigarette ash on Lanza's rug while he consumed endless cups of espresso.

Sitting by herself in another corner, reading a newspaper and looking several times tougher than any of the men, was a stern-looking blonde in her midthirties named Alberta Biliato, brought in by Di Lenardo from the Udine brigade to do escort duty.

"Listen, suppose the general pulls a gun?" Vanzi asked, but the phone rang before Savasta could reply. He allowed it to ring five agonizing times before answering. The room went deadly still.

"Pronto?"

"Ciao!" It was Di Lenardo, calling from his station in a telephone booth near Dozier's downtown office. There was an excited edge to his voice. "I think tonight would be a good night to have a chicken for dinner!"

"It's about time we had chicken," replied Savasta, his eyes meeting Vanzi's. He nodded slowly. At the moment, Savasta could not remember why or when they had begun to call Dozier "the chicken," but if the police had somehow managed to intercept this call, a conversation about having *pollo* for dinner would not arouse any suspicions.

"See you soon then," agreed Di Lenardo and he rang off without further comment.

Gently, Savasta replaced the receiver. "Chicken for dinner," he announced to his team in a matter-of-fact tone. "He's just left for home." There was a bustle of activity as people got to their feet and assembled equipment and disguises. There were no cheers. Savasta watched as Emilia slipped her Beretta into her handbag. There was no expression on her face.

"Suppose he resists?" Pietro Vanzi repeated his question.

"If he pulls a gun," Savasta said as he took his Browning automatic out of the desk drawer and slapped a clip of shells into the handle, "then we kill him. Let's go."

BOOK II

THE
KIDNAP

1

"Buona sera, Di Nardo," said the general as he stepped out of the staff car, his mind on other things.

"Signor Si!" responded the sergeant. "Buona sera, Signor Generale."

It's been a darn tough week, Dozier thought as he strode toward the entrance to number 5. The Polish situation was tense. General Jaruzelski was putting most of Solidarity behind bars, and the intelligence reports looked bad. If the Russians invaded Poland, the cold war could warm up in a hurry.

Then, at the beginning of the week, there had been a last-minute decision to send him to a NATO meeting in Naples. There were two senior Italian officers assigned to LANDSOUTH who might have gone, but the Italians did not enjoy conferences where the principal language was English, and Dozier had been deputized to attend in their stead. And while he was in Naples, the work had continued to pile up on his desk back in Verona, and his briefcase was now filled with letters that needed answering.

On the elevator car, Dozier remembered that there was a meeting tonight of the Verona Community Activities Association, of which he was president. Looking after the small American community in Verona was a job he liked, but it was still work.

Ah well, perhaps they could escape early. Getting out on the top floor, Dozier put his key into the lock and pushed open the door to his apartment. In his years as a soldier, he had lived in apartments and houses and tents and tiny rooms in officers' quarters all over the world, and he knew that when the day came to retire and go home to Florida, he would always remember this lovely flat in Verona with unusual affection.

It was his sanctuary in an unruly world. On the lower floor were the kitchen and a sprawling living room that opened out

63

onto a balcony. Their bedroom was in the penthouse proper, and from the window they could see the Alps.

"Hi, hon?" he called. There was no answer, which meant that his wife had not yet returned. Dozier glanced at his wristwatch, calculating the maximum lateness that could be integrated into the evening's program. He was a methodical man, who had long been obliged to live a systematic existence, a life measured out in allotments of minutes and hours.

It was only twenty after five, which meant that there would be time for a drink and a fast dinner, assuming that Judy was not more than ten minutes late. He climbed the circular staircase to their bedroom, where he traded his class A uniform for a pair of trousers; a long-sleeved, black turtleneck knit shirt; and a pair of Hush Puppies. He was back in the kitchen, mixing himself a vodka martini, when he heard a key in the lock.

"Sorry, hon, have I made us late?" his wife asked, entering the kitchen. Judy was dressed with her usual stylishness, a blouse-and-sweater combination over a skirt and boots. Impulsively, she dropped her packages on the table and kissed him.

"We won't be late," he assured her, putting his arms around her waist and giving her a substantial hug. "Want some wine?"

"A little of the red, maybe," she replied, stepping back and inspecting him. "You know, those trousers don't go with that shirt. In fact, those trousers will never go with anything!"

"Un-huh," he said, wondering how anyone could work up any emotion over an ordinary pair of trousers in which dark blue, maroon and white were integrated into an intricate checkered pattern.

He poured her a glass of red wine. They had celebrated their twenty-fifth wedding anniversary in June and Dozier was certain that their happiness over the past quarter-century was the result of certain protocols that had been tacitly negotiated between them. It was her wifely privilege to inform him when his civilian clothes failed to meet her sartorial standards; it was his prerogative to overrule her when he felt like being comfortable.

"Oh, I met Aldo Marulli coming in," Judy remarked as Jim settled into a chair at the kitchen table and spread the accumulated mail out before him.

"Good!" The general had always marveled at his wife's ability to establish solid new friendships no matter where the army sent them. Aldo and Franca Marulli, who lived downstairs, had assumed the task of introducing Jim and Judy to Verona. "Are we still scheduled to see that art show on Saturday with him and Franca?"

"It's still on. Look, let me get some dinner started and I'll help with that mail."

While he worked, Judy slid some frozen fish into the microwave oven and then put some fresh carrots and potatoes on to boil. Then she took a sip of her red wine and joined him at the table.

"Are we going to be late?" she asked.

"Don't worry," he smiled. "We've got all the time in the world."

2

5:25 P.M., 17 DECEMBER 1981
VIA LUNGADIGE CATENA, VERONA

Antonio Savasta checked his image in the rearview mirror. The false beard itched like hell.

"There they are," muttered Pietro Vanzi, who was lounging in the passenger seat of the Fiat 128, looking resplendent in a similar set of false whiskers. Savasta steered the car into the parking lot on the east bank of the Adige where Di Lenardo and Marcello Capuano were standing under a tree. It was twenty-five minutes after five, and at this hour there was a lot of coming and going. No one was likely to take any notice of a quick conversation among four men wearing workmen's overalls.

Savasta had divided his forces into three separate teams. He and Vanzi were prepared to make the critical entry into the Dozier apartment. Cesare Di Lenardo and Marcello Capuano would join them once the prisoner had been secured, and Giovanni Ciucci and Emilia Libera would remain with the Fiat van, with Ruggiero Volinia at the wheel. Everyone was armed. In the event that an alarm was somehow sounded and the Carabinieri arrived, the team down on the street had the responsibility of holding them off long enough for the four men inside the building to make their escape.

"Our chicken entered the apartment at five-fifteen," Di Lenardo reported. "His wife came in seven minutes later."

"That Carabiniere sergeant?" Vanzi asked.

"Gone!" Di Lenardo shrugged. "As far as we can see there's no surveillance at all, and there shouldn't be anybody inside the apartment but the two of them."

"*Mi senti?*" The powerful military walkie-talkie lying on the seat purred with Emilia's voice. "Can you hear me?"

Driving the rented Fiat 127, Emilia and Ruggiero Volinia were only a few minutes away now, and it was time to wave them off if the operation were to be aborted. Savasta bent down to conceal what he was doing from any idle passerby.

"Okay," he responded, speaking into the microphone of the walkie-talkie. "*Tutto bene.*"

Emilia clicked the push-to-talk button at him in acknowledgment and went off the air. The operations plan was now rolling. Emilia would guide Ruggiero to a designated spot behind the Dozier apartment. They would park the 127 there and leave it, because Savasta liked having spare wheels available during an operation. If everything went according to plan, the 127 would be abandoned. Emilia and Ruggiero would then transfer to the Fiat 238 van, which had been parked on the Via Magellano behind the Dozier apartment building several hours earlier.

Emilia and Ruggiero would wait in the van, staying out of sight until they were needed, and monitoring both Polizia di Stato and Carabiniere transmissions for advance warning. Meanwhile, Giovanni Ciucci was circling the block on the Lambretta motor scooter, maintaining surveillance and waiting for the others to get into position.

"*Andiamo,*" breathed Savasta, glancing up at Cesare Di Lenardo. The big former soldier nodded and called to Marcello Capuano, who was still sitting silently on the bank of the Adige, smoking. When Capuano heard Di Lenardo's voice, he flicked his cigarette toward the river, and the two of them headed across the bridge on foot.

This is going to be the tricky part, Savasta thought, starting the Fiat. There must be no delay when we all meet in front of that door or somebody will get suspicious. It must all look natural!

He swung the car out of the parking lot and took it over the bridge, passing Di Lenardo and Capuano midway. At the foot of the bridge, he paused, seeing Giovanni Ciucci approach from the opposite direction on the Lambretta and park in front of the Dozier residence.

"He's going in," Pietro Vanzi said as Ciucci approached the door and pushed the bell for the Sports Systems office on the ground floor. Giovanni would make an inquiry about the price of body-building equipment and then leave.

The time sequences were critical. Savasta slid past the Total station on the corner of the Via Lungadige Catena and parked the Fiat around the corner, just out of sight. He stepped out of the car, leather plumber's bag in hand. Vanzi joined him a second later, and they walked around the corner past the bar and the stationery shop, seeing Di Lenardo and Capuano strolling up on the river side of the avenue. As Savasta and Pietro Vanzi approached the entrance to number 5, they spotted Giovanni Ciucci on the other side of the glass door and picked up their pace.

"Buona sera," Ciucci spoke in a matter-of-fact tone of voice as he opened the condominium's main door and stepped out, giving no sign that he had ever seen Savasta or Vanzi before.

"Grazie, signore," responded Savasta, catching the door before it could close and engage the lock. Without a backward glance, Ciucci strode off down the Lungadige Catena, heading for the Fiat van where Emilia and Ruggiero were waiting. Meanwhile, Savasta and Vanzi walked casually into the condominium, but before the glass door could close behind them it was caught by Cesare Di Lenardo and Marcello Capuano, who followed them into the foyer.

There had been repair crews in this apartment building all week, and Savasta was assuming that no one would pay any attention to them. We are merely four proletarian plumbers coming to fix the leaky pipes of the bourgeoisie, he thought with dark humor.

The lobby was empty. Wordlessly, Di Lenardo and Capuano started up the stairs. Vanzi opened the doors of the elevator and got on with Savasta. The big Roman pushed the button for the third floor. The old carriage jerked upward a few inches and then stopped.

"That's all we need," said Savasta. Vanzi poked the button a second time and the elevator obeyed. When they reached the third floor, Savasta paused and then took it down to the second. He then climbed to the sixth floor, giving Di Lenardo and Capuano a chance to get into position. The building seemed quiet. Seeing Di Lenardo and Capuano catch up to them on the sixth floor, Savasta pushed the button for the seventh.

As they reached Dozier's landing, he dropped to one knee and opened his leather plumber's bag, extracted a Beretta nine-millimeter automatic pistol with an aluminum silencer, and handed it to Vanzi. There was a second silenced automatic in the bag, identical to the first. Snapping off the safety, Savasta inserted it into the pocket of his overalls. His usual Browning automatic was tucked into the back of his trousers as a reserve.

Vanzi opened the door to the elevator wide enough to take a quick look at the hallway. There was no one there. Marcello Capuano and Cesare Di Lenardo were hiding just around the corner of the staircase, armed and ready to intervene if Savasta and Pietro ran into anything they couldn't handle.

"Let's go!" Savasta spoke in an undertone, putting a hand on Vanzi's shoulder. "Quietly!"

"Suppose he won't open up?"

"Then we shoot him through the door," Savasta told him, and he rang the bell.

3

5:30 P.M., 17 DECEMBER 1981
VIA LUNGADIGE CATENA, VERONA

That's the inside bell, Jim Dozier realized, looking up from a letter. Not the *citofono* on the street. There's someone out there—

Theoretically, this was not supposed to happen. Visitors were meant to ring from the street level and identify themselves before getting access to the lobby. Of course, one of their neighbors from within the condominium itself could be calling on them, perhaps Franca Marulli from downstairs, but it was unlikely at this hour.

The general rose and walked toward the door.

"That makes me uncomfortable," Judy warned. "Maybe you shouldn't—"

"Don't worry." Like most West Pointers, Dozier moved into

situations with a sense of physical self-confidence. He was not an arrogant man, or a violent one, but even in his fiftieth year he tended to open doors with the implicit assumption that he could deal with anything he found on the other side.

"*Chi è?*" he called out.

"*Generale, siamo idraulici incaricati di riparare una perdita,*" Savasta responded from the other side of the door. It took Dozier a few seconds to digest the message. An *idraulico* is probably a hydraulic engineer, or a plumber, and *perdita* means a leak somewhere. His first concern was their evening schedule. How long would it take two *idraulici* to locate and repair a *perdita*?

He opened the door, facing two young men with full beards and floppy moustaches. They were both wearing workman's uniforms. One was a hulking man with heavy, black, bushy eyebrows, and impressive muscles. His colleague, who was carrying a leather bag and gave the impression of being in charge, was a short, slender guy, about five foot ten.

"*Da una tubazione del suo apartamento filtra acqua di sotto,*" Savasta explained.

"We've sprung a leak," the general translated in a matter-of-fact tone as Judy looked questioningly from the kitchen door. "They say there's water trickling into Pio and Mariagrazia's place downstairs."

Judy nodded and ducked back into the kitchen. Dozier led the way into a combination bathroom and utility room where the washing machine and drier were kept and dropped to his hands and knees to look for the leak.

As he inspected the tubing, Judy appeared in the doorway. "Honey, I used the washing machine today," she volunteered.

"*Niente,*" Dozier reported, looking up at the two visitors. "The floor is dry as a bone."

"*Il termosifone?*" Savasta inquired.

"What's a '*termosifone*'?" the general asked; it was not a word he could immediately bring to the surface of his consciousness. "I'll get the dictionary."

He sprang to his feet and followed Judy down the corridor to the kitchen.

As the general flipped through his dictionary, Savasta grabbed him from behind, throwing him momentarily off balance as he tried to pin his arms. Absurdly, Dozier's first thought was that this had to be an exercise of some kind, some macabre drill organized by an insane army security officer to test his level of preparedness. In front of him, Pietro Vanzi pulled out a silenced automatic and waved it at him.

"We are the Red Brigades!" Savasta said from behind him. The words came in a garbled English, but the general's first reaction was that the smaller man had demanded money. In that corner of his mind that always kept ticking away even in emergencies, Dozier somehow found time to observe that the silencer on Vanzi's gun had never been used, because the padding inside was still new and clean.

Then Savasta pushed him violently forward and Dozier's temper flared. Ignoring Vanzi's pistol, he struck out at the big Roman, charging into the hallway with Savasta clinging to his back and Pietro Vanzi retreating.

"I don't have any money!" he roared. "What do you want? This is stupid!"

"Be careful or we will kill you!"

In the middle of one of those fragments of time when the room was spinning and everyone was shouting in at least two languages, Vanzi stood his ground and swung furiously in Dozier's direction. The general never saw the punch coming, but Vanzi hit him hard enough to split the skin over his left eye.

He did not quite lose consciousness, but he went down on his hands and knees, rolling into the corridor and landing on the hallway rug. In the kitchen, Savasta tackled Judy Dozier, flinging her to the floor.

An instant later, Vanzi landed on top of the general, straddling his body and pounding him in the face again, taking advantage of his helplessness. Instinctively, Dozier fought back, but as the heavy fists crashed into his face, again and again, he realized that whatever this was, it could not be a drill. Nobody would beat a general half to death to bring verisimilitude into a training exercise.

"Do as they say!" Judy called.

"Shut up or we kill your 'usband!" Savasta growled.

For a moment, Dozier lay still, dazed, blood trickling from the open wound on his forehead. Moving fast, Vanzi rolled the American on to his side, bending his arms behind him, and slipped his wrists into a pair of handcuffs. The room was still spinning, but Dozier's mind was working furiously. The Red Brigades, he was thinking, they said they were from the Red Brigades—

There was blood obscuring the vision in his left eye, but his right was clear and he could see that Savasta was standing over Judy, pointing the pistol at her head while he forced her to crouch on her hands and knees on the kitchen floor. The fight seemed to be over.

"Honey! Do as they say," he cried.

"Shut your mouth!" Vanzi's fists started flying again. Dozier twisted, trying to avoid the punishment, but the guerrilla belted him several times hard in the stomach.

"Listen," he gasped, deciding to identify himself in the vain hope that his assailants had perhaps attacked the wrong man. "Senti, io sono . . ."

"Shut up!" Vanzi ordered. "Stay calm!"

Right, let's all stay calm, Dozier thought, realizing that his attempts to negotiate were futile. Stay calm, Judy. Stay calm, honey, and we'll get out of this. I've survived worse than this, he promised himself. And I'll survive this too.

4

5:40 P.M., 17 DECEMBER 1981
VIA LUNGADIGE CATENA, VERONA

Savasta climbed to his feet, feeling sudden fatigue and breathing hard, even though Pietro Vanzi had done most of the real fighting. The instinctive violence of the American's reaction had astonished both of them. Despite the two guns pointing in his direction, the *generale* had fought back aggressively, displaying more courage and more sheer physical strength than they had anticipated.

"Is he breathing?" Dozier was lying so still that Savasta wondered whether they had inadvertently killed him. Vanzi put a finger beneath the general's nose and then nodded as he felt the man's breath.

"Good, let's get to work!" Savasta ordered. Vanzi opened the plumber's bag, extracting a heavy roll of plastic packing tape and the kind of rubberized elastic bandage athletes use to support sprained knees.

Holding Judy Dozier down with one hand while he covered the general with his pistol, Savasta watched as his colleague trussed up the unresisting American, taping the general's ankles together and putting a piece of plastic packing tape across his mouth. To reduce the chance that he would overhear something they did not want him to know, Vanzi inserted flexible wax ear-plugs in each of the general's ears. Then he fitted the elastic bandage over the man's head as a blindfold.

"And now, the Signora." Vanzi slid the plumber's bag over to him and Savasta pushed Judy Dozier face-down onto the floor. Quickly, he tore off a length of packing tape and plastered it across her mouth to keep her quiet. Then he twisted her arms behind her back and looped the chain around her wrists, securing it with one of the Yale padlocks. Next, he removed her high leather boots and passed a second length of chain around her ankles, fastening it together with a second lock.

When she was bound hand and foot, he ran a third chain between her wrists and her ankles and fastened it with another Yale lock, leaving Judy lying on her side, totally immobilized. Savasta then pulled her out of the way, sliding her body under the kitchen table with her head facing the wall. He left the key half-turned in each of the Yale locks, wanting Mrs. Dozier to free herself later, after they had made their escape.

"Set?" he asked his colleague, who was on his feet, pistol in hand, guarding the hallway. "Get the door."

Savasta covered Dozier while Vanzi moved down the hallway to admit the second team. Marcello Capuano knew what to do without being told. His pistol in hand, the Roman moved up the circular staircase from the living room to ensure that there was no-body hiding in the penthouse bedroom. He returned a moment later to report that the apartment was empty and then went back upstairs to begin a methodical exploration of the Dozier residence.

"Is the hallway outside clear?" Savasta asked Cesare Di Lenardo.

"The building's quiet," Cesare reported. He was excited but under control. "Are we ready for the refrigerator?"

"Tell them to get ready."

"*Pronto, pronto?*" Di Lenardo murmured into a walkie-talkie.

"*Va bene!*" An instant later, they heard Emilia Libera's husky voice, asking whether everything were proceeding according to plan. She sounded calm.

"*Va bene,*" Di Lenardo assured her. "I'm coming down." This was the signal for the street team to drive the van around the corner and into a courtyard behind the apartment complex. Cesare turned off the walkie-talkie and headed for the door.

Five minutes later, he returned with a mover's dolly that they had rented together with the Fiat van. On the dolly rested what appeared to be a cardboard-and-wood packing crate for a small refrigerator. The word FRAGILE was printed prominently on the side, together with the usual Italian-language versions of "This side up" and "Handle with care."

No one needed to talk. Savasta and Di Lenardo knelt next to the prostrate American while Vanzi swung open the hinged top of the packing case. Inside was a large steamer trunk padded with a thick layer of foam rubber.

The two men eased the general's body into the crate. He's conscious, Savasta reassured himself, watching the American curl up inside the steamer trunk. Di Lenardo lowered the top and they heard it click closed. Savasta sprang to his feet, turned the crate onto its bottom end, and pushed the dolly beneath it.

"Remember to warn us if there's a problem down there," Vanzi said. Savasta nodded. Capuano and Vanzi had been assigned to stay behind, guarding the woman and searching the apartment for documents while the prisoner was taken to Padua. If something went wrong, they would be trapped.

"We won't forget you," Savasta promised and they shook hands. After giving the transport team enough time to reach the safety of Emanuela's flat in Padua, Vanzi and Capuano would change into State Railroad uniforms, drive to the Verona train station in the Fiat 128, abandon it, and travel to Milan with whatever important papers they might find in the Dozier flat. They would be met in Milan by Francesco Lo Bianco, who would take the documents back to the Via Verga headquarters for analysis. The Romans would stay overnight in a safe house near the Stazione centrale, call the Milan newspapers in the morning to claim the kidnapping of General Dozier for the Red Brigades, and then go back to Rome.

Savasta wheeled the mover's dolly out of the apartment and into the hallway. The elevator carriage had disappeared, and below them in the elevator shaft they could hear the sound of people talking and then the groaning of cables as the carriage began to rise. Savasta withdrew his automatic while Di Lenardo followed suit. If it were the police . . .

The elevator stopped at the sixth floor. A family got off and the building went quiet. Savasta sighed with relief as the elevator finally responded to their call.

"Let's get this chicken home!" He put his pistol away and pushed the refrigerator crate into the elevator. As they started their descent, he looked at his watch. The operation had taken thirty-five minutes.

5

6:05 P.M., 17 DECEMBER 1981
VIA LUNGADIGE CATENA, VERONA

Ruggiero was sweating despite the coolness of the early evening air. Characteristically silent, Emilia Libera was sitting in the passenger seat to his right, alert to the possibility of the police's arriving to disrupt their operation. A Sterling machine gun in his hands, Giovanni Ciucci was crouched in the rear of the van, watching for danger. The radio was now tuned into a frequency used by the State Police, and every now and then the speaker would crackle with static as a dispatcher sent patrol cars off on a series of routine errands.

Everything has gone according to plan, Ruggiero reassured himself. But anxiety had begun to gnaw at him after Di Lenardo had come down from the seventh floor to pick up the mover's dolly and the refrigerator crate. Earlier in the year, Savasta had kidnapped a man named Taliercio, whom he had later executed. Should they decide to shoot today's prisoner, then Volinia would be an accessory to homicide and liable to a life sentence.

He was imagining how it would feel to go to prison when the walkie-talkie crackled. Emilia Libera responded.

"*Senti?*" It was Cesare Di Lenardo's voice again. "We're on our way down with the chicken!"

They all exhaled simultaneously, Giovanni Ciucci slid an

ammunition clip into a Sterling, tapped it into place with the palm of his hand, and passed it to Emilia Libera. The woman inspected the weapon expertly and handed it to Ruggiero. If the police should arrive now, it would be the task of the people in the van to radio a warning to the team on the seventh floor and then hold off the police with machine-gun fire until Savasta and the others could kill the chicken and escape. Ruggiero looked in the rearview mirror and watched Giovanni Ciucci slide two more Sterling machine guns into a brown paper bag.

"They're coming!" Ciucci cried. There were two middle-aged women standing at the back door to the condominium, chatting in the fast-fading light. Then the door opened and Antonio Savasta maneuvered the refrigerator crate through the narrow opening.

The ladies moved aside to allow Antonio and Cesare to pass. Giovanni Ciucci pushed open the rear doors of the van and jumped down onto the pavement. Together, Ciucci, Di Lenardo, and Savasta hoisted the refrigerator crate into the back of the van. With his shopping bag full of machine guns, Ciucci strode off toward the parked Lambretta, kick-started it into life, and let it idle while Di Lenardo climbed into the back of the van.

Savasta slammed the rear doors shut and then strolled off to the motor scooter, where Ciucci passed him the shopping bag. The two men on the Lambretta would now ride shotgun through the city behind the van, ready to intervene should the police appear.

"Are we ready?" Volinia asked while Emilia checked in the rearview mirror to ensure that their convoy was prepared to leave. There was hysteria in his voice, and he heard it himself as he spoke.

"Yes, let's go." Ruggiero jumped as he felt her hand touching his shoulder. The Fiat's engine fired on the second try. Gently, Ruggiero pulled out of the courtyard and into the Via Lungadige Catena.

When they reached the foot of the street, Ruggiero turned left over the Catena Bridge, pointing them toward downtown Verona and away from Padua, their real destination. Any witnesses to their departure would testify that the van had headed into Verona, which is where Savasta wanted the police to think they had taken the *pollo*.

★   ★   ★

On the east bank of the Adige, Ruggiero made his way into a residential district, not far from where Lisa and Alessandro Arcangeli lived, eventually turning into an alleyway that led to an underground parking garage. It was dark in the garage and just before Ruggiero killed the headlights on the van, he noted with relief that the other two vehicles were already in place.

One was Savasta's Fiat Ritmo, recently modified by the removal of the backseat and the addition of a powerful radio. The second was Alberta Biliato's white Fiat 127, in which the blond woman sat smoking and reading a magazine. Locating the transfer point had been Ruggiero's responsibility, and he congratulated himself on finding a place where they could switch vehicles without any danger of being observed. In the rearview mirror, he could see the lights of the motor scooter as Ciucci drew up at the entrance to the garage.

Changing vehicles was an important part of Savasta's plan. A witness who observed the van's leaving the Via Lungadige Catena might describe it to the police. Hence, the Fiat 238 would be deserted in favor of the Ritmo, which had been deliberately kept away from the scene of the operation. Once they had transferred their prisoner into the smaller vehicle, Savasta would ditch the van in the city center, providing even more evidence that the Red Brigades were hiding in Verona itself. After Savasta had dumped the van, Giovanni would pick him up with the Lambretta and carry him to the train station, where the two of them would catch the evening *rapido* to Padua.

"Let's get going," Di Lenardo said from the back of the van, swinging the rear doors open. Volinia sprang down from the driver's seat and helped Di Lenardo transfer the refrigerator crate from the van into the Ritmo.

"Ready?" Emilia Libera was already settled in the Ritmo's passenger seat when Ruggiero took his place again at the steering wheel. Behind him, Di Lenardo was squeezing his big body in beside the refrigerator crate. As soon as Ruggiero started the engine, Alberta Biliato put down her magazine and swung her 127 out of the underground garage with Ruggiero behind her.

Until they reached Padua, Alberta would act as their lightning rod. If there were a police roadblock waiting for them, Alberta would run into it first and it was her responsibility to radio a warning, even if she were in danger of being captured. In a few minutes, they were in open countryside. It was now dark, and all

Ruggiero could see was the faint amber glow from the taillights of Alberta's car.

"What happens if we run into a police patrol?" Ruggiero asked.

"We'll take evasive action," Emilia Libera answered.

"Suppose we can't get away, like if—"

"Then we execute the prisoner and make our way cross-country on foot," Libera responded, as if the answer were obvious. "*Va bene?*"

"Yes," he stammered, feeling the fear come back. "Sure."

6

6:40 P.M., 17 DECEMBER 1981
THE COUNTRYSIDE BETWEEN VERONA AND PADUA

I need air, General Dozier was thinking. There are a lot of things I could use right now, but oxygen is the one thing I cannot do without.

Calm down and concentrate on breathing, he told himself, fighting for self-control. He shifted inside the cramped space, trying to find some comfortable position. There wasn't one, so he gave up and let his body go slack, trying to cut back on his oxygen requirement.

The handcuffs were standard police issue, and every time he rolled on them they grew tighter, cutting off the circulation in his hands. The inside of the box was foam-covered for his comfort and safety, but there wasn't enough space, and his legs were cramping badly.

Is Judy okay? The question pounded in his brain.

Think! Had they wanted to kill us, they could have shot us both dead at the door. Therefore, this is about captivity, but not about death, at least in the short term. This is a kidnapping, something political. Didn't they say they were the Brigate rosse? Of course, it was me they want as a hostage, and they could have killed Judy after they took me out of the flat to eliminate a dangerous witness.

It wasn't much fun thinking about that and he prayed, asking

God to guide his Judy. Send us all some guidance, Lord, and inspire the folks in the front seat to remember that all living creatures need oxygen, even American generals.

Then he tried to process what little data he possessed. Besides tying him hand and foot and taping his mouth and putting a mask of some kind on his head, they had inserted plugs into his ears. Why? Sensory deprivation?

Then, just as he had begun to recover from the pain and grogginess that came with being beaten, they had forced him into this crate and taken him down the elevator and into a vehicle. His sense of direction had lasted long enough for him to determine that they had then turned left over the Catena bridge, and then left again up that hill by the hospital. Then, for a while, there had been a rapid series of turns before they had stopped and transferred him to another vehicle.

It's a light passenger car, he calculated from the way it handled on curves and bounced over bumps in the road. And the muffler is loose. Despite the earplugs, he could hear incoherent fragments of conversation. One woman seemed to be talking into a radio, and another woman seemed to be answering, saying "Va bene, va bene," in response to questions from the first.

Suddenly, he heard the catch being worked, and the top of the crate was opened.

Air! He inhaled, feeling his body's reacting gratefully to the sudden availability of oxygen. Although he could see almost nothing through the blindfold, the caliber of the darkness around him changed. A woman's hand reached into the crate, seeking one of his wrists and taking his pulse. This was good news because it suggested that they were concerned about his well-being, that they intended to keep him alive.

The woman's hand moved to his chest and rested there for a moment, checking his heartbeat, and then withdrew.

Use the senses they haven't taken away, he told himself. Knowing where I am could become important later in formulating an escape plan. For a moment he thought he could smell a bakery, and then, a little later, the harsher scent of petroleum came to his nostrils. A refinery would mean that they were headed toward the Adriatic Sea because there were petrochemical factories along the coast.

Clearly, they were in the countryside, because the air was cool and fresh. And they were traveling on a narrow, winding country road because the car changed direction every few minutes and there was very little other traffic.

His body was cramping and there was blood in the back of his throat that made it difficult to swallow. Dozier tried to raise his head, partially to get a better feeling for his environment, and partly to try to find a more comfortable position because he was losing the circulation in his legs.

"*Giù, giù!*" the woman commanded, forcing his head back down into the box with her hand.

"Listen," he began.

"*Silenzio!*" the woman's voice was sharp and Dozier settled back down into the crate.

"*Senti? Senti?*" a metallic voice came over the radio.

"*Si?*" replied the woman who had taken his pulse.

"*Tutto va bene!*" replied the caller. Everything goes well, the general translated dully. I can't move my legs.

7

7:15 P.M., 17 DECEMBER 1981
VIA LUNGADIGE CATENA, VERONA

Who are these people? What do they want?

There were no answers. Judy Dozier was lying on the kitchen floor beneath the table, her legs bent behind her and her face against the wall. Earlier, there had been a big box of some kind in the hallway, and she wondered whether they had taken Jim away in it. The intruders were still there! They were all wearing shoes with soft soles and their movements were difficult to detect, but she sensed that they were still roaming around her apartment, sifting through her clothes and her books, violating her life.

She squirmed, trying to find a less uncomfortable position, but there did not seem to be any way of lying hog-tied on a kitchen floor that was not disagreeable. She began to investigate the chains and locks holding her prisoner. To her surprise, she found that at least one of the locks still had a key in it. She touched it, trying to guess why such competent professionals would make such an elementary error. Or do they want me to escape?

Eventually, maybe, but not now! One of the strangers entered the kitchen, the taller of the two men who had come to the door posing as plumbers.

Handling her body as if she were a sack of potatoes, he pulled her out from under the kitchen table, produced another elastic bandage, and fitted it tightly over her head, blinding her to the world. The coarse elastic material covered her nose and mouth, making it difficult to breathe. She panted to communicate her discomfort, but he ignored her. With a smooth, powerful movement, he swung her body around on the tile floor and began hauling her out of the kitchen on her stomach. He did not seem to be trying to hurt her, or trying not to hurt her; as far as she could tell, he was perfectly indifferent to her welfare.

Am I being taken away too? Have they got a box for me? It was frightening enough being pulled around on the floor from room to room, but being blindfolded made it that much worse.

Suddenly the man lowered her head and shoulders to the floor. She heard his steps crossing the room and then there was the click of a light switch. The darkness deepened. There was a faint thud as a door closed and locked.

She was alone, unsure where in the apartment she had been taken. For a long time, nothing happened and she waited in the darkness, her mind whirling back and forth between worry about her husband's safety and concern about her own situation. Muffled sounds in the distance suggested that she still shared the apartment with these strange and violent men, but she could hear nothing distinct. Then the door opened again and she heard the light switch click on.

She gasped loudly, making it clear that she was having great difficulty pulling enough air through the blindfold. The intruder dropped to one knee beside her, and moved the bandage up on her head so that it continued to obscure her vision but left her nose and mouth free. Then, he rose and left, again turning off the light and locking the door behind him.

Several times someone returned, opened the door, and turned on the light, checking to see that she was still securely bound. After each visit, he closed the door again and went away.

It was difficult to estimate the passage of time, but after what seemed to be a long wait, the door opened again, and someone entered. Without speaking, he turned on a radio, tuning in an all-music station and cranking up the volume until the noise level was disagreeably high. Then he placed the radio out of reach above her.

Is this to prevent me from hearing them, she wondered, or to prevent anyone from hearing me? Does it mean that they are going away?

The man's hands lifted her head and fastened more packing tape around her mouth. When he lowered her head, she found that a cushion or a pillow of some kind had been placed beneath her cheek. He wants me to be comfortable, she thought. A gentleman and a terrorist.

The unknown man began winding the same packing tape around the chains attached to her wrists and ankles, making sure that she could make no noise. She felt his hands on her waist, unzipping her skirt. No, she thought, not— He released her, and she realized with a flood of relief that he had merely been loosening her skirt in a quixotic attempt to make her more comfortable.

He disappeared, leaving her alone again in darkness. This time she sensed that he would not be coming back.

She waited, indecisive. She heard the phone ring for a long while. Perhaps someone from the Verona Community Activities Association was wondering why Jim and Judy had missed that evening's meeting.

Will it occur to them that something has gone wrong? Jim never forgets an appointment, and he's never late. Of course, they will hardly come around tonight and break down the door. Perhaps tomorrow, when Jim fails to turn up at the office.

Maybe yes, maybe no, she told herself. It would be sensible to assume that nobody is going to come anytime soon. Jim is gone, and unless he can escape, nobody will know I'm here. If I don't get free then I stay here, until . . . until I don't know. I'd better get to work on those padlocks!

Explore! She strained her arms, stretching back to touch the padlocks. One key seemed to give a little when she twisted it, but nothing happened. A second key would not budge, and if there were a third, she could not find it.

Keep at it, she told herself after a rest, and tried again. She managed to undo one of the locks and felt a chain fall away, the link that had been attaching her ankles to her wrists. Her arms were still fastened together behind her back, and her feet were also still hobbled, but for the first time in an hour, she was able to unbend her knees. It felt wonderful!

She concentrated next on the blindfold, rubbing her face against the pillow. Slowly she pushed the bandage up over her cheeks and uncovered one eye.

The room was still pitch-dark, but Judy could detect a blue flame a few feet away from where she was lying, the pilot light from the water heater. She was back in the same place where this nightmare had begun, in the combination utility room and bathroom, near the washing machine and the drier.

It was difficult to raise her body with both arms still bound behind her back, but she rolled onto one side, sat up, and managed to work her way across the floor on her bottom. When she got to the wall, she dropped down on her back and raised her feet until she could reach the light switch with her heels.

Lights! Her morale began to soar as she oriented herself in this familiar part of the world. Impatiently, she tried to work the door handle with her toes, but the door was locked from the outside.

I can't get out, she was forced to admit, realizing that her one hope of escape now lay in attracting the attention of a neighbor. She worked for a while on the plastic tape across her mouth, but without being able to get at it with her hands, it was impossible to remove, and she could only make inarticulate groaning noises.

Percussion, she decided. She sat back up and inched her way over to the side of the washing machine. Swinging her legs sideways, she pounded her knee against the thin sheet-metal side of the machine.

It made a hollow, resounding thud, and she did it again, harder. She was still not clear about what time it was, but there were people living downstairs, Pio and Mariagrazia Scudellari, and if they were not there now, they had to come home eventually!

"*Aiuto!*" she tried to shout for help. The plastic tape distorted her cry, but every little bit of noise helped. She gathered her strength, doubling up her legs and slamming her knees against the side of the washing machine, trying to produce as much racket as possible. It hurt, but she did it again, and again, and again.

8

7:30 P.M., 17 DECEMBER 1981
THE OUTSKIRTS OF PADUA

"What's happening?" Ruggiero cried out. A fancy white sports car had suddenly appeared in his rearview mirror, honking furiously at him. It must be the police, he thought, and stepped on the accelerator. Now the shooting starts—

An instant later, a powerful NSU Prinz passed him and then cut back in between the Ritmo and Alberta's Fiat. Out of the corner of his eye, Ruggiero caught a glimpse of a diminutive young woman at the wheel of the Prinz. She had dark curly hair and she was wearing a fur coat. Whoever she was, she was not the police.

"Easy, easy, it's the hand-over," Emilia Libera assured him. "Slow down, okay? Slow down!"

"Right," he muttered, cutting his speed, furious that he had once again displayed his nervousness and ineptitude. Emilia Libera reached for the microphone of the radio on the dashboard.

"Grazie, 'Anna,' " she said. Ruggiero saw Alberta Biliato flick her headlights, acknowledging Libera's thanks. A moment later, the blond woman slowed and pulled her 127 off the road to let them pass.

"That woman in the Prinz," Ruggiero began. "Wasn't that—"

"Don't worry about who it is. Just follow her. We're almost there." Emilia reached back and closed the cover of the refrigerator crate. She had left the top open in the countryside to give their captive some air, but now they were passing through the outskirts of Padua.

That's Emanuela Frascella, Ruggiero thought as he followed the Prinz through a succession of back streets. Michele Galati recruited the two of us at about the same time and I met her at a Veneto column conference. Is she another big secret I'm not supposed to know? And this is the Via Guizza! I could have taken us here without having Emanuela nearly run us off the road!

A few minutes later, Ruggiero slowed to follow Emanuela into the underground garage beneath number 2, Via Pindemonte.

"Park by the elevator," growled Di Lenardo from the backseat.

"What happens now?" he asked as he killed the motor.

"We wait," Emilia Libera told him. "That was really good driving."

Ruggiero felt a vague sense of anticlimax. The prisoner lay quietly in his crate while Di Lenardo and Libera stared at the dimly illuminated subterranean garage.

I'll be glad to get out of this place, he thought. It was getting cold with the motor off, but he imagined that they would soon be going upstairs for a celebration. After a glass of spumante, he would go back to Lisa's house and get into bed where it would be warm.

"*Difficoltà!*"

Ruggiero jumped as a dark figure in a uniform appeared by the car door. For a moment, he thought of the machine gun on the floor beneath the seat, but he could hardly get to it in time, assuming that he wanted to try, and besides—

Besides, it was Savasta, wearing a train conductor's uniform but minus his false beard. Giovanni Ciucci was beside him.

"No, niente," Ruggiero stammered. The chief of the Veneto column must have timed it all perfectly, synchronizing his operation with the train schedule so that they could all arrive in Padua together.

No one was telling him what to do, but Ruggiero contented himself with opening doors as Di Lenardo and Ciucci carried the refrigerator chest to the service elevator. They all crowded on and Savasta took them up to the top of the building, and then back down to the underground parking garage, and then up to floor 5. No one spoke.

He's doing it to confuse the chicken, Volinia understood. Why bother? How could the prisoner even know what city he's in, much less what floor or what building?

Finally, they stopped on the second floor and Savasta and Ciucci carried the refrigerator chest into an apartment. Ruggiero followed them past a kitchen and a living room and into a bedroom where a camping tent had been erected on the floor.

"What's the tent for?" he asked. The tent had one chamber in back, containing what looked like an army cot. This space could be closed off with a canvas flap, leaving a kind of veranda area, where a folding lawn chair had been set up.

Savasta looked up with an expression of perplexity, as if he were surprised to find Volinia still there. He took him by the arm and walked him back to the door of the apartment.

"You've done well tonight," he whispered. "Your job now is to forget that this place exists. Go back to your father's home in Verona and continue looking for work."

"Who did we kidnap tonight?"

"When the Organization decided to take out Aldo Moro, Mario Moretti had me chasing all over Rome, stealing cars, delivering messages, and picking up packages. Nobody ever told me what it was all about because I didn't need to know, and after it happened, I read about it in the newspapers like everybody else. Tonight, we told you what you needed to know to do what you had to do. Now, listen carefully! Lisa and her brother—"

"They're reliable people!" Ruggiero began to feel his anger coming to the surface, but Savasta leaned forward and took his arm.

"They've been on the fringes of the Organizzazione for years and they were both involved in protests and demonstrations at the university," Savasta told him. "So their names could be on a police list somewhere. I don't want you with them if they're picked up for questioning. So you need to stay away from the Arcangeli place until I give you the word that it's safe. Understand?"

"How . . . how long?"

"There's no way of telling. A month, maybe. Maybe longer. I'll be in touch at your father's place. Don't try to contact me, and don't ever come here, understand?"

Ruggiero stepped over the threshold into the corridor. A month without Lisa! No, there had to be some arrangement they could make! He turned back to explain his objection, because even though Savasta was a member of the Esecutivo and a field commander for major Red Brigades operations, he was still a man who had to be able to understand that . . .

Savasta was gone. The door was closed and the lock had clicked into place, shutting him out. There was a bus stop on the corner, and Ruggiero stood for a long time in the cold, waiting for the bus to come.

9

There was light!

The bandage was still snugly drawn over his head, but General Dozier could see brightness as the top of his tiny prison opened.

So we're here, he thought, discovering that his legs were still numb. And where is here?

His sense of time could have been distorted, but the general guessed that they had been on the road for about an hour and a half. This put them forty or fifty miles from Verona.

And I'm in a relatively tall building, he calculated, six or seven stories high, at least, because they ran me up and down an elevator several times to disorient me. I can't be anywhere close to the top because the last trip was down and it was a long ride.

"Bene, bene," someone was saying as they took him by the arms, lifting him from either side. Even without knowing what was going to happen next he felt an enormous sense of relief in leaving that box.

"What's happening?" he demanded, but they ignored him and he felt himself being stretched out face down on a cot. Their hands were neither rough nor gentle but merely impersonal. They slid the blindfold off his head. The sudden light dazzled him for a moment, but when his eyes finally focused, he saw that he was in a tent. The three men were wearing ski masks to conceal their features.

There was a fresh bloodstain on the mattress, and he realized that he was still bleeding from the scalp wound he had suffered during the fight in Verona.

Wordlessly, the team went to work and Dozier noted the disciplined efficiency with which they secured him. First, Savasta leaned over him with a sharp pair of scissors and carefully sliced away the packing tape they had used to cover his mouth. Then he circled the cot to deal with the packing tape holding Dozier's ankles together.

They were taking no chances with him. At the foot of the cot, there was the hulking, menacing figure of Cesare Di Lenardo, pointing a Beretta nine-millimeter automatic in his direction. The third man, Giovanni Ciucci, picked up his left foot and circled it with a chain, which he then fastened with a padlock. The other end of the chain ran to the frame of the cot, where it was fastened with a second padlock.

Savasta opened the lock on the handcuffs, releasing Dozier's left hand but quickly securing his right wrist to the frame of the cot. Once they had immobilized him, the team seemed to relax. Savasta searched him, taking his watch, wallet, belt, and shoes and then going through his pockets and confiscating his change.

As the search ended, Emilia Libera squeezed into the tent. Like the men, she was wearing a shapeless jogging suit and her hair was tucked up inside the ski mask, but the general could see her ample breasts moving beneath the fabric of her jacket.

"Listen, folks, do you want to tell me what's going on—" he began, speaking in English in an attempt to establish the principle that negotiations would take place in his native language.

"We communicate with prisoners only in Italian," replied Savasta, speaking in his own language.

"Io . . . uh . . . non comprendo . . . italiano," Dozier countered, deliberately worsening his accent.

"That won't work," snapped Savasta. "We have observed you speaking Italian fluently in public."

The others had stepped back now and were sitting cross-legged on the floor of the tent.

"Scusi," Dozier asked. "What happened to my wife?"

"First, the prisoner will give us his name and rank."

"All right," he agreed, wondering whether it was possible that they had kidnapped him without knowing who he was. "My name is James Lee Dozier. I am a brigadier general in the United States Army. I am deputy chief of staff for logistics and administration, Allied Land Forces, Southern Europe. Now who the hell are you?"

"We are members of the Brigate rosse." There was pride in Savasta's voice.

"Va bene; what about my wife?"

"She has not been harmed. We will arrange for her release."

"How? Where is she now?" Dozier sighed with relief at the news that Judy was unhurt. Of course they could be lying, but why would they bother?

They ignored him and Emilia Libera produced a first-aid kit. With surprising gentleness, Savasta applied a dab of iodine to the general's wound and covered it with a bandage. When they finished, Savasta produced a pair of heavy padded earphones, the kind that serious music lovers use.

"Wear these!" he instructed the prisoner. "It is better if you do not hear anything."

He slipped the earphones over Dozier's head. They were attached to a cord that ran from the prisoner's section of the tent to a portable tape recorder on a chair in the outer chamber. Pounding through the foam-rubber earphones was the kind of heavy-metal rock music that the general detested.

Why? Was this meant to be torture?

"Too loud! Too loud!" he complained, waving his free left hand at the kidnap team, but they ignored him and all left.

Okay, get organized, he told himself, anger pumping adrenaline into his blood. He sat up on the couch, feeling a dull ache in his head and right ear. His wrists and feet still tingled from the aftereffect of being held motionless for so long. He massaged his legs, noting that there did not seem to be any permanent damage. This was important; he wanted those legs in good working order.

Time for reconnaissance. The tent was made of light blue canvas with a blue plastic flooring, and there was the smell of newness about it. His section was about six square feet and sparsely furnished. The light was coming from a bare forty-watt bulb clipped to the ceiling of the tent near the flap, with an electric cord running out under the side of the tent along with the extension cord from his earphones. He was sitting on a steel-framed folding cot, on which had been placed an inner-spring mattress covered with a light tan wool blanket. Curiously he lifted the blanket and discovered that there were no sheets. There was, on the other hand, a pillow, with a pillowcase.

And the bathroom? It consisted of a white plastic portable chemical toilet that sat in one corner of his space, smelling of disinfectant.

Well, he asked himself with a shrug, what did you expect? Color television and a swimming pool?

Okay, how do we get ourselves out of here? Dozier examined the chains attaching his leg to the cot. The links were robust steel, unlikely to be bent or broken. With his right arm still handcuffed to the frame of the bunk, movement of any kind was going to be tough. Because the cot folded up in the middle, it might be possible to jettison the mattress and hobble out with the cot frame in his arms. It would be noisy and awkward, but if they left him alone, it would be worth a try.

Access to the outside was through a doorway flap that opened and closed with a zipper. At the moment, it was open and pulled back. Dozier could see a folding chair in the tent's outer chamber. Di Lenardo was on guard, watching him.

He flopped back on the cot. For a long time, he lay there, looking at the ceiling as he sorted through an extraordinarily short list of options and opportunities.

West Point was tough, he reflected. Vietnam was tough. This could be very tough.

10

8:30 P.M., 17 DECEMBER 1981
VIA LUNGADIGE CATENA, VERONA

There was a pounding at the door.

Aldo Marulli looked at his wife, Franca, in puzzlement. In the polite Verona society they inhabited at number 5, Via Lungadige Catena, neighbors occasionally tapped at one's door. Nobody pounded.

"That could be trouble," said Franca. They had lingered over dinner, Aldo thought, looking around at the company, but it had been such a pleasant evening. Franca's sister, Daniela, and her husband, Mario, had joined them for a meal, and there had been some good family gossip, and . . . and now, there was some kind of emergency.

"I'll go," Aldo volunteered. As a retired Italian army officer, he was in charge of emergencies, domestic and foreign, but his brother-in-law loyally followed him to the door.

"Who's there?" Aldo demanded without opening the door.

"It's us, Pio and Mariagrazia!" came a familiar voice. Aldo drew back the bolt and opened the door. Pio and Mariagrazia

Scudellari had been their neighbors at number 5 for some years now. Pio was a civil engineer and a solid citizen.

"What's happened? Come in!" Aldo said, but Pio held back, pointing up the stairs toward the seventh floor.

"Look, we've heard a pounding. . . ."

"I think it's coming from the Dozier bathroom," interrupted Mariagrazia. "We went up and knocked at the door, but no one came. They're friends of yours, and we thought that perhaps . . ."

"Maybe *il generale* is hanging pictures," Mario suggested from over Aldo's shoulder.

"They should be there," Aldo said. "I talked to the *Signora* Judy before dinner. We're going to an art show together on Saturday."

"It's been happening for fifteen minutes now," insisted Pio Scudellari. "You can hear it from our bathroom, a kind of rhythmic pounding, and sometimes you can hear . . . it sounds like someone moaning."

Terroristi, Aldo speculated. He had sometimes wondered whether the revolution would ever come to his peaceful little Verona.

"What are we going to do?" Pio Scudellari asked.

"You call the police," Aldo ordered. "Mario, go down to the street to let them in."

"Suppose it's Judy hanging pictures?" Franca demanded.

"Then we'll be appropriately embarrassed. Meanwhile, I'll go up there and see what we can do." In the year since Jim and Judy had arrived in Verona, the Marullis and Doziers had become close friends. If there was the slightest chance that anything was wrong . . . He left the thought unfinished. He rang the Doziers' bell and waited impatiently, his ear pressed to the door. Then he pounded, rattling the sturdy wood paneling. Silence.

Diavolo! he thought, reconstructing the geography of the Dozier flat in his mind. They can't be up in the penthouse bedroom because Pio could never have heard that noise from there. And if they're on this floor, they must have heard the bell and my pounding. So why aren't they answering the bell? Unless . . . unless what?

"Signore!" Aldo turned to find that a Carabiniere patrolman had answered Pio Scudellari's call with record speed. "This is the American general's apartment?"

"Yes, and I'm worried," Aldo said. "I think we need to force an entry."

"I'll go with you," decided the Carabiniere. The two men raced up the staircase to the rooftop patio and pushed open the metal door that led to the eighth floor. Stumbling through the combination porch and utility area, the two men climbed into the Doziers' patio. The drapes were open, but it was dark inside the bedroom, and they could see nothing.

"How do we get in?" asked the Carabiniere.

"That leads to the bathroom." Aldo balled his fist and broke the windowpane. The sound of the shattering glass crashing to the tile floor of the bathroom seemed deafeningly loud in the quietness of the rooftop. The Carabiniere boosted him through the open space.

He moved gingerly into the darkened bedroom. There was no one on this floor, but it occurred to him that if there had been terrorists or burglars in the Dozier apartment, there was no reason why they should not still be there, perhaps lurking in the darkness with their guns. It was a sobering reflection, and he was pleased when the Carabiniere joined him, armed with a pistol and a flashlight.

At the top of the staircase, Aldo looked down into an utterly black living room, realizing that the blinds must have been drawn to eliminate even the glimmer of light from the streetlamps. Cautiously, he made his way down the spiral staircase, orienting himself in the living room and finding the light switch. The front was locked, but after a moment's fumbling, he managed to open it.

To his surprise, there was already a crowd. Another Carabiniere had arrived, and Pio Scudellari's son, a physician, had turned up with his doctor's bag in response to a call from his father. Less welcome, there was a mob of curious neighbors from other apartments in the building.

"Did you see anyone?" Pio Scudellari asked.

"The place has been ransacked," Aldo told him, turning and leading the way back into the Dozier apartment. There were drawers pulled out of desks and closet doors hanging open and clothing strewn around on the floor.

"Terrorists!" Pio announced publicly what everyone was thinking privately. "There have been terrorists here. Dozier is a NATO general!"

One of the Carabinieri, his revolver out, looked nervously around. It struck everyone that there could still be danger here. Or a corpse. If they had come to kill the general . . .

"Let's get going!" Aldo Marulli said. "Let's find whoever is still here to be found."

11

8:45 P.M., 17 DECEMBER 1981
VIA LUNGADIGE CATENA, VERONA

Hitchcock, she thought looking up from the laundry-room floor at the crowd of strangers who had burst in on her. This is like a scene from a horror movie!

She tried to ask them who they were but the plastic tape was still stretched across her mouth.

"Signora!" a squat, heavyset man with a military-style hat and a heavy leather jacket knelt beside her. It took her a moment to realize that he was a policeman. He was trying to undo the chains, but the two remaining locks continued to resist.

"*Andiamo, andiamo,*" she heard him say, conferring with another patrolman. The two men carried her down the corridor and into the kitchen, where they positioned her uncomfortably on a chair, her wrists still bound behind her back.

"*Va bene,*" one of the policemen said, waving back the crowd. To her relief, she saw the friendly face of Aldo Marulli, approaching her with an implement that resembled a giant pair of pliers. They turned her around brusquely. She heard the crack of steel against steel and felt the chains falling away. Her muscles ached, but for the first time in three hours she could move.

"Oh, Judy, Judy!" Franca Marulli, her friend from downstairs, was hugging her. With a shock, she realized that only a few hours ago she had been standing at the front door talking to Aldo about plans to visit an art gallery.

"Franca," she groaned as Franca removed the packing tape from across her mouth, pulling it away bit by bit to minimize the discomfort.

"Where's Jim?" asked Aldo, taking one of her hands.

"I don't know." She heard a flat, leaden quality in her voice as she spoke. "I don't know. They put him in a box and took him away."

She stood, feeling shaky. Franca took her arm and led her out of the kitchen and into the living room. Her normally tidy apartment was a wreck. Clothes and Jim's personal papers were strewn all over the floor. There were people she had never seen before wandering around her home and she felt violated. First the terrorists, and now this crowd of curious strangers, she found herself thinking. *They have no right. . . .*

"We've got to leave," Franca told her. "The police need to take you somewhere to make a report."

"No," she refused, fighting off hysteria. "I've got to stay here. When Jim comes back . . ."

"No, listen, you should pack a bag of things. Some underwear . . ."

Judy shook her head, aware that she was being foolish. Jim had been kidnapped by terrorists. He was not coming back any time soon. Certainly not tonight. With a sigh, she allowed Franca to take her upstairs to pack an overnight bag.

"What were they looking for?" she asked as she surveyed the wreckage of her bedroom. Her clothing had been pulled from the dresser and slung on the floor. She noticed that some of her jewelry was missing.

"They've taken grandma's ring." She sighed. "And that broach-and-necklace combination and . . ."

"Judy, we've got to go."

She found a suitcase lying by the bed and threw a few basic items into it, a nightdress, a change of underclothing, a fresh blouse and skirt combination. Then she located her toothbrush and a packet of makeup before following Franca back down the circular staircase.

Someone had brought her boots into the living room, and she was allowed to sit down on the couch long enough to put them back on. The two policemen were clearly nervous, wanting to get her and everyone else out of the apartment before any evidence was destroyed.

This is worse than when he went to Vietnam, she thought, following them to the door. When the men all had to go to

Vietnam, there were other wives left behind, and Judy remembered how important they had been to one another.

But this time, Jim went off alone. *And now I have to wait alone.*

12

4:30 P.M. (EASTERN STANDARD TIME), 17 DECEMBER 1981
THE WHITE HOUSE, WASHINGTON, D.C.

In Washington, the afternoon was gray and overcast. President Ronald Reagan was in the middle of a heavy schedule. He had worked in the Oval Office that morning and then gone off to host a White House luncheon for a delegation of lobbyists from the automobile industry.

Beginning at three-thirty, the White House had staged one of Mr. Reagan's rare press conferences. The former governor of California resented these unstructured, unrehearsed, and uncontrolled encounters, but today things had gone well. There had been no serious gaffes, and Mr. Reagan stepped back from the lectern with the air of a man who had turned in a satisfactory performance.

As the president walked out of the Press Room, followed by his aides and several reporters, he was intercepted by his acting national security adviser, Admiral James Nance.

A few minutes earlier, the NSC had received a cable from the American embassy in Rome, announcing that Brigadier General James Lee Dozier, deputy chief of staff for logistics and administration, Allied Land Forces, Southern Europe, had been kidnapped from his home in Verona by a team claiming to represent the Italian Red Brigades. There was no further information concerning Dozier's safety or whereabouts at this time. The Italian police were investigating. It was the first major terrorist crisis for the Reagan administration.

Nance handed Mr. Reagan the cable and stepped back while he scanned it.

This was an awkward moment for such a crisis. Mr. Reagan's

senior advisers had not yet decided which branch of the government would deal with high-profile acts of terrorism against American citizens abroad. Theoretically, it was a State Department function, but the secretary of state was the volatile Alexander Haig, who had never been trusted by the conservatives among the president's backers. The CIA was now being run by Mr. Reagan's trusted friend, William Casey, but the Agency was not ideally organized to handle the public and diplomatic aspects of counterterrorism.

And the National Security Council staff itself was in a shambles. Mr. Reagan's first appointee as national security adviser had been a foreign policy expert named Richard Allen, but Allen had been accused of accepting a thousand-dollar bribe from some Japanese businessmen and had been put on administrative leave while investigators probed the incident.

The decision had already been made to replace Allen with Judge William Clark, an old Reagan crony with no discernible familiarity with international relations, but Allen was not yet out and Clark was not yet in. For the interim, Nance was doing his best to fill the gap, relying on military specialists such as the navy's John Poindexter and Oliver North from the Marine Corps.

"They've kidnapped one of our generals," Nance explained to the others. "It's General Dozier in Italy. The Red Brigades . . ."

"What are we going to do, sir?" asked a reporter. "I mean, this kidnapping?"

"The United States will do everything possible to secure the safe release of the general," Reagan said woodenly, making an attempt to contain the anger brewing within him.

"What can we—" another journalist began, but Reagan cut him off.

"This is, I think, a terrible situation," he said. "It's a most frustrating situation because I would like to be able to stand sometime—I'm sure we all would—and say to the people who did these things, they are cowardly bums."

"Mr. President?" There was a chorus of attempted interruptions, but Reagan rolled on.

"They aren't heroes and they don't have a cause that justifies what they're doing! They wouldn't have the guts to stand up to anyone individually in any kind of fair contest!"

"Sir?"

"Cowardly bums!" shouted Reagan. Several reporters wrote "Cowardly bums" in their notebooks and raced for the Press Room telephones.

13

11:15 P.M., 7 DECEMBER 1981
VILLAGE OF MAROLA, NEAR VICENZA

The phone rang. It's hardly ever good news after 10:00 P.M., Colonel Bill Reed thought. From her side of the couch, Judy Reed turned down the television, sending him a look that was somewhere between a sympathetic smile and a grimace. Nurses make good wives for intelligence officers, he reflected, as he reached for the phone, because they understand the etiquette of emergencies. On the other hand, intelligence officers make lousy husbands. I must advise my daughters never to marry one.

"*Pronto?*" he barked.

"Look, Bill, there's ah . . . sort of a problem," came the voice of a senior staff officer from Vicenza. "It's about General Dozier, over in Verona."

"What is it?" demanded Reed. "Do I need to come in?"

"The police say that he's been kidnapped," the caller blurted out. "Something about a refrigerator box and uh. . . ."

"I'm on my way!"

"Bill, what—"

"I warned the wrong general! The Red Brigades have just picked up Jim Dozier!"

"Is Judy Dozier okay?"

"I dunno." Reed took his forty-five out of the drawer and put it into his pocket. "I'll be in touch!"

He kissed her farewell. Judy Reed knew better than to ask when he would be back. At the entrance to their apartment, Reed cocked the automatic and switched off the safety as he opened the door and peered out into the darkness. There was a streetlight not far away, casting light and shadow through the night mist. It looked as if there might be rain before dawn. Reed shivered and ran for his car, the pistol in his hand.

The Pentagon must be chasing its five-sided tail over this one, he thought, flinging himself behind the wheel of his car. He had already begun to compose a mental list of tasks that would need to be accomplished within the next few hours. NATO and U.S. commands would have to be informed and a crisis command post established at SETAF.

Who will control the investigation? he asked himself. Us? The Carabinieri? The Polizia di Stato? Or will we all fight over it?

As he approached SETAF's front entrance, Reed saw that SETAF Security had already heard about the kidnapping. The American MPs guarding Camp Ederle were normally casual and relaxed. Tonight they were wearing flak jackets and combat helmets and carrying loaded weapons.

It occurred to Reed that there would be some anti-Italian antagonism within the American community. Dozier occupied a NATO billet, which meant that his personal security was Italy's responsibility. The average Yank would accuse the Italians of carelessness, or maybe worse, and the Pentagon was not always sensitive to the national pride of our NATO allies. The American ambassador in Rome was going to need his diplomatic skills to keep the sometimes thin-skinned Italians and the frequently abrasive Americans from turning this into a diplomatic feud.

"Your ID, sir!" said the sentry. The MP knew precisely who Colonel Reed was, having seen him a thousand times before, but tonight everybody was playing by the rules. Once inside the gates, Reed parked his car in front of the Vicenza Headquarters of the Sixty-sixth Military Intelligence Group and dashed past the sentry at the reception desk. Reed's own desk was covered with notes from the Sixty-sixth's duty officer, telephone calls from the local police that needed to be returned, and a few incoming cables from the CIA station in Rome.

The two patrolmen who had helped rescue Mrs. Dozier had radioed a report to their central offices in Verona. When Judy Dozier had arrived a few minutes later at LANDSOUTH headquarters in the Palazzo Carli, a senior Carabiniere investigator was waiting to take her initial statement.

Almost simultaneously, the Carabinieri had informed the

defense minister, who in turn had telephoned Prime Minister Spadolini's office in the Chigi Palace in Rome. Spadolini had been hosting a banquet for a visiting French dignitary, but he had broken away immediately and informed his staff that the Dozier affair was their first priority until the general was rescued. There were to be no deals, no negotiations, and no concessions made in exchange for Dozier's life.

If this had to happen, Reed decided, it couldn't have happened under a better prime minister. Spadolini had begun his career as a university professor, becoming famous with a series of scholarly books on the twentieth-century history of Italy. He then branched out into journalism, ending up as editor-in-chief of the *Corriere della sera*, Italy's most prestigious newspaper. As a politician, he had revitalized Italy's tiny Republican party before becoming the nation's chief executive officer the previous summer.

But terrorism had destroyed promising political careers before, Reed reminded himself. In fact, by now there was a kind of macabre ritual about it. The Red Brigades would kidnap an important man. The prime minister of the moment would announce his indignation and intention to act resolutely, but the police would be unable to make arrests. After four or five weeks of public humiliation, either the government would make concessions to secure the safe release of the hostage or the Red Brigades would execute their victim. With a vote of "no confidence," the Italian parliament would angrily dismiss yet another governmental coalition.

"From the embassy, sir," announced a sergeant from the message center, laying the document on the cluttered desk. Reed scanned the message: Max Rabb had heard the news while making a speech in Genoa, but the American ambassador was driving through the night to Rome and would be in touch with the Italian government in the morning.

Rabb had been a controversial figure ever since President Reagan had appointed him to the embassy in Rome. Rabb had been graduated from Harvard Law in 1935 and ever since had divided his time between the management of a successful law practice and high-level government service as a negotiator for every Republican president from Eisenhower to Reagan.

In many respects, Rabb was ideally qualified to be America's emissary to the Italian Republic. He had been in and out of the country since World War II, and knew most of the top people well. He was a brilliant negotiator and a hard-driving "hands-on" executive.

On the other hand, the new ambassador sometimes behaved with the abrasiveness of an imperial proconsul. Never having learned a word of Italian, Rabb often seemed perplexed that the Italians should persist in speaking their own peculiar language when it would be so much more convenient for the United States of America if they would all learn English.

Reed was trying to decide where to begin when his wife called.

"How does it look?"

"Mrs. Dozier was not hurt," he said, aware that he could tell her nothing classified over this uncleared line. "She's giving a statement to the police now, so we'll know more in a while, but it is clearly a Red Brigades operation."

"What do you think the general's chances are?" As Reed pondered the question, he remembered a study compiled by Army Intelligence in Washington. According to the antiterrorist experts, the Red Brigades had released about half of their kidnap victims alive after the government had paid ransom or made some other humiliating concession. Other hostages, like Aldo Moro and Giuseppe Taliercio, had been executed.

There was not one recorded case of a kidnap victim's being successfully rescued from the Red Brigades in their ten-year operational history.

"Not terrific," he said. "Not really very good at all."

14

11:30 P.M., 17 DECEMBER 1981
VIA PINDEMONTE, PADUA

Just in time, he heard the movement of sweat socks on canvas and saw the rustle of the tent flap. Dozier pushed the earphones back into the approved position over his ears. Then he sat expectantly on his cot, the model prisoner.

The woman entered, still wearing her jogging suit and ski

mask. She was carrying a plate and a plastic cup, which she put on top of the porta-potty.

"I've brought you some food," she announced. "Do you like spaghetti?"

"Ah, yes," he said, a little amazed that they should be having this civilized conversation. Was she armed? They seemed to consider him a dangerous person and yet she was allowed to enter his tent alone and unprotected. If she was armed, there was always the chance that he could take the weapon away from her the first time she became careless. He glanced covertly at her body, but there was no sign of a concealed weapon. Then, out of the corner of one eye, he saw that they were being watched by Giovanni Ciucci, the short, heavyset man whom Dozier had nicknamed "the soldier" because everybody seemed entitled to give him orders.

"What happens now?" he asked.

"You eat. Then sleep." For a moment she hesitated, as if she would have liked to say something more, but instead she turned and left.

Eat, he told himself. Early in his career, every soldier learned to eat when the opportunity presented itself, so he lifted the plate onto his lap and ate. A glass of wine would have been nice, but there was only water in a Styrofoam cup sitting on the floor next to the toilet. It was awkward eating with one arm handcuffed to the frame of the cot, and when he noticed Ciucci watching him, he rattled his handcuffs.

He had just placed the empty plate back on the porta-potty when the tent flap was lifted for a second time and the three men appeared. The awkwardness of the handcuffs had apparently been acknowledged; Savasta removed them, using a two-foot chain as a replacement.

Wordlessly, he secured both ends of the chain with key-operated Yale padlocks. Then Savasta removed the white forty-watt light bulb and replaced it with a blue bulb that gave out a dim, restful light.

It must be late, Dozier realized, irritated that they should have taken his watch. There was no sound from the outer chamber of the tent except for the occasional sound of a page being turned as Ciucci read a book to keep him awake through a long shift of guard duty.

The lack of privacy bothered him. Apart from having no bathroom door to shut, it took some athletic skill to use a toilet with one leg and one arm attached to a cot. He managed, however, feeling silly about perching on this absurd plastic contraption with his trousers around his ankles, making a tinkling sound in the silence of the room.

When he was finished, he put the top down on the porta-potty and stretched out on the cot again. The air around him was cooling, as if the heat in the apartment had gone off for the night. He covered himself with the army blanket, feeling tired, and eventually managed to find a comfortable position without entangling his arms and legs in the chains.

An unemotional, pragmatic man, Dozier had long since recognized that there came a point every day when you had accomplished just about everything you were going to get done. Some days, it wasn't very much, but when that moment arrived, there was nothing to do but get some sleep.

He prayed briefly, asking guidance for himself, enlightenment for his captors, and protection for his wife.

Good night, Hon, he told her silently. Wherever you are.

BOOK III

THE
HOSTAGE

1

There was the faint swish of tire track against wet cobblestones and an automobile stopped on the street below.

Police Commissioner Salvatore Genova stirred in the warmth of his bed and opened his eyes. He wondered whether noises like this would always awaken him or whether someday, when the *brigatisti* were all in prison or dead, he would be able to sleep through the night the way normal people did.

He looked at his woman in the faint light from the hall, wondering whether Rina were really asleep or shamming. When he was summoned in the middle of the night, it was often easier for her to pretend to be asleep. They both knew that he might be back in ten minutes, or ten days, or that an accident might occur. It was better to avoid melodramatic farewells.

Down on the street, a car door closed. The commissioner slid out from between the warm blankets, groping for his jeans and tennis sneakers, his sweatshirt and leather jacket. He glanced out the window and something about the quality of the darkness over the Tyrrhenian Sea told him that it was still very early, perhaps two-thirty, surely no later than three. He finished dressing and put his pistol into his leather jacket. Outside in the corridor, there was the sound of footsteps as his visitor reached the top of the stairs. For a moment, Salvatore Genova stood at the doorway, looking back at the bed and thinking what an odd couple he and Rina had become. In a few hours, she would awaken, pack her textbooks and corrected essays and red pencils, and spend the day teaching literature to adolescents.

He moved toward the front door, cocking the revolver. It was almost certainly Blondie on the other side, but it did not pay to take chances.

"Commissario!" The whisper was familiar and Genova opened the door. Blondie was one of the few people Genova had ever trusted with the address where he lived with Rina.

105

"What's up?" Genova asked as they walked down the stairwell to the street. There was cold fog shrouding the commissioner's white Alfa Romeo but the inside of the car was warm.

"There's a cable from Rome that says we've got to be in Verona by morning."

"Do I get to take the boys?" Genova's first concern for his men. The "boys," as he always called them, excelled at undercover operations, dressing and talking like street people. They worked together like a team of athletes, instinctively knowing each other's moves.

"The cable said you could take anybody you want," Blondie told him. "I told Nico, Amadeo, Giacobbe, Ivano, and Massimo to meet us at headquarters."

"They'd only get in trouble if I left them behind," the commissioner grunted as Blondie guided the big Alfa downhill toward the dark waters of the harbor where the Polizia di Stato offices were located.

"Do we know what it's about?" Genova asked. He was not enchanted by the idea of being sent again halfway across northern Italy to operate in someone else's territory. He was still seeing Fulvia Miglietta almost every day, and the woman was talking more and more, sometimes about everyday things and sometimes about the growing strength of her religious convictions. He was confident that some day soon, she would tell him what he needed to know to dismantle what was left of the local Red Brigade establishment.

"There's an American general missing," Blondie said. "He was assigned to that NATO command in Verona and his wife says the kidnappers identified themselves as Brigate rosse. They were led by a skinny guy who sounds like he might be Savasta. The Carabinieri think the Yank is being stored somewhere in downtown Verona."

Genova winced. Not Savasta again! Genova and his boys had been called away from their home city earlier in the year to search for Savasta when the Veneto column chieftain had kidnapped the chief executive officer of the Montedison Chemical Company, Giuseppe Taliercio. They had spent several months in the Venice area and come home empty-handed, after Taliercio's body had been discovered, riddled with bullets.

Savasta was a hard case. There were no recent photographs of him. He didn't seem to make mistakes. Nobody even knew much about him beyond the fact that he tended to shoot his way out of life's little difficulties.

"The Carabinieri will go crazy over a missing American general," Genova said, his mind turning immediately to the bureaucratic implications of the case. From the Polizia di Stato perspective, the glamorous Carabinieri tended to concentrate their energies on a few spectacular high-profile cases and leave the State Police to handle the undramatic but hard-to-solve mysteries of everyday criminal life. Since the beginning of the "years of lead," the Carabinieri's Carlo Alberto Dalla Chiesa had been linked in the public mind with the government's war against the Red Brigades. The Polizia di Stato caught just as many terrorists, but the Carabinieri had a way of capturing most of the publicity.

In front of State Police Headquarters on the Corso Aurelio Saffi, there was a middle-aged Fiat sedan containing the five other members of Commissioner Genova's team. In the harsh glare of the streetlight, they all looked sleepy and irritable. Genova got out of his Alfa and strode over to the Fiat, exchanging some friendly banalities with his team before sending them on their way with instructions to meet him in front of the Verona Questura, the central State Police station in Verona.

Then he wandered back to his car, thinking about Rina and wondering whether she were awake and worrying or still asleep. The day ahead looked long and unpredictable; it might be days before he could get a call through to her. Would they ever be allowed to share a normal life?

The commissioner tried to work up his usual enthusiasm for a new case, but it was cold and optimism was hard to achieve at this hour. Could anyone possibly catch Savasta this time, when they had failed so often in the past? Genova and his boys were good in Genoa because they knew their city brick by brick. But Verona was foreign territory to them; they would be the outsiders there, resented by the local Polizia di Stato cops and shunned by the Carabinieri, who would try to dominate the case. It would be a lousy, cold, miserable Christmas spent in a cheap rented apartment in somebody else's city.

Blondie was standing by with the Alfa Romeo. Silently the two of them drove off, looking for coffee.

2

6:45 A.M., 18 DECEMBER 1981
VIA PINDEMONTE, PADUA

He awoke, remembering instantly all that had happened, and found the hint of a depression lurking somewhere within his brain, a sad and unfamiliar presence. Judy, he thought, where is Judy now? The kids . . .

The general had spent a lifetime disciplining his emotions, and he ordered them back into formation. He sat up. During his slumber, the earphones had slipped down around his neck, but he pushed them back into position to avoid irritating his captors. At some point in the night, they had changed the tape, but the music was still hard rock and he still hated it.

He began the day by leaving a trail, realizing that he could at any moment be moved to another location, perhaps even out of the country. First, he made several clear imprints of his thumb and index finger in order to establish his identity, at least to a police forensic squad. Then he selected a portion of the plastic flooring of the tent concealed by the bunk and with his fingernail, he scratched "James Dozier, 18 December" into the rubberized material. It was a desperate measure, he realized. Dozier was here. Kilroy was here. Did anybody ever find Kilroy?

What time is it? The stiffness in his body told him that he had slept longer than usual. It was perhaps six o'clock, and he reminded himself that he needed to establish a strenuous regimen and stick to it. At some point, in fifteen minutes or fifteen days, these people were going to make a mistake, and when they made it, he needed to be strong enough to exploit it.

Get limber! He rolled out of bed and began a strenuous series of deep knee bends. For years, he had suffered from low back pain, and he knew that keeping his abdominal muscles in peak condition was essential to mobility.

Assuming that the Red Brigades would not let him out for his morning jog, he decided to compensate by running in place. His chains clattered, and a moment after he started, Di Lenardo entered his tiny space.

"That's too much vibration." The big man was dressed in jeans and a T-shirt. In his hand there was a sheaf of papers that he offered to Dozier. "Anyway, now you need to study and prepare yourself for our meeting."

"Can you tell me what has happened to my wife?"

"This topic will be discussed during our *conferenza*. Read, and I will answer any questions you have."

The general took the document and scanned it. There were six pages of single-spaced text, a wordy, rhetorical political tract of some kind. At the top of page 1, there were the words RISOLUZIONE STRATEGICA printed in capital letters.

Indulging himself in a minor act of defiance, he placed the document under the cot and finished his exercises. Then he retrieved the *Risoluzione strategica* and began to work his way through the text. Dozier's knowledge of Italian was oriented toward practical military matters, and the document before him was filled with abstract political philosophy. The reading was slow and heavy.

As nearly as he could make out, the *risoluzione* was a basic exposition of Marxist-Leninist thought as applied to contemporary Italy. According to the Red Brigades, Italian-style capitalism was crumbling. When the suffering of the proletariat became unbearable, a rebellion would inevitably break out. There needed to be a vanguard movement like the Red Brigades, capable of guiding the proletariat into the Communist future by striking into the heart of the state.

In the meantime, the revolutionaries were unhappy about the American military presence in Italy, the U.S. Cruise missiles scheduled for Sicily, and what they regarded as economic dominion over Italian life by American-owned multinational corporations. The general was still working his way syllable by syllable through his assigned reading when Savasta, Giovanni Ciucci, and Emilia Libera joined Di Lenardo in the tent.

"My wife?"

"We wish to discuss the contents of the document given to you this morning for study," Di Lenardo insisted. The woman and the three men were sitting cross-legged on the plastic floor of the tent while Dozier perched on the edge of his cot. Ciucci was stationed in the doorway, holding an automatic pistol. Savasta was fussing with a tape recorder, since this interview was apparently destined to be preserved for revolutionary posterity. The woman was staring at him with a mixture of hostility and curiosity.

"I want some assurance that my wife has not been harmed," Dozier repeated. He could hear an inappropriate I-am-a-general-giving-you-orders tone slipping into his voice, but at the moment he was too angry to care.

"Show him the picture!" snapped Savasta. Emilia Libera produced a newspaper clipping and handed it to the general. It was from the 18 December edition of a Milan daily called *La Notte*. On the front page there was a photograph of a haggard, distraught Judy Dozier, being led from the front door of what was plainly number 5, Via Lungadige Catena. She appeared unhurt. Dozier exhaled heavily. Oh, thank God, he thought, thank God. . . .

"Okay, all right," he said, putting the clipping on the cot next to him. "Well, let's get on with it. I assume that you represent the KGB; is that correct?"

"What?" Di Lenardo responded but they all seemed stunned. "Who?"

"The KGB," Dozier repeated. "Don't you people work for Soviet intelligence?"

"We are independent Italian Communists," Savasta said. "We have nothing to do with the Russian social imperialists and we dislike the Warsaw Pact as much as NATO! You must understand that we wish our nation to be controlled neither by the Russians nor by you Americans!"

"Okay, what do you want with me?" He hoped they were telling the truth. If these folks are really domestic Italian terrorists, he thought, then there is no point in trying the old name-rank-and-serial-number defense. I'd better chat with them and establish some kind of dialogue. But they get nothing serious out of me. No classified information. Nothing damaging to the United States or to the army.

"You were supposed to have studied our Strategic Resolution," Di Lenardo said.

"I studied it. My Italian isn't much good and it didn't make a lot of sense to me."

"Then I will explain it to you," Di Lenardo enthused, and Dozier felt his mind slipping into neutral as the masked ideologue sat down next to him and started a detailed explanation of the document. The gist of his argument was that there existed some kind of conspiracy among the big multinational corporations, NATO, the American government, and the Italian Christian Democratic party, all of whom were seeking to oppress the workers, or—to use the expression Di Lenardo favored—the proletariat.

"What proletariat?" Dozier interjected.

"The Italian proletariat! The poor people of Italy—"

"The poor people in Italy are not going to stage any kind of Marxist revolution," Dozier told them. "People who are starving will rebel, but nobody in Italy is that hungry, and besides the economy is expanding. It's not going to happen here."

"The revolution is inevitable once the necessary and sufficient conditions of impoverishment have been reached...." Di Lenardo corrected him, but Dozier smirked and shook his head.

"Do you find this amusing?" Di Lenardo reacted.

"If we can't convert you, maybe we can at least make you neutral in our struggle," Savasta said.

"Look, maybe it would help matters if you guys would say precisely what you wanted from me."

"You have been brought here for two purposes," Savasta said. "First, we hope to use you as a hostage to force our government to release some of our colleagues who have been captured and imprisoned."

"Then hadn't you better get in touch with the Italian authorities and start negotiating?" Actually, Dozier's feelings about negotiating with terrorists were mixed. In the Aldo Moro case, the Italian government had refused to negotiate, convinced that the Red Brigades would never dare to execute the celebrated statesman. After Moro's murder, however, the Italian authorities had conducted negotiations with terrorists several times to secure the safe release of hostages.

As far as American policy was concerned, Dozier had always opposed making concessions to terrorists, and he was sure that the new Reagan administration would never surrender. The Italians could do whatever they wanted but he would prefer to be rescued or—even better—to escape.

"No, it is much too early," Savasta said. "This kidnapping is merely the beginning of our Winter Campaign, and there are several more operations to be carried out. Right now, both your government and ours think that they can liberate you with policemen or your CIA spies. We must first allow them to try and fail, and we will open negotiations when they realize that it is their only choice."

Dozier nodded, digesting the unwelcome news that this vacation was likely to be a lengthy one.

"Secondly," continued Savasta, "we want you to explain to the Italian people your plan for the economic, military, and political subjugation of Italy."

"What?" All those boring cocktail parties, he thought, and all along I was supposed to be out subjugating Italy!

"NATO is the instrument of American imperialism in Italy," Di Lenardo added. "And you are the general in command of NATO!"

"Look, did you guys get the right general? I am deputy chief of staff for logistics and administration for LANDSOUTH. This is only one of several NATO commands in Italy, and I'm not even in charge of LANDSOUTH. There are two Italian generals above me! There is no American plan to subjugate Italy!"

"That's a lie!" said Savasta. "The Italian command structure is window dressing for the reality of American hegemony over a puppet government. It all began after World War II, when you Americans produced the Marshall Plan, which was your scheme to dominate the whole of Europe!"

"I thought the Marshall Plan was about feeding hungry Europeans." Dozier was growing tired of the argument. It seemed to him that his captors did not enjoy a close relationship with reality.

"Was it not the same when you attempted to subjugate Vietnam?"

"Vietnam was about freedom not subjugation." They've had a look at my service record, Dozier thought. I need to be careful. What else do they know about me?

"Tell us about Vietnam," Savasta invited. "Did you go there voluntarily?"

"Yes . . . yes, I went there voluntarily. It seemed to us then that there was something that we could accomplish there, a people who could be rescued."

"And what were your responsibilities there?" Savasta's voice was taking on a harsh inquisitorial tone that Dozier was beginning to find offensive. I'm not going to be put on trial for Vietnam, he thought. Not by you. Not by anybody.

"I served with an armored cavalry regiment. One of our jobs was to intercept enemy units as they infiltrated from Cambodia into South Vietnam."

"And why did you fail?"

"Militarily we didn't fail! We won every major battle we fought!"

"Your country lost the war! You can't deny—"

"Somebody failed, but it wasn't the army." Dozier decided that it would be better to keep the discussion at the technical level. "The supply routes from the north were never successfully interdicted. Because of political considerations, Washington kept interrupting the bombing of the north, and enemy logistics were never seriously disturbed, and in the final analysis—"

"The American people got tired of the war!" Di Lenardo intervened.

"I suppose so. The politicians never managed to explain what we were doing, and some of the folks back home got impatient. In the end, the same thing will happen to you. People will get tired and what little support you have will dry up."

"We will win!" Savasta's voice was a low hiss. "It may take a long time, but in the end, we will triumph."

"You don't have a long time. Maybe that's what we learned in Vietnam."

"Did you kill people in Vietnam?" It was the woman's voice, her first contribution to the discussion. For a moment their eyes met, and then she looked away. Somehow, the American sensed that she wanted him to say: no, I served at a desk a hundred miles behind the front lines, sorting mail.

"Of course I killed people," he told her.

"We will conduct another interrogation of the prisoner soon," announced Savasta, turning off the tape recorder. Emilia Libera looked at him with disappointment, and then they all left.

3

It was a cold morning with a moody, overcast sky. Dressed in faded jeans and sneakers and a heavy woolen jacket, Ruggiero Volinia was taking the long way to the newspaper stand, circling around the corner from his home on the Via Magellano in order to walk down the length of the Via Lungadige Catena.

He had not reached home the previous night until very late and had slept badly. Now, he was thinking about ways to propose to Antonio Savasta that he be allowed to end his active service with the Red Brigades, not betraying anyone but retiring honorably from an organization whose aims he continued to support, albeit externally.

In front of number 5 there were half a dozen police cars and Ruggiero was instantly tempted to go back the way he came before anyone saw him. No, he thought, steadying himself. I live legitimately in this neighborhood and I've got documents to prove it. I'm on my way to the kiosk on the corner because I'm looking for work and I need the Help Wanted section from the morning paper.

But the fear of arrest stayed with him and he tormented himself with a vision of his capture. If they broke his spirit in some awful dungeon, what could he safely tell them? He decided that he would never betray his own people, but he could give the police the location of that arms depot in Mestre, near Venice, the guns they got from the Palestinians. . . . At the end of the street, he dug into his pocket for four hundred lire and bought the morning edition of *L'Arena*, Verona's daily paper.

THE RED BRIGADES KIDNAP AN AMERICAN GENERAL! screamed the headline.

An American general! Ruggiero shook his head in disbelief. He had assumed that the *pollo* was an Italian. Why did we have to pick on an American general? This means bringing the Pentagon down upon us! If Savasta was right about the Americans' controlling Italy behind the scenes, then the police reaction will be horrible!

His hands were trembling as he folded the newspaper and put it into the back pocket of his jeans. For a moment, he thought about running across the bridge and up the hill to Lisa's house on the Via Monte Ortigara. While there was still time they could get her money out of the bank and take the train across the border into Switzerland.

No, if they are following me, I would be leading them directly to her. And if they've found her name on a list somewhere, then they will be there waiting for me. Savasta told me he would be in touch when it was safe.

I've got to wait it out, he told himself, turning back toward his home. Oh Christ, why did I get involved?

4

8:05 A.M., 18 DECEMBER 1981
VERONA QUESTURA (STATE POLICE HEADQUARTERS)
VIA LUNGADIGE PORTA VITTORIA, VERONA

The locals called it the Cops' Bar. It was close to the Verona Questura and so grubby that nobody but a State Policeman would be found dead there. Commissioner Genova hesitated at the door, but the "boys" had driven through the night without food, and they were all facing a twenty-four-hour shift.

"Who wants what?" he asked, studying the array of food on offer behind the counter.

"Beer!" somebody groaned.

"All right, we'll have an early lunch," the commissioner decreed. The middle-aged Fiat had not come equipped with much of a heating system and the men were cold.

About as cold as General Dozier's trail, Genova thought as his men ordered cheese sandwiches and beer. For himself, he ordered a righteous double espresso, flooding his system with industrial-strength caffeine in preparation for a long day after a mostly sleepless night. The commissioner had already spent an hour at the Questura in a senior officer's meeting where the principal investigators had been briefed on the abduction.

The case was going to be tough, because they were starting with very little to work on. The Carabinieri had found a Fiat 238 van with forged plates near LANDSOUTH headquarters and were dusting it for fingerprints, but the commissioner already knew they were not going to find any. If Savasta had fingerprints, he had never left them lying around on abandoned vehicles.

On the other hand, it did look like the best team of State Police investigators ever assembled for one crime. In command of the whole operation was a canny old Sicilian named Gaspare De Francisci, who had often been compared to John le Carré's George Smiley. With his dry, self-contained manner, De Francisci had worked in police intelligence ever since the end of the war, staying out of politics but rising steadily to the top of the secret world.

De Francisci would be spending most of his time in Rome, dealing with the politicians and leaving a DIGOS superstar named Umberto Improta in Verona to provide on-the-scene technical direction. Umberto had accepted the assignment on the condition that he be allowed to bring in three commissioners whose work he admired.

As a result, Commissioner Oscar Fioriolli and his team had been ordered up from Florence, arriving in the early hours of the morning. An old friend of Genova's named Luciano De Gregorio had slipped into Verona with a mob of heavyweights from the Bologna DIGOS. The third *commissario* on Improta's list had been Genova himself.

The commissioner finished his coffee, and when the boys had gulped their beer, he marched them all out of the Cops' Bar and into the Verona Questura, a tan, three-story building with green shutters. The sky was still gray and the temperature trembled a few degrees above freezing. On the other side of the Via Lungadige Porta Vittoria was the Adige River, and the water looked rough and menacing in the faint morning light.

The office assigned to them was on the Questura's second floor. Genova had been hoping for a window overlooking the river, but instead they had been given a view of the parking lot. There was a stale tobacco odor in the room, which had only three chairs. In one corner were a desk and what looked like the first Olivetti ever made.

Genova took the chair behind the desk while the others hunkered down on the wooden floor, resting their backs against the soiled gray plaster walls. Somebody passed around a pack of Muratti cigarettes. Behind the desk there was a shelf jammed with hundreds of pink cardboard folders, each with a name and an archival number written in bold letters on the front.

"We've drawn the records detail," the commissioner announced and his men groaned.

A records search was necessary but often boring. The fact that the Veneto column had staged a major operation in Verona suggested that there was a Red Brigades infrastructure in place here. Most *brigatisti* had edged slowly into the revolutionary movement, becoming terrorists only after joining radical youth groups or taking part in protest marches or demonstrations. Hence the names of Savasta's local support people might well be on the covers of these dossiers.

Hence, they would pore over old files, going as far back as the late 1960s when demonstrations against the war in Vietnam were common. Once a list of possible *brigatisti* had been drawn up, selected individuals would be placed under surveillance; their movements would be followed, their telephones tapped, and their mail intercepted until it was clear that they were not involved in subversive activities.

"Why were we brought in?" grumbled one of the men.

"Because we're the best!" Genova tried to project an air of confidence, but inwardly he was pessimistic. *That Yank has been gone for twelve long hours with nobody but dumb Carabinieri looking for him,* he thought. *Dozier could be over the border into Austria or Yugoslavia by now or in a submarine headed for Libya. Or he could be a kilometer from here, hidden in a secret subbasement in downtown Verona. Or he could already be dead.*

Somebody in one of these dossiers might know where he is, but only if Savasta made the silly mistake of trusting an old Verona lefty with a police record.

And if Savasta made mistakes like that, the commissioner was thinking sourly as he began to pass out the dossiers, *we'd have nailed him a long time ago.*

5

"To those who have taken my husband and the father of our children, I appeal to you for humane treatment." Judy Dozier spoke simply, gazing into the television camera.

She had worked hard on this public appearance, powdering over the bruises on her face. She had been resistant to the notion of a press conference but ultimately decided that it was important to give a public impression of calmness and confidence. She was tired; the night had been spent working with the police and contacting her children, Cheryl and Scott.

The frantic character of the night had been punctuated by one moment of absurdity. President Reagan had called LAND-SOUTH from the White House to say that Judy would have all the support she needed. The call had been taken by an Italian official who failed to recognize the significance of a *casa bianca*, and told the caller that the Signora Dozier was too busy to come to the phone. When all this is over, she thought, we will laugh at the day I was too busy to take a call from Ronald Reagan.

"Jim is very important to us," she spoke through the television to the kidnappers. "He is everything to us. I hope you will return him safe and well."

She glanced over at Cheryl, and her daughter smiled encouragement. As soon as the Air Force had received word of Jim's abduction, Cheryl's commanding officer at Rhein Main Air Force Base in Germany had put her aboard a medical evacuation plane for Verona. Scott would be flying in from Florida on the first available flight.

Judy plunged into the portion of her statement that was designed to bolster Jim's morale, if he was allowed to listen to her words.

"Honey, if you are watching this, then you know that we are fine. We're waiting for you to come home, and we need you.

Cheryl is here with me. Our prayers are with you. Come home. We love you."

The press conference finished. Cheryl took her arm, and the two women left the room.

6

It was past quitting time. The offices of the Sixty-sixth Military Intelligence Group were dark, except for a solitary light glowing on Colonel Bill Reed's desk.

We're getting nowhere, he thought, sorting through the pile of documents on his desk and pausing to reread the transcribed text of the phone call made by a Red Brigades spokesperson to ANSA, the Italian national news service.

"We take responsibility," the text said, "for the kidnapping of NATO's chief executioner, James Dozier, who has been confined to a people's prison where he will be subjected to a trial by the proletariat."

Why had they picked on General Dozier? Jim must have shot the occasional Viet Cong during the war in Southeast Asia, but he had never functioned as an "executioner" for anyone, least of all NATO.

How would the Italians respond? Publicly and privately, Prime Minister Spadolini was insisting that there would be no deals with the Red Brigades. Not only was Italian intelligence forbidden to negotiate for the general's release but Spadolini had ordered the police to prevent anyone else—including the American CIA—from making a payoff to the Red Brigades in order to secure the release of the hostage.

Reed knew that Dozier himself would be the first to rule out a dirty deal. But they were only fifty hours into the crisis and everybody was still feeling brave. Suppose they began torturing him? A Calabrian gang had once kidnapped John Paul Getty's grandson and opened the bidding by cutting off the boy's left ear and sending it to the family. If portions of Jim Dozier began arriving in the morning mail, how long would everybody stay brave?

Or suppose they broke him with torture? There was no question that Dozier was tough, but with sophisticated interrogation techniques anybody would crack eventually. What could Jim Dozier give away if he started talking?

Reed winced at the prospect. The general knew as much as anyone about NATO's wartime strategy. He was an expert in tank warfare and the employment of tactical nuclear weapons. He was familiar with the nation's intelligence system and had been receiving regular briefings at the supersecret code word level, which meant that he understood spy satellites and communications intercepts and aerial photography.

There was only one conclusion: a detailed and successful debriefing of Dozier would constitute a major national security disaster for the United States.

To make matters worse, some idiot on the LANDSOUTH staff had told a reporter, "General Dozier knows everything, but we are certain that he will not talk." This piece of carelessness could increase the pressure on Jim to reveal classified information. The embassy had quickly leaked stories to friendly journalists that the general was actually a minor administrative official with no access to classified data, but it remained to be seen how much of the damage could be repaired.

The phone on Reed's desk rang. It was Judy Reed. "Can't you come over for just a few minutes? You've been there for two days!"

"What's wrong?" The colonel tried to remember where he was supposed to be.

"Bill, it's the Christmas party," she reminded him. "Come relax for a few minutes, okay?"

Reed agreed, but he was still reviewing the case in his mind as he wandered off in the direction of the officer's club.

There might be too many cooks in the kitchen, he thought. Several rival Italian intelligence agencies were already competing with one another, and the Carabinieri were not sharing their information—assuming they had any—with anyone. The Polizia di Stato had stormed into Verona with a collection of mysterious

DIGOS heavyweights who were saying nothing about their investigation.

Even worse, the Pentagon was already feuding with the State Department! Representing the Foreign Service, Ambassador Max Rabb had taken the reasonable position that only the Italians were capable of finding Jim Dozier. Although there were several dozen American intelligence groups that wanted a piece of the action, Rabb had promised Prime Minister Spadolini that he would keep the Defense Department and CIA at arm's length as long as the Italians seemed to be making progress.

The Pentagon, on the other hand, was enraged by what had been done to Jim Dozier and did not believe that the Italians had the resources to find him. Point man for terrorism in the Pentagon was a handpicked Reagan appointee named Noel Koch, who had reacted to Dozier's disappearance by ordering a Delta Force team at Fort Bragg to get packed and leave for Italy.

Noel Koch had apparently not bothered to ask the American ambassador's permission; Rabb had burst into fury when he read in the morning papers that the Delta Force had entered "his" country without permission.

The colonel strolled into the Officer's Club and followed the music to the party. Judy Reed was presiding over the punch bowl. There was a Christmas tree, and people were consuming drinks and hors d'oeuvres and Christmas cookies, but nobody seemed very festive.

"How's it going?" he asked.

"I've had more fun at funerals," Judy Reed confessed. "Is there any word?"

"No. Mrs. Dozier has been on television to plead for Jim's release. She's been terrifically brave."

"The poor woman! What do you think is going to happen to the general?"

"We'll get him back."

"Good," Judy Reed sent a whom-do-you-think-you-are-kidding look in his direction. "Do you want a drink?"

"Ah . . . I'll have a coffee."

"It'll keep you awake."

"I know," he replied, his mind returning to the documents on his desk. "Awake is what I've got to be for a while yet."

7

"He's my son," Judy Dozier announced, identifying the young man with the beard and long hair.

The policeman at the door gazed critically at Scott Dozier before stepping aside to allow the Dozier family to enter the apartment. News of his father's disappearance had reached Scott at home in Florida, where he was working part-time and studying art at a community college. The young man had caught the first flight to Italy but arrived to find that he had no apparent function beyond comforting his mother, who was coping magnificently with the stress. Feeling useless, Scott was now searching for a way to contribute something practical to the hunt for his father.

Judy pushed open the door. It seemed a lifetime ago that she and Jim had sat in the kitchen, sorting their mail and debating the demerits of his gray trousers. The apartment seemed oppressively silent, and she wandered through the living room and out onto the balcony. Cheryl and Scott followed her and they stood in the fresh air. It was cold but sunny, the first clear day in weeks.

"Mrs. Dozier! Signora!" There were shouts from below, and Judy looked down to see a cluster of journalists and photographers who had gathered on the street below. "We take your picture?"

Judy nodded. The kidnappers would see these pictures in the press, she thought, and there was even a chance that Jim himself would be permitted to look at them. He needed to see that his family was together.

When the cameras had clicked, they went back into the living room, and Cheryl disappeared into the kitchen to make coffee. Judy sank onto the sofa. Scott paced the floor, his face pale with jet lag and anxiety.

"Is our government doing everything it can?"

"I think so," she told him. "There was some confusion at first, but afterward . . . I think they're working hard."

"How about the Italians?"

"They're doing their best. I've never seen so many policemen on the streets, and their detectives questioned me until I was blue in the face. Yesterday, just before you arrived, I spent hours helping their police artist attempt to draw portraits of the two plumbers."

"How did they come out? I mean, did the results look anything like what you remember?"

"Not much. Listen, why don't we give it a try? You draw and I'll describe!"

"Let's do it!" Scott located a supply of blank white paper and some pencils in his father's desk. "I'll sketch some faces, and you tell me what needs to be changed, okay? Let's start with the shorter of the two men, the one you thought was in charge."

"Okay! He had a long, thin face, as I remember. . . ."

"Do you think they'll do a trade?" Scott asked as he began to work. "Will they negotiate with the Red Brigades?"

"I don't know. I don't think Mr. Reagan will make concessions to terrorists."

"So, it's going to be hardball all the way?"

"I think so." In her heart, she knew that she would pay any price to get him back, but hardball had always been Jim's favorite game. He would not want a deal done.

"That's good," she said, watching a face emerge on Scott's pad. "His nose was a little longer."

8

11:30 A.M., 21 DECEMBER 1981
VIA PINDEMONTE, PADUA

Today is Monday, he calculated. Friday is Christmas.

On his first day in captivity, Dozier had found an empty matchbox under his cot and had begun to use it as a calendar, making a deep fingernail impression in the soft cardboard every morning to mark the date.

Where is Judy now? Would the authorities have allowed her to remain in their apartment? Or had they moved her to a secret location for her protection? And where are my kids? Are they protecting Cheryl up in Germany? What is Scott doing?

And how about Judy's Christmas present? That necklace with the Lion of Saint Mark pendant was still sitting in my desk. Could I ask Savasta to ring up NATO Headquarters and tell somebody to take the pendant around to Judy in time for Christmas?

That's ridiculous, he told himself. Why don't I concentrate on getting out of here so I can give it to her in person?

And where is here? He was in an apartment building somewhere in northeastern Italy. From below, he could hear an indistinct rumble during the day, but upstairs there were occasionally the footsteps of children. From outside, he thought he could hear the rumble of traffic, quite loud during the day and softer by night.

Was any of this useful? He was being held captive by at least four professional terrorists, one of whom was a woman. The place was apparently a headquarters of some kind: someone was doing a lot of typing and his hosts seemed to come and go frequently. Whenever they opened the door of the apartment, the movement of air made the wall of his tent billow, and this happened several times a day.

The telephone rang occasionally, but Dozier could never hear an actual conversation. Usually, the phone would ring three times and then stop, and he guessed that this was a code. Once in a while, it rang six times and then stopped, conveying some different message.

Who were his captors? There seemed no reason to doubt their assertion that they belonged to the Brigate rosse, despite the fact that Italian terrorists had never before targeted the American community. They seemed bright and professional; they did not appear to be sadistic or gratuitously cruel. They had never permitted him to see their faces; optimistically, Dozier thought this implied that they did not wish to be identified after his eventual release.

Physically, he was still in reasonable shape, although he was worried about a possible loss of hearing from the constant pounding of rock and roll in his ears. His hosts had provided him with a toothbrush and toothpaste, but he had not been given the opportunity to wash or shave since his arrival.

Was it possible to remove his chains? If he could get free, he could tear a length of cloth from his shirt to use as a garrote and then jump the guard in the middle of the night. . . . The general turned on his side to conceal his movements and began to force the chain down over his hand. The process scraped some skin away, but with a burst of happiness, he found that he could remove his arm chain entirely.

Quickly, he replaced the chain around his arm and went to work on the three-foot shackle attached to his ankle, accepting a certain amount of pain as the links bit into his flesh.

The loop refused to slide down over his heel and there were footsteps outside, forcing him to abandon his efforts. Hurriedly, Dozier pushed the earphones back into place as Savasta entered with lunch.

The food generally had not been bad, although today the meat and beans seemed to have come straight out of a can. For lunch and dinner, there was usually a meat, a vegetable, and either potato or pasta, with an occasional side salad.

"Do you like wine with your meals?" Savasta asked as he put the plate on the chemical toilet.

"Yes," said Dozier, surprised at this concern for his comfort. Did terrorists get Christmas spirit like everyone else? "Wine would be nice, but what I really need is a wash. I smell bad."

"You do."

"And I need fresh clothing."

"After you have finished your lunch," the guerrilla promised, ducking out of the tent.

Dozier ate, feeling the tension rising within him. To allow him to change his clothing, they would have to unchain him, at least momentarily. Would there be a careless moment, a chance for fight or flight? Or would the chains be less tight afterward?

When lunch was over, Savasta and Ciucci entered; in the background, Dozier could see Di Lenardo's powerful figure holding an automatic. They were going to take no chances.

It was a fast wash. Savasta threw some light blue jockey shorts, an undershirt, black socks, and a new black track suit onto the cot, and then undid the chain around Dozier's wrist. Ciucci placed a bowl of warm water on top of the porta-potty, together with a bar of soap and a clean towel. The three men then retreated to the outer chamber of the tent, but Dozier realized that he was still too closely observed to make a bid for freedom.

When the general finished washing his face and torso, Savasta replaced the arm restraint and then unlocked the ankle chain, allowing the general to slip out of the gray trousers that Judy hated so much. It was embarrassing to perform his ablutions under the nonchalant gaze of three terrorists, but Dozier did a thorough job, not knowing when he would again be permitted this luxury. Then Savasta reattached the ankle chain to the frame of the cot, once again securing both ends with Yale locks.

Was the chain around his ankle less tight? It was difficult to say, and it would have been foolish to look down, but it felt less restrictive, and a slender hope invaded the general's mind.

And now what? The burly Di Lenardo shouldered his way into Dozier's space with a large sheet of heavy paper that he pinned to the tent wall over the cot. On the sheet was a big red, five-pointed star enclosed within a circle. In large red letters, the words BRIGATE ROSSE were printed on either side of the star. Dozier recognized the star as the emblem of the Red Brigades, but he did not understand what was happening until Savasta handed him a piece of white cardboard, about two feet wide, on which a propaganda statement had been printed with a felt-tip pen.

"The crisis of capitalism generates imperialist war," the text began. It was the usual demand for a proletarian uprising against American capitalism.

"You need to hold this up so we can take your picture," Savasta said. Behind him, Di Lenardo was now holding a camera.

"No!"

"This is the only way your family will know you are alive," Savasta insisted. Dozier realized that he had no real choice. If the price of communicating with the outside world was displaying this silly propaganda statement, then the outside world would have to understand his motives. Holding the paper under his chin, he casually extended the middle fingers of each hand in the classic "Up yours!" sign. Di Lenardo put his eye to the viewfinder and focused, but Savasta groaned.

"No, not like that. We know what that means even in Italy."

Dozier withdrew both of the offending fingers and concentrated upon giving the camera a sardonic half-smile. When Di Lenardo had snapped a few pictures, the revolutionaries took down the sheet with the red star and removed the propaganda statement from his hands.

"Look, can I have a razor?" Dozier demanded. "I need to shave."

"No!" Savasta's reply was unhesitating.

"Why?" demanded Dozier, wondering how it would advance the cause of the revolution for him to look like a polar bear.

"We will need occasionally to demonstrate that you are still alive. A growing beard is the best proof."

The guerrillas departed, leaving Dozier alone. Instantly, he attacked the chain around his wrist. It was still loose enough to slip over his hand!

The full use of both hands meant that he was halfway to freedom, but when he experimented with the chain around his ankle, the hope died. The lower chain was as tight as ever, or maybe tighter.

For a moment, he sat on his cot, disappointed. Savasta had made it clear that they intended to keep him prisoner long enough for his beard to grow.

Curious, he peered at his bearded reflection in the blue disinfectant fluid at the bottom of the chemical toilet.

An aging hippie with wild hair and white whiskers stared back at him, a man he hardly recognized, and Dozier closed the top of the porta-potty with an angry gesture.

9

5:15 P.M., 24 DECEMBER 1981
VIA PINDEMONTE, PADUA

It was nearly dark. Savasta, Di Lenardo, and Emilia Libera were sitting at the kitchen table, preparing for the next round of discussions with the prisoner. Emanuela Frascella was cooking beefsteaks for their Christmas Eve dinner. She was burning them severely, as was her custom.

There was a sharp knock at the door and the four of them froze. Police?

"Wait," muttered Savasta. He took Emanuela's arm to prevent her from acting precipitously and felt her slender body trembling. As he withdrew the automatic pistol from his belt, he nodded to Emilia and Cesare, who walked to the bedroom, where the heavy weapons were kept. They paused to warn Giovanni Ciucci, who was on duty in the tent room.

Savasta raised the Browning and stepped behind the door to conceal his presence. Emanuela had installed an elaborate anti-burglar system on this door, including steel bars to strengthen it against unwelcome intruders. She undid the lock and opened the door.

"Buona sera, Signorina." It was the building superintendent. "We've got the usual problem about the chimney. The people upstairs are complaining about the smoke. I'll just have a look at it."

Savasta lowered his pistol, remembering that the smoke from Emanuela's stove rose into a flue and then into a ventilation pipe that passed through all the apartments above them. When Emanuela incinerated their dinner, the excess smoke poured into other apartments above.

"I'm sorry," Emanuela responded, blocking the door and nailing him with her I-am-a-rich-man's-daughter look. "We're cooking steaks for dinner and we'll be finished in a minute. I won't let it happen again."

"Va bene, Signorina," the superintendent said as Emanuela closed the door in his face.

"You were fine," Savasta told her warmly, congratulating himself on his decision to make the quiet, reliable Emanuela a member of the team. She and Cesare Di Lenardo were constant companions, but if they were having a love affair, they were keeping it to themselves. With five guerrillas and a captured general all living in one small apartment, nobody was having much of a sex life.

They dined on well-done steaks, preparing themselves for the continuing interrogation of the prisoner. The Executive Committee did not intend to bargain with the Italian government over the fate of the captured *generale americano* until after the successful conclusion of the other major Winter Campaign operations. Savasta intended to hold discussions with Dozier over perhaps a two- or three-month period, giving his team plenty of time to extract from the general what they wanted to know.

There was a rigid Red Brigades policy against using physical violence during an interrogation, but it was legitimate to use psychological techniques to break down the prisoner's emotional defenses. Savasta had decreed that any reading material given to

Dozier would be censored to eliminate any reference to his abduction, making him feel that he had been forgotten and abandoned by the outside world.

The rock and roll in his ears was intended to keep him isolated from the routine of everyday life, and the tent was meant to complete the task of cutting him off from the world. Savasta and his colleagues were also confusing Dozier's sense of time, shortening his days by changing the bulb in his tent from white to blue thirty minutes earlier every twenty-four hours, and then bringing him breakfast earlier each morning. In sixty days or so, they would have him psychologically disoriented. By that time, they should have no difficulty extracting admissions about American guilt for Vietnam and about the imperialist nature of American policy toward Italy.

But it was going to take some time to break this prisoner, Savasta reflected as he led his team into the tent. Dozier was still incredibly active, doing a marathon round of exercises every day and keeping himself in top physical condition. He seemed alert and unafraid of them, prepared to exploit the slightest act of carelessness on their part.

"Today we will continue the interrogation of the prisoner," Savasta announced, seating himself on the plastic floor of the tent and switching on the tape recorder to preserve the discussion for the Esecutivo.

"Great, listen, can you people come up with something to read and a deck of playing cards? The boredom is killing me."

"Yes . . . of course," conceded Savasta, irritated at the way the man always seemed to be able to establish his dominance.

"And this music is too loud! It would be nice if you could find something else for me to listen to. This stuff is driving me nuts."

"Yes. And now we must talk." Savasta saw that he had to redirect the whole tone of the encounter. "Do you understand why you have been brought here?"

"I am afraid that I do not," Dozier replied stiffly.

"Do you know what the Red Brigades are?"

"Urban guerrillas of some kind. I had the impression that you were strictly an Italian problem. I now see that I was wrong."

"Let me explain why you have been locked up in a people's prison. Through you, we're going to put on trial the whole structure of your military occupation of our country and American imperialism since 1945. Your own military career is a microcosm of CIA state terrorism in which you have been an accomplice!"

"Accomplice? Listen, I'm not sure what you want out of me."

"We need to know about American atomic bombs in Italy."

"Atomic bombs?" Dozier looked at him blankly. "Then you've got the wrong general."

"This peninsula is a virtual launching pad for your nuclear weapons! There are planes with bombs in Aviano, and Nike Hercules missiles with atomic warheads all over Italy!"

"Could be," Dozier shrugged. "I never got involved with that side of the operation."

"What would be the function of the 599th Artillery Group?" A recent issue of an Italian newsmagazine had published a list of all of the American-controlled nuclear sites in Italy. If Dozier would confirm that these U.S. units controlled nuclear weapons, the Esecutivo could prepare a propaganda offensive. Most Italians were nervous about American hydrogen bombs on Italian territory.

"I don't know." Dozier frowned. "Are you sure that it's an American unit?"

"How about the Sixty-second Engineer Battalion? The Sixty-seventh Ordnance Group?"

"Look, nuclear weapons were never part of my job," Dozier said. "I was assigned to LANDSOUTH, and we don't have any atomic bombs."

"Where does the American military keep its nuclear weapons?" Savasta glanced at his notes. "Are some of them stored at Site Pluto?"

"I don't know." The general looked at him steadily. If he had ever heard of Site Pluto, he was giving nothing away.

"How about Camp Darby in Livorno?"

Dozier shrugged.

"How is it possible that you don't know?"

"It wasn't my job to know. We compartmentalize classified information."

There are six thousand policemen out looking for him, Savasta thought. And he wants us to believe that he was so insignificant that he never got to know any secrets!

"I don't believe you," Savasta told him.

"There are some things I am not going to be able to tell you about," Dozier said bluntly.

"There is something you can tell us!" Di Lenardo cut in. "We need to know what kinds of special forces and commando troops are going to be used against us when we make the transition to full-fledged guerrilla warfare. How well is the government prepared to combat guerrilla forces?"

"Reasonably well prepared. The junior officers all receive classes in small-unit tactics."

"What kind of unconventional warfare training do the Carabinieri receive?"

"I don't know."

"How about the Alpine regiments?"

"They seem to have good morale," Dozier conceded.

"What kind of weapons do they have?"

"Oh, rifles, that sort of thing," Dozier said dryly. "I don't know exactly."

Savasta looked down at his notes. Beyond Dozier's devastating admission that the Alpine regiments had rifles, they were getting nowhere.

"If you want to go home, you have to answer some of our questions." Savasta looked at the prisoner sharply as he uttered the threat, but Dozier simply glared back at him.

"We will continue the interrogation of the people's prisoner on another occasion." Savasta snapped off the tape recorder, finding that he disliked this prisoner in a way that he had never disliked any of the others. Dozier was apparently not afraid of them or worried by what they might do to him. He seemed to regard the whole episode as a temporary inconvenience, like a delayed flight or a mechanical failure in one of his tanks. And he was treating them with contempt, as if they were juvenile delinquents rather than guerrilla warriors.

Did he understand what was likely to happen to him? This abduction would have to serve the revolution in some way. Either the Italian government would release Red Brigade prisoners, or Dozier would make valuable propaganda statements, or . . . or he would be executed as a war criminal!

10

At the end of December, the darkness in northern Italy comes down at night like a hammer. In the fast-fading light, Colonel Bill Reed stood on the tarmac, watching an overloaded Beechcraft U-21 lumber into the air like a vulture with arthritis. Once it was airborne, the plane turned northeast and disappeared into a cloud, flying toward the U.S. Air Force Base at Aviano.

In order to confuse anyone who might be curious about the presence of a National Security Agency (NSA) aircraft in northern Italy, the pilot had filed a spurious flight plan, giving Aviano as his destination. As soon as he reached his desired cruising altitude of one thousand feet, the aircraft would bank to the west and fly toward Verona. At that height, the pilot would escape detection by Italian air traffic control radar. Special noise-suppression gear on the motor would prevent him from being heard on the ground. With darkness closing in, the aircraft would soon be invisible, which was NSA's favorite color.

The pilot's solitary passenger was an Italian-language intercept operator. Once the Beechcraft was on course, this technician would lower an array of signal collection gear into the night sky. When the antenna was deployed, the translator would slip on his earphones and begin scanning the airwaves. For the next four hours, he would troll the skies over the Veneto region, fishing for sound.

There was no point in waiting for him here in the cold, because the plane would not return for hours and the translator's report would not be available until morning, unless he managed to overhear the Red Brigades' sending out for a pizza with extra cheese for someone named Dozier.

Thus far, unfortunately, the NSA team had picked up nothing of importance, despite the fact that Italy's *brigatisti* were known to use several different kinds of radios and Judy Dozier had heard a woman's voice on a walkie-talkie during the kidnapping. Either NSA was having some seriously bad luck or the Red Brigades were staying off the air.

"Let's go back to the office," Reed told his driver. We are doing everything we can think of, he told himself as the staff car rolled toward Camp Ederle. Eventually, we will have to get lucky. In the meanwhile, everybody was getting into the act, even Italian astrologers. On the basis of a fortuitous conjunction of Mars and Jupiter, Madam Liliana Colla of Verona had just announced that Jim Dozier was developing stomach problems and could be getting an ulcer. The general was being held in a deserted house in the hills somewhere to the northeast of Verona, Signora Colla assured the public. One of his guards was a beautiful young woman with short brown hair who was falling in love with him.

As if we do not have enough real problems. . . . Reed slammed the door of the staff car and marched into his office, anxious to resume his study of the second Red Brigades communiqué on the Dozier abduction.

The second communiqué contained, in the form of a photograph, the first hard evidence that Dozier was still alive. The general was pictured sitting in front of the five-pointed star that was the symbol of the Red Brigades. In his hands he was holding a large sheet of paper, on which was written: "Capitalist war generates imperialist war! Only anti-imperialist civil war can bring an end to war."

There was a bruise under Dozier's left eye, apparently acquired during the struggle in his apartment, and he was sporting a week's growth of gray whiskers. The text of the communiqué was not very comforting. After the usual rambling propaganda statement, there was a brief announcement that Dozier's kangaroo trial had begun.

Comrades, proletarians! The people's trial of the pig Dozier has begun. This pig, this murderer, is a hero of the American massacres in Vietnam where he won various decorations for his "merits." His long career as a pig has taken him to wherever the imperialists found it necessary to strangle popular national liberation struggles. His last task, interrupted by our revolutionary forces, was the actual command of Allied Land Forces in Southern Europe. The pig Dozier must answer to the international proletariat about the function of troops and weapons under his command in Verona.

The repetitious use of the word *pig* suggested that Jim's captors were dehumanizing their victim, making it psychologically easier for them to butcher him like a real pig when the time came.

Damn! The number of imponderables in this case was growing every day. The Bonn office of the Italian news service ANSA had received a cable that seemed to be a series of mysterious code words. It ended with the words, "With best regards by and for another victim, (signed) Dozier." What could this possibly mean? Was it the work of a crank, or a serious attempt to send someone a message?

Equally mysterious was a classified ad that had appeared in a Rome newspaper: "Dozier, Monna Lisa asks another hearing."

And there had been a distressing flood of anonymous calls claiming that Jim was already dead, sometimes even giving directions for finding his body. A few were obviously from cranks, but others demanded to be taken seriously. For example, a Lebanese Arab was calling ANSA's Beirut office with information about the Red Brigades only an insider would know. When he had predicted that Dozier's body would be found on 22 December, everybody had been frantic with worry.

Christmas had come and gone without the macabre discovery, but another group called the Movement for African Liberation telephoned to say that General Dozier would be liquidated for his crimes against African people. In fact, there had been several announced executions a day since the abduction, and Reed wondered whether the authorities were managing to shield Judy Dozier from their grisly impact.

Thus far, the announced executions had all turned out to be false. Some of the calls had probably been made by the Red Brigades as a way of encouraging the police to waste their time and energy. But the situation was objectively not very encouraging. The Spadolini government was still refusing to make concessions to the terrorists, and unless the police got lucky soon, one of these death threats was going to be true.

Impatiently, Reed swept the paperwork from his desk and locked it in his office safe. Taped to the top of the four-drawer steel cabinet was a form he had to sign, certifying that all of Uncle Sam's secrets had been locked away for the night.

We should worry this much about our generals, he thought.

11

Emilia was a long time returning from her walk. The weather outside was foul, with sleet tumbling out of the sky and freezing on the pavement.

It was New Year's Eve and Antonio Savasta was worried. In the days immediately after the kidnapping, the police had concentrated their energies on Verona, but now they were beginning to flood Padua with men, even stopping pedestrians for document checks. Savasta had been arguing that they should not leave the apartment unless it were operationally necessary, but Emilia insisted that she needed to escape from time to time.

Savasta sat in the living room with Di Lenardo and Emanuela Frascella, waiting impatiently. Cesare was performing his tireless maintenance on one of the Sterlings, coating the machine gun with a light oil and then wiping it with a lint-free cloth. Cesare still took everything a little too seriously; recently, he seemed fidgety and irritable.

Emanuela sat cross-legged on the carpet, working her way through a stack of *Panorama* magazines with a scissors, removing every reference to the Red Brigades or the Dozier abduction before the magazines were given to their prisoner for reading.

Savasta noticed that her hands were not very steady. Twice over the past week, Emanuela had broken into bouts of silent crying and Savasta guessed that she was feeling the strain of sharing her apartment with five other people, one of them a kidnapped American general. Or was her relationship with Di Lenardo under some kind of stress?

Think positively, he ordered himself. Thus far, the Executive Committee was delighted with the Dozier operation. For the planned abductions of Fiat's Cesare Romiti and Nicola Simone of the Rome DIGOS, Luigi Novelli was planning to imitate Savasta's technique from the empty refrigerator crate to the use of a tent to isolate the prisoner.

Furthermore, the Dozier abduction had been successful in

drawing thousands of policemen into the Veneto region. The Italian government had thrown greater resources into the search for James Dozier than had been dedicated to the missing Aldo Moro. The Italian and American governments were treating Dozier's disappearance as an international emergency, conclusive proof that Dozier was the authentic behind-the-scenes commander of NATO in Italy.

And every cop transferred here to the north was one less policeman patrolling the streets of Rome. When Novelli's operations were launched, the police forces would face a devastating shortage of manpower.

Spadolini would then be forced to order the army into the cities to maintain essential services. The presence of armed infantrymen, patrolling streets and piazzas with automatic weapons, would convince the population that the government was losing control. Inevitably, there would be firefights breaking out all over the peninsula as workers and soldiers stumbled into conflict with one another. The transition to full-fledged civil war would then be an inevitability.

But the future hinged upon the present. Savasta's responsibilities to the Executive Committee were taking him away from Padua for days at a time. When he was gone, Emilia was in charge of the Via Pindemonte safe house, and yet she insisted on taking these long walks at night. . . .

Restlessly, Antonio walked into the tent room where Giovanni Ciucci was on guard. Ciucci always had his nose in a book, but today he had put aside the profundities of Marx or Lenin to read a collection of Bob Dylan's lyrics.

Ciucci glanced up at him and nodded, without offering a smile. The two men did not know each other well. Nor had they ever worked together before, because Ciucci's small organization in Tuscany fell under Barbara Balzarani's operational control. Giovanni was regarded as reliable and dedicated to the cause, although at thirty-four he was old for a revolutionary. Savasta could not remember the last time that Ciucci had smiled or laughed.

A key turned in the lock and Emilia Libera stumbled in, obviously distressed. Her hair was wet from the rain, and her cheeks were flushed with cold. She pushed him aside as he tried to put his arms around her.

"What's wrong?"

"The police are everywhere!" she gasped. "I had to walk miles to get back here without running into a patrol!"

"Okay, it has nothing to do with us!" Savasta tried to reassure her. "It's New Year's Eve! There will be drunks on the road and wild parties—"

"I'm telling you that there are thousands of police in Padua!" Emilia hissed at him.

"But no one knows where we are!"

"There are dozens and dozens of police outside this building!" she insisted. "The Carabinieri are turning Padua upside down! They're stopping every car on the Via Guizza! They could be starting house-to-house searches!"

"There is no reason . . ." Savasta began, but he went silent as they heard a shout from the floor below. It was a man's voice. Was he speaking English?

". . . General Dozier! We know . . ." There were footsteps on the staircase, the sound of many men coming up to this floor.

"*Cristo!*" Savasta picked up one of the Sterlings and chambered a round while Di Lenardo rushed up with a second machine gun.

"Is . . . is this . . . are we . . ." stammered Emanuela, coming into the corridor, her eyes wide with fear. Emilia Libera drew the younger woman into the kitchen, out of the line of fire. Savasta noticed that Emilia had not gone for a weapon.

More shouts came from the stairwell, louder and closer.

"Come out, General Dozier! We know you're here somewhere!"

It was a young man's voice, clearly speaking English. Every time he shouted Dozier's name, there were peals of riotous laughter coming from others who seemed to be with him. Was this the American army?

"Let's go!" The footsteps passed their landing and headed for the third floor. "We're gonna be late!"

"They're medical students," Emanuela Frascella spoke up suddenly. "When they can't get into American medical schools, they come to the University of Padua. There's a bunch of them living on the fourth or fifth floor. I think they might be a little drunk."

Exhaling heavily, Savasta put down his Sterling. From high

above them on the stairwell, the American students were still shouting gleefully for General Dozier. Eventually, their voices became faint, and finally there was silence.

Neither of the two women spoke, but for a moment there seemed to be an understanding between them. Holding her hand like a little girl clinging to her mother, Emanuela followed Emilia Libera down the corridor into the bathroom. The door closed behind them, and Savasta stood in the corridor listening to them cry.

12

12:40 P.M., 31 DECEMBER 1981
PIAZZA BRÀ, VERONA

"What do you see?" whispered Salvatore Genova. It was late, and the commissioner was pulling in his troops.

He could see next to nothing himself because his eyes were not adjusted to the darkness. The rain had stopped, but a thick mist was rolling in to take its place.

"Not much," Blondie admitted. The two men crouched in an alley behind some cardboard boxes. The four-apartment palazzo under surveillance was a mere dozen meters away but only the bare outline of the building was visible in the fog. "He got home just after ten, and the television went on. He watched until eleven-thirty and then turned out the lights. Doesn't look like he's going to a party either."

"What's he do?"

"He sells automobile insurance."

Genova nodded. The DIGOS was certain that there had to be a Red Brigades infrastructure in the Veneto region, and they were concentrating on anybody who had once been a rebellious student. But it was turning out that a lot of people who had admired Che Guevara in 1968 were selling automobile insurance in 1981.

"What was in his file?"

"The usual student stuff. He wrote 'Down with Nixon' on a wall about ten years ago."

Cristo, so did I, Genova thought, suddenly overcome by the futile irrationality of it all. Here I am, a creature of the sixties prowling around in the fog searching for other sixties people who have now turned to violence. We were all on the same side once. Now they have become murderers and I have become the garbage collector for my generation. . . .

"*Capo?*" Blondie pulled him out of the fog. "What happens now?"

"Tomorrow we start with the next name on the list," Genova said. "Come on, we can get something to eat in the Piazza Brà. Rina and the others are meeting us there."

"Do you think we're ever going to find this general?" The two men slipped out of the alley and walked to Genova's car.

"With this fog, we'll be lucky to find the Piazza Brà."

Blondie could always find a place to eat when he was hungry, and a moment later the Alfa emerged into the great emptiness of the Piazza Brà. Most of the other restaurants were closed, but their dinner party was waiting in an old pizzeria on the corner. With school closed for the holidays, Rina had come over to Verona for a few days, and the commissioner slipped into an empty chair beside her. Somebody had ordered a large number of pizzas and other customers were drifting in to find company at twelve o'clock on New Year's Eve.

Genova wondered how the restaurant's other guests would feel if they knew that they were sharing this particular midnight with a group of undercover detectives. Early in the investigation, there had been public enthusiasm for the rescue of General Dozier. But this was the third week of the hunt, and the citizens of northern Italy were getting tired of gun-toting cops demanding their identification papers several times a day.

Even Italy's drug addicts were suffering, because the Mafia had decided that running heroin into this part of the country was unacceptably risky. With the supply of illegal narcotics drying up fast, thousands of junkies were doing involuntary cold turkey in hospital emergency rooms all over the north.

It was midnight, and the restaurant exploded with conviviality. Commissioner Genova kissed his Rina, reminding himself that she was the most beautiful woman he had ever known. She kissed him back, and for a moment, they forget about the others.

"When are you coming home?" she whispered.

"When I find this wretched general!"

"Find him soon, okay?" she murmured, leaning forward to kiss him again. "Find him real soon."

13

3:55 A.M., 3 JANUARY 1982
GALLIATE CARABINIERE BARRACKS
VILLAGE OF GALLIATE, PROVINCE OF NOVARA

Major General Carlo Alberto Dalla Chiesa looked up at the old-fashioned wooden clock on the wall. It was almost four. Outside, a freezing rain was pelting down, but in the corner of this shabby old office, borrowed from the chief warrant officer who commanded this obscure Carabiniere station, an electric fire was glowing.

In a little town like Galliate, four in the morning was a good time, he reflected. The roads were empty, except for the occasional patrol car. The burglars had all gone home to bed. The town drunk had consumed his nightly bottle of grappa and arranged to be arrested for public intoxication so that he could snore the night away in a warm cell. The little town was quiet.

"Is he here yet?" the Carabiniere general asked a staff officer.

"Just pulled in, sir."

Dalla Chiesa had not seen Galati since September when the prisoner had warned them about a possible attack on an American general. Galati was still reluctant to reveal information that could jeopardize his own situation in prison or his family's safety in Verona. The Red Brigades had established a firm policy about executing traitors, and Michele had no desire to be next on the list.

Shortly after Dozier's disappearance, Dalla Chiesa had met with Ambassador Rabb's people from the American embassy and told them about his September interview with Galati. He had explained Galati's fears but insisted that Michele could—if he became brave enough—provide them with enough data about Veneto column safe houses and infrastructure to lead them to Dozier.

In General Dalla Chiesa's opinion, Americans shared a common conviction that there was no difficulty in life that could not be solved by the generous application of dollar bills. Instantly, the men from the embassy had proposed a financial solution. The U.S. government would provide enough money to keep Michele Galati and his entire family happy forever in the foreign country of their choice, if the prisoner would reveal the information needed to locate Jim Dozier. It only remained for Dalla Chiesa to tell them how much money he needed.

Dalla Chiesa had mentioned a modest sum. The Americans doubled it and sent the proposal back to Washington, where the figure was doubled again.

Then a snag developed. The State Department discovered that it was illegal under American law to use taxpayers' money to pay a bribe to a convicted murderer. Hence, the money could not come from official U.S. sources.

The solution had been found by a young Marine Corps officer assigned to the White House National Security Council (NSC) staff. Major Oliver North was not a senior official at the NSC, but he had managed to win the trust of a patriotic American billionaire who had written big checks in the past to get fellow Americans out of difficulties.

H. Ross Perot had been eating in a Dallas restaurant when the call came through from the White House. Without interrupting his dinner, the businessman had telephoned his bank in New York and left instructions for the equivalent of five hundred thousand dollars in Italian lire to be delivered to the American embassy in Rome.

The money was now resting comfortably in a safe at the embassy on the Via Veneto in Rome where Max Rabb's staff had instructions to hand the money over to Dalla Chiesa or anybody else who could produce Jim Dozier. The embassy had announced that Dozier's wealthy friends had put up the reward.

"Shall I bring him in, sir?" The aide appeared again in the doorway. Dalla Chiesa nodded and a moment later Michele Galati walked in, digging in his pocket for a cigarette. Dalla Chiesa looked at him impassively, waiting until the convicted terrorist got his Nazionale lit.

"The subject is Dozier," began the general.

"Look, I don't give a fuck about Dozier! They can kill him four times over as far as I'm concerned. I detest Americans!"

"All right, all right, although at this point, the subject is not how you feel about Dozier, but about whether or not there is any possibility of an arrangement." Dalla Chiesa had once spent a pleasant evening drinking wine with Jim Dozier at a party in Verona but decided that it would not help matters to admit that he and the American general were friends.

"This Dozier is as good as dead!" Galati insisted.

"Do you know where he is?"

"I don't."

"This Savasta," the Carabiniere persisted, "is he using the structure you built in the Veneto? Your safe houses, your logistics people? He couldn't have rebuilt the whole Veneto column from scratch, could he? There hasn't been time!"

"Look, we're cut off in the Prison Front," Galati said. The "Prison Front" was the organization of unrepentant men and women who were serving long prison terms for terrorist crimes. "Savasta doesn't send me progress reports."

"You've heard about the reward?" Dalla Chiesa inquired. "This money is real, and we could make a package deal for you and your family, fresh identification papers for you and your brother and a girlfriend, and then some cash in a bank account and all the protection you'd need! Think about it!"

Galati thought about it.

"They'd know it was me," he said finally. "If Savasta were arrested in one of my safe houses, they'd all know it was me."

"We could protect you and your family from them!"

"The way you protected Robert Peci?"

Dalla Chiesa recognized that Galati's fears were justified. A year earlier, Dalla Chiesa had coaxed a full confession out of a senior Red Brigades leader named Patrizio Peci. During the resulting wave of arrests, the Carabinieri had protected Peci and smuggled him into the government's Witness Protection Program under a new identity.

Frustrated at their inability to punish the informant himself, the Red Brigades had kidnapped Peci's younger brother, Roberto, and executed him. And a few days before Dozier's kidnapping, a group of Red Brigades prisoners had caught another one of their traitors in a penitentiary courtyard and slit his throat. And Michele Galati had a younger brother, a guileless kid named Paolo.

"Why hasn't somebody made us an offer for Dozier's safe return?" The general had been wondering why the Red Brigades had not proposed an exchange of prisoners. "What's it going to take to get him back in one piece?"

"*Generale*, the Prison Front has been thinking about the Dozier case and the reward money. If that money could be offered directly to the Red Brigades, a message could be sent to Balzarani—but they'd want more than money. As things stand, it's impossible to let him go, unless an exceptional offer is made on his behalf."

"Such as?"

"The price for Dozier will keep going up until the Winter of Fire campaign is over. They'll wait until you've realized that you can't get him back through your own efforts, and then they'll ask for the liberation of some prisoners. And not just Italians!"

"They want some kind of international deal?"

"When the negotiations begin, the request will be the following," Galati leaned forward in the chair and counted off the conditions on his fingers. "Ten of our people, Italians, plus ten Red Army Faction prisoners in Germany, and ten Irishmen from the Provisional IRA or maybe ten from the Basque ETA group. Plus, you've got to close the American Air Force Base at Comiso where the Cruise missiles are and shut down the Pianosa Maximum Security Prison."

"We can't release any important prisoners and no money can go to the Red Brigades," Dalla Chiesa told him. In fact, Prime Minister Spadolini had specifically ordered that no money was to go to the terrorists. Ross Perot's half-million could only be given to Galati if the man broke completely with the Red Brigades and provided information leading to the rescue of Dozier.

"Then your American general is dead." Galati shrugged and both men fell silent. After a pause, Dalla Chiesa pressed a button on the desk, summoning Galati's escort. The terrorist trudged out of the room, not bothering to say good-bye.

This conversation never happened, thought Dalla Chiesa, switching off the tape recorder he had hidden in a desk drawer.

Sorry, General Dozier, he said to himself. If we gave them all that money, they'd have the financial resources to fight for another decade.

Sometimes people have to come second and countries have to come first, he thought. This time Italy comes first.

14

It was cold on the Via Mazzini. A cruel wind swept down the prison wall and into the piazza where the jail guards were standing with their machine guns, stamping their feet to keep warm.

Sergio Segio stood in front of the bar, facing the piazza, the Via Mazzini running off to his right. I don't give a damn about the Red Brigades, he thought, watching the street. He was tired, an idealist turned cynical. There had been too many winter campaigns, too many losses, too many defeats. It was time to rob a bank for the pension fund and then get over the border into France with a new name and a fresh passport. But without Susanna, exile would be unendurable. . . .

Sergio studied his watch. This was a high-risk operation and Savasta had insisted, as the price of logistics support from the Veneto column, that there be no civilian casualties. The timing had to be perfect.

The piazza was almost deserted. In a little while, the bars would open again for the evening, and the traffic would start to flow, but at thirty minutes after three, nothing very much was happening in downtown Rovigo.

On Sunday afternoons in the Rovigo Penitentiary, the exercise period ran from three to four. Susanna and Maria and Loredanna and Federica would be near the gate that led to the courtyard, clustered around a guard whose friendship they had been cultivating.

Sergio reached into his pocket for a packet of cigarettes. As he lit one, an old Fiat 112 made its way down the Via Mazzini. One hundred meters from where Sergio was standing, the driver eased his vehicle up over the curb, brought it to a halt next to the prison wall, and climbed out, lounging by the side of the car as if he were waiting for someone. On the other side of the wall, the courtyard would, at this hour, be empty.

Now! Sergio threw the cigarette away, and on this second signal, four men with automatic rifles began firing from con-

Cadet James Dozier at West Point, 1953.

Brigadier General James Dozier and his wife, Judy.

Doziers' penthouse apartment located in ona on Via Lungadige Catena 5.

Colonel William Reed, U.S. Army, 66th Military Intelligence Group, Vicenza.

Salvatore Genova and Rina. (ANSA)

Francesco Lo Bianco, Red Brigade leader, Genoa column. (ANSA)

Antonio Savasta, Red Brigade column leade Verona, member of the Executive Committee (AP/WIDE WORLD PHOTOS)

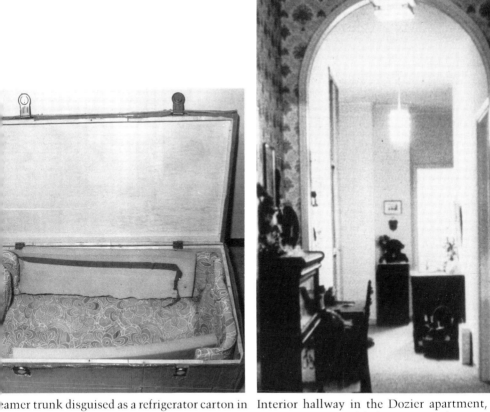

Steamer trunk disguised as a refrigerator carton in which Dozier was transported.

Interior hallway in the Dozier apartment, where the general led Savasta and Pietro Vanzi who were disguised as plumbers.

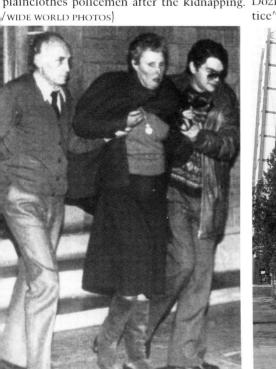

y Dozier being led out of the Verona apartment plainclothes policemen after the kidnapping. (WIDE WORLD PHOTOS)

The apartment building in Padua where Dozier was held, dubbed the "Palace of Justice" by the Red Brigades.

Photo of Dozier left by the Red Brigades in a trash can in Milan, December 27, 1981.

Major Dozier (right) in Vietnam, 1969; part of t[...] "imperialist crimes" for which the Red Brigad[...] "tried" him.

Judy Dozier and the Doziers' daughter, Cheryl, await news of the general.
(AP/WIDE WORLD PHOTOS)

Giovanni Senzani, a historical leader of the [...] Brigades in Rome escorted by police after his [...]ture, January 9, 1982.

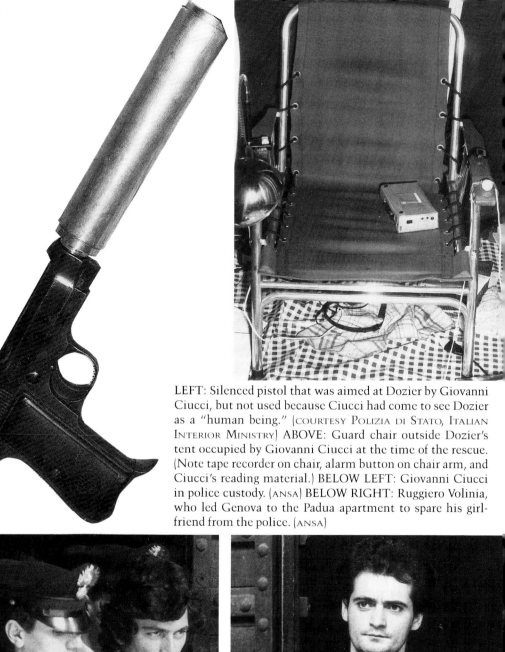

LEFT: Silenced pistol that was aimed at Dozier by Giovanni Ciucci, but not used because Ciucci had come to see Dozier as a "human being." (COURTESY POLIZIA DI STATO, ITALIAN INTERIOR MINISTRY) ABOVE: Guard chair outside Dozier's tent occupied by Giovanni Ciucci at the time of the rescue. (Note tape recorder on chair, alarm button on chair arm, and Ciucci's reading material.) BELOW LEFT: Giovanni Ciucci in police custody. (ANSA) BELOW RIGHT: Ruggiero Volinia, who led Genova to the Padua apartment to spare his girl-friend from the police. (ANSA)

Antonio Savasta in police custody. (ANSA)

Emilia Libera, Savasta's common-law in police custody. (ANSA)

Emanuela Frascella, whose apartme Padua served as the Red Brigades' "Pal. Justice." (ANSA)

Cesare Di Lenardo in police custody. (ANSA)

ozier, at a Frankfurt press conference, rejoicing
earing news of her husband's rescue, January
2. (AP/WIDE WORLD PHOTOS)

Dozier in the Padua police station shortly
after his rescue.

s first meal after captivity—a hamburger, Coke, and fries.

Dozier and wife, Judy, reunited, waving to reporters from their Verona balcony. (AP/WIDE WORLD PHOTOS)

RIGHT: Francesco Lo Bianco and the leader of the Red Brigades, Barbara Balzarani, after their capture. (ANSA) BELOW: Salvatore Genova and Rina get married and celebrate with the "boys."

cealed positions on the far side of the piazza, aiming at the front gates of the jail. The guards responded to what they took to be the beginning of a frontal assault, taking cover and blazing back.

It's happening! If everything were going on schedule, Susanna and her three friends should now overpower their guard and take the key to the courtyard. Meanwhile, the driver of the Fiat 112 reached through the window of the car with a cigarette lighter. He ignited a short fuse and ran for his life.

Thirty seconds later, the Fiat 112 exploded, shattering windows for half a mile around. His ears ringing, Sergio leapt into his own car and careened through the rubble on the Via Mazzini until he saw the gaping hole in the prison wall created by the explosion. A split second later, as bricks and mortar continued to tumble from the wall, Susanna Ronconi and the other three prisoners rushed out and threw themselves into the back of his car.

"I love you!" he cried, turning and looking to see whether the years in prison had left a mark on that beautiful face. In two minutes, they would be in Savasta's safe house.

"Then drive!" said Susanna. "Drive!"

15

9:00 A.M., 4 JANUARY 1982
VIA PINDEMONTE, PADUA

Life in the people's prison was improving.

For a week, Dozier had been asking them to change the music, arguing that a demented general would do them no good as a hostage. On the fourth morning of 1982, he awoke to hear a majestic dum-dum-dum-DUM, three graceful ascending notes followed by a plummeting fourth, the beginning of Gershwin's *Rhapsody in Blue*.

He was humming along when Emilia Libera came in with his tray. For breakfast, they had been serving him warm milk with a sugar cube in it, supplemented by dry toast or crackers.

"*Fiocchi d'avena*," she announced. Cornflakes!

He was being given reading material now, newsmagazines like *Panorama* and *L'Espresso* and even the overseas edition of

Newsweek. Somebody was attacking the periodicals with a scissors to remove any references to his case, but the censor routinely forgot to snip out the table of contents, allowing him to observe that the *Sequestro Dozier* was still making the headlines.

And there were some books as well, used student editions of English-language classics. Thus far, his hosts had produced a Jack London novel called *Martin Eden*, Shakespeare's *Coriolanus*, and Jerome K. Jerome's *Three Men in a Boat*. They had also given him two decks of American-style playing cards. After a few marathon games of solitaire, he developed a version of bridge in which one corner of his brain played against the other three corners simultaneously.

"Buon giorno!" Savasta entered his section of the tent with a newspaper. "You're an important guy. Your friends are offering us a half-million dollars for your release!"

"A half-million dollars?" I don't know anyone with that kind of spare change, he thought.

"An organization called the 'Friends of Dozier' put up the money!"

"Are you going to accept their offer?"

"We aren't mercenaries and we didn't kidnap you for money!" Savasta seemed offended at the idea. "Besides, we haven't finished our questioning yet."

Dozier shrugged. From his point of view, his "trial" was going well. The Red Brigade team seemed to have no sense of the kind of secret information an American general was likely to have. A Soviet-trained interrogator would have known what to ask, but Savasta seemed to accept Dozier's assertions that he was ignorant about a vast range of sensitive issues.

"When are you going to contact the Italian authorities?" Dozier asked.

"We have several more operations to carry out before we can begin negotiating," Savasta told him. "Yesterday, the second phase in our Winter of Fire campaign was successful. A commando team of revolutionaries rescued four women prisoners from the Rovigo State Prison. This gave us great pleasure."

"I am so happy for you," said the general dryly. Antonio Savasta left, smiling, and Dozier finished his cornflakes.

16

9:50 P.M., 4 JANUARY 1982
VIA DELLA VITE, ROME

Luigi Novelli sniffed the evening air, trying to sense danger. It was almost ten in the evening, but there was still a crowd of foreigners in the Piazza di Spagna.

After months of planning, Novelli's people had come for Cesare Romiti. The chief executive officer of the giant Fiat Corporation lived with his family in the northern city of Turin, but his work brought him so frequently to Rome that he maintained an apartment here on the Via della Vite. He was expected to arrive at any moment.

Aware that there might be surveillance over Romiti's residence, the chief of the Rome column had organized his assault team so that it would blend into the background. A few steps away from Romiti's front door, a nondescript blue Ritmo was parked by the curb. The good-looking young man sitting on the hood of the car was Stefano Petrella, Novelli's brother-in-law and closest friend. His colleague, Ennio Di Rocca, was lounging at the Ritmo's wheel, smoking casually but ready to move the moment they had taken their prisoner.

Two other teams, each with two men and a woman, were strolling up and down the Via della Vite so that one of them was always close to Romiti's front door. A hundred feet away, mixing with the tourists in the Piazza di Spagna, there was a backup squad of four men, armed and ready to intervene if they were needed. Novelli himself stood on the corner of the Via della Vite and the Via Propaganda Fede, from where he could superintend the operation.

The attack would take place on the street, because Romiti's Rome apartment was well equipped with security devices and the Fiat executive was unlikely to open his door to anybody with a story about a leaky pipe.

Romiti would be vulnerable for only a few seconds while walking from his armored car to his door. There would be bodyguards, of course, but Novelli's twelve people were prepared for a quick, violent operation. The necessity of shooting the escort had been accepted as inevitable. Once captured, Romiti would be smuggled out of Rome in a series of escape cars, one of which was already equipped with an empty refrigerator box. The "proletarian prison" had been prepared in a beach house a few miles down the coast.

The plan was simple, flexible, and forceful. It would take some extraordinarily bad luck for it to go wrong.

Just after 10:00 P.M., extraordinarily bad luck began to occur. A State Police squad car cruised down the Via della Vite. Novelli observed it calmly, guessing that it was a routine patrol. He lit a cigarette and strolled a few steps farther away from Romiti's front door.

In the patrol car, one of the officers saw that the Ritmo was standing in a no-parking zone. He was about to stop and tell Ennio Di Rocca to move when his colleague noticed that there were at least six other people walking with unnatural slowness up and down the street, not far from Romiti's door.

After the Dozier abduction, the Polizia di Stato had stopped believing in coincidences. The driver of the squad car continued down the Via della Vite, while his colleague reported the situation to DIGOS headquarters. The senior DIGOS officer on duty was Commissioner Nicola Simone, who ordered every police car in central Rome to converge on the Via della Vite.

Novelli got almost no warning that his operation was coming unglued. At twelve minutes after ten, a patrol car rolled slowly into the far end of the street. Novelli walked back toward the Ritmo, where Stefano Petrella and Ennio Di Rocca were still awaiting Cesare Romiti's arrival, noticing for the first time that Ennio had placed the car in a no-parking zone.

Another squad car sailed around the corner from the Piazza di Spagna end of the Via della Vite. Novelli halted, realizing that Stefano and Ennio were trapped.

Stefano jumped down from the hood of the Ritmo but hesitated to reach for his pistol, still hoping that this was just a coincidence and wanting to avoid an unnecessary shoot-out. Moving fast, one of the State Policemen attacked him from behind, spinning him around and kneeing him in the testicles. Two policemen from the other car seized Ennio and dragged him from behind the Ritmo's wheel.

The sirens started, violating the night like curses, and dozens of police cars began to descend upon the Via della Vite. Following their orders, the rest of Novelli's team scattered, disappearing down side streets.

"You! Hold it right there!" As Luigi Novelli watched Stefano and Ennio being handcuffed a few dozen feet away, a squad car approached and Novelli realized that the policeman behind the wheel was talking to him.

Novelli spun into the Piazza di Spagna, knowing that the police would not risk shooting into a mob of tourists. There were at least two policemen behind him as he sprinted through the crowd and up a long marble stairway toward the Trinità dei Monti Church.

"Stop!" He heard a warning shot, fired into the air, but he kept on going.

His chest was heaving as he raced up the steps, but at the top he spun to the left, where he had left a stolen car, one of several vehicles that he had deployed on the periphery of his zone of action. With a final burst of speed, he flung himself into the driver's seat, his lungs in agony, the taste of vomit in his throat. Two policemen had just reached the top of the steps as Novelli got the motor started and raced off into the darkness.

He was deeply depressed. This failure would be analyzed and he would have to explain the disaster to the Esecutivo and then again at the next plenary meeting of the Strategic Directorate, which might decide to remove him from the Executive Committee.

Worse, he would have to tell Marina, his wife, that the brother she loved was in prison.

The sirens were far away now. Luigi Novelli turned into a side street and parked the car. He got out and leaned against it for a moment, rolling a cigarette and feeling his hands go steady as he performed the familiar operation.

This will crush Marina, he thought. He would try to comfort her, but there was a level at which husbands were never as important as brothers.

17

2:45 P.M., 6 JANUARY 1982
VIA LORENZO IL MAGNIFICO, ROME

It was the middle of the afternoon on Wednesday of a good week. The Polizia di Stato commissioner, Nicola Simone, the tall, bearded deputy commander of the Rome DIGOS, was eating pasta and prosciutto in his bachelor apartment.

Things were going well even though his DIGOS colleagues in Verona still could not find that American. Here in Rome, Simone had just arrested Ennio Di Rocca and Stefano Petrella. Di Rocca was already talking and secrets were tumbling out, names and the addresses of some local safe houses. Ennio had only been a spear-carrier and it remained to be seen whether he held the key to any of the crucial mysteries, such as where Savasta had hidden his prisoner or where the Esecutivo held its meetings. And if Stefano Petrella should confess . . .

The doorbell rang.

Commissioner Simone was worried; someone had bypassed the *citofono* security system at the front door, mounting to the third floor and pressing the bell outside his apartment door. If that's the Red Brigades, he reflected, they must think I'm brainless. He picked up his P-38 Special and went to the door.

Through the spy hole, Simone saw a young man named Massimiliano Corsi, wearing a postman's uniform and holding a telegram. Because Corsi had never been arrested or even identified by the DIGOS, Simone had no reason to know his name or to recognize his face. Both of Corsi's hands were visible and there was no sign of a gun. He was apparently alone; behind him the hallway was empty, at least as far back as the stairwell.

"Si?" Simone said.

"Telegramma per il Commissario Nicola Simone."

"Let me see it!" said Simone, his suspicions easing and the P-38 still clenched in his hand. The postman could have legitimately gained access to the interior of the building because he had first delivered a telegram to one of Simone's neighbors. Or someone could have left the door ajar.

Corsi held up the telegram so that Simone's name and address were plainly visible. The telegram was authentic because Corsi had sent it to himself that morning and then replaced his name with the commissioner's.

Simone opened the lock, lowered the P-38, and reached for the telegram.

Suddenly Corsi threw his full weight against the door, tossing Simone off balance. There was a muffled shout as Luigi Novelli and two other Red Brigade operatives named Giovanni Alimonti and Loris Scricciola surged around the corner of the stairwell and sprinted down the corridor toward Simone's door.

Corsi had a gun in his hand now and Simone fired at him wildly. He missed, but the postman tripped in his attempt to dodge the bullet. Simone was about to shoot him when Giovanni Alimonti fired from the stairwell.

The bullet caught Simone in the chin like a punch and spun him around. He dropped to his knees. He was dimly conscious that he had been hit in the face, but there was no pain yet. He saw Alimonti, Scricciola, and Novelli running toward him. The commissioner fired and Alimonti screamed as the bullet sliced into his shoulder.

Luigi Novelli took aim from the corridor and shot Simone in the head. The bullet seared across the side of the commissioner's skull, tearing the skin but bouncing off his skull. Novelli fired again, catching him in the side of the neck.

Simone fired back, one shot after another, forcing Novelli to take cover in the stairwell. With a last burst of desperate strength, the policeman kicked his door shut.

There was a confusion of shouts and cries in the corridor, as Novelli, Scricciola, and Massimiliano Corsi carried the wounded, hysterical Giovanni Alimonti down to the street where a car was waiting.

His own wounds were starting to hurt now, and Commissioner Simone found himself hoping that one of his neighbors would call the police. Unable to stand, he propped himself up in a corner, blood pouring from his head. They shot me, he was thinking as consciousness oozed out of him. I shot one of them. I defended my fort. . . .

18

4:15 A.M., 9 JANUARY 1982
VIA DELLA STAZIONE
TOR DI SAPIENZA, PROVINCE OF ROME

"Senzani!"

The professor woke up fast, instantly realizing that this was the end. He was being arrested. His heavy body went cold.

"Get up, Professor!" a policeman shouted at him. "Get your hands out where we can see them!"

"I declare myself to be a political prisoner." Senzani sat up in bed, pulling the covers up over his groin. He was a fat man and he hated the idea of standing naked before these lean young cops. "I am an official of the Red Brigade organization."

A few more days, he thought as he climbed out of bed, and I could have made the Winter of Fire campaign a triumph. On the appointed day, there would have been bombs going off all over the city, blocking traffic, creating chaos. There would have been machine-gun attacks on the Central Police Station and parliament. And then we would have launched our historic attack against the Christian Democratic Party Congress with mortars and antitank weapons and rockets—

"Let's get some trousers on you, Senzani," said a senior Polizia di Stato officer.

"How did you find me?" They ignored him, but Senzani had already worked out the answer. Ennio Di Rocca had known this address. And Di Rocca had been arrested on Monday.

Ennio must have been treated badly, perhaps even tortured, Senzani thought. But a certain standard of fidelity had to be maintained. He made a mental note to have Di Rocca executed.

"How is Commissioner Simone?" the professor asked as they led him to a waiting car.

"He'll need some plastic surgery, but he's out of danger."

"We'll get him next time," Senzani said. The Winter Campaign is over, he thought, as they put him in the backseat, his hands shackled behind his back.

"Somebody might get him next time, Senzani," said the officer as the car pulled away. "But it isn't going to be you."

19

6:45 P.M., 10 JANUARY 1982
VIA PINDEMONTE, PADUA

The general shifted restlessly on the cot, wondering how long the interrogation was going to continue. They had been at it for hours already, with no signs of giving up. Savasta specialized in asking questions that were really lectures in disguise, demanding that Dozier admit American culpability for everything that had gone wrong since the Declaration of Independence.

"You went to Vietnam primarily for economic motives; is that not the case?" Savasta was saying. "To secure access to rice, oil, mineral wealth. . . ."

The general forced himself to concentrate on his answer, trying to frame his response in reasonable Italian. They seemed desperate to force him into an admission of guilt for Vietnam; it had become important to Jim Dozier not to give them what they wanted. Under the circumstances, he wasn't going to win any major battles, but he was determined never to lose a skirmish.

"I went to Vietnam because I was sent there by my superiors," he told them, wondering whether they really thought that the United States had spent several billion dollars to control some rice paddies. "American policy toward Vietnam was motivated by a desire to prevent Communist conquest of Southeast Asia."

"And the oil?" Di Lenardo snapped.

"There is no oil in Vietnam! If we wanted oil that badly we'd have invaded Saudi Arabia!" He watched carefully, observing how they reacted to his defiance. Savasta was always cold and self-contained, no matter what happened, never fidgeting or displaying frustration. Di Lenardo, on the other hand, frequently let his anger get the better of him, sometimes cursing under his breath and stalking out of the tent in an obvious fury. Giovanni Ciucci, on the other hand, seemed more sympathetic than any of the others. When Ciucci was on guard, Dozier routinely convinced him to lower the volume on the rock and roll, an indulgence he won from no one else.

"How many people were killed in Vietnam?" Savasta returned steadily to the attack. Dozier noticed that the young revolutionary seemed capable of sitting cross-legged and motion-less for hours, dedicating total concentration to his interrogation. I've got to be as disciplined as he is, Dozier decided. The guy is a total professional.

"We lost about fifty-five thousand of our men. I don't know how many people the other side lost."

"Several million!" Di Lenardo informed him. "Was this not a deliberate attempt to depopulate Vietnam? Like the genocidal war waged by the Nazis in World War II?"

And this is the guy I have to watch, Dozier reflected, looking into Di Lenardo's angry eyes. If the order for my execution comes down from their higher headquarters, he will obey with en-thusiasm.

"People get killed in wars," he grunted. "But we were not monsters and we did not commit the kind of war crimes attrib-uted to the Nazis."

"How about the massacre at My Lai?"

"My Lai was the exception that proved the rule. Our troops hardly ever committed atrocities, and the incident at My Lai was halted by an army warrant officer."

"Do you feel any remorse for what you did in Vietnam?" It was the woman speaking. Libera often seemed to have more common sense than the men. He wondered what she looked like behind the mask.

"There is a lot of savagery in combat," he told her. "I was a soldier, fighting according to our code of conduct and obeying legal orders. I do not feel remorse for what I did."

"But you would concede that the war against the Vietnamese people was a regrettable error?" Like a lawyer, Savasta seemed to be trying to find an acceptable verbal formula.

"We did not fight a war against the Vietnamese people," Dozier said. "We were fighting against you Communists, and our only error was going home before the job was done."

It was the wrong answer. Savasta permitted himself a gri-mace, glancing sideways at the others to see whether they wanted to pursue the matter further. Di Lenardo was too furious to speak; the big man hurled himself to his feet and stamped out of the tent. Libera shook her head and followed, pausing to exchange a word with Giovanni Ciucci, who returned to the guard's position.

"This is a trial, you know," Savasta said quietly, turning off the little Sony he invariably used to record these sessions and closing his notebook. "As in any courtroom, a sign of *pentimento,* of repentance, could be important—"

"This is not a trial," Dozier corrected him. "You are not judges and I am not guilty of anything."

"Your refusal to admit your guilt—"

"I'm not guilty," the general said, realizing that a warning was being delivered and wondering precisely how serious Savasta was. Had they arrived at the stage of direct threats? He had war-gamed a variety of scenarios, and several of them ended with his execution. . . .

"Our view of the war—"

"Look, when are you going to get in contact with the Italian authorities?"

"The time is not yet right." Savasta looked away, his eyes troubled.

"When I was captured, you said I would be used as a part of a prisoner exchange."

"When the appropriate moment arrives." The young Roman shook his head and rose, his tape recorder and his notebook in hand.

It's all gone to hell, hasn't it? Dozier watched as Savasta departed. Your wonderful Winter of Fire has fizzled, and you have nothing to negotiate with, except me. Nobody wants to do a deal and there isn't going to be a prisoner exchange.

Am I playing this right? he asked himself, suddenly beset by doubts. I'm trying to be a tough, courteous model prisoner who refuses to make admissions of guilt but doesn't antagonize his jailers any more than necessary. Am I being brave enough? Or should I have stuck to the old name-rank-and-serial-number routine?

No, that would be crazy. Maybe I'm being too brave! Should I be more conciliatory? But suppose he gets me on tape saying that we were butchers in Vietnam. . . . No, I couldn't live with myself afterward!

So what's my role model, anyway? The rules for regular prisoners-of-war situations have been pretty clear since the Korean War, but these guys have never heard of the Geneva Convention. How am I supposed to deal with this predicament?

I hang tough, I guess. Remember that first year at West Point? That was worse than this. There was a rustle of feet in the outside compartment, and Dozier pushed his earphones back into place.

He cheated routinely, and his captors became upset whenever they caught him defending his sanity and his eardrums by avoiding the direct blast of rock and roll.

"Dinner," announced Emilia Libera, setting a plate down on the top of his chemical toilet and then stepping back expectantly. "It's *sepiola*."

Sepiola turned out to be squid, and Dozier took a mouthful on his fork, finding it fresh and tasty.

"Do you ever have nightmares about the war?" she asked, watching him as he chewed.

"No, I seldom have nightmares."

"Some people suffer terribly from nightmares," she remarked. "Do you like the *sepiola*?"

"It's very well prepared," he said sincerely and he saw her eyes crinkle as she reacted to his compliment with pleasure. "I like it."

"Thank you," she said, ducking beneath the tent flap. "I'm glad you like it."

Weird people, he thought as he settled into his meal. Lousy grasp of global politics. Wonderful with seafood.

20

9:35 P.M., 12 JANUARY 1982
SIXTY-SIXTH MILITARY INTELLIGENCE GROUP
HEADQUARTERS, SOUTHERN EUROPEAN TASK FORCE
CAMP EDERLE, VICENZA

On the surface of it, there was really nothing useful.

Colonel Bill Reed doggedly read the third Dozier communiqué again, looking for some hint beneath the banalities of the text. If there is a message here, I don't want him to die because we failed to decipher it, he thought. There has got to be something here, something we have all missed.

     ... the first phase of the interrogation of the dirty Yankee has produced evidence of personal guilt in his long career as a butcher. He is collaborating with us because he is aware that the balance of power has shifted against him. But he has not repented. We want all proletarians and all revolutionaries to know the significant aspects of this interrogation.

Do you know why we captured you?

No, I don't know. I don't understand.

Good. Now we will explain to you why you have been captured and shut in a proletarian prison. Through you, we intend to prosecute the structure of NATO's military occupation and the imperialist policy of America toward the Italian proletariat. The history of your government is the history of state terrorism, constructed by the CIA, from the Marshall Plan to enslavement under Reagan's policies. In order to avoid staining yourself with new crimes, you must cooperate with the forces of the revolution to unmask the American project for dominion and for war against the international proletariat. Yet you continue to defend and support the policies of imperialism and this makes you an accomplice.

Accomplice? No, I understand what you are asking. I am telling the truth.

Let's begin to talk about your military career. For each step, specify the dates, the places, and the key personalities.

I understand. In 1952, I entered West Point. In 1951, I had been a student in Florida and a member of the National Guard. That was the period of the Korean War. In September, there was an opportunity to enter a preparatory school for West Point. . . .

Reed sat back in his office chair, closed his eyes, and tried to concentrate. Following past practice, the Red Brigades had left copies of the communiqué in a refuse bin in Rome and then called a newspaper editor with instructions for finding it.

This communiqué contained no picture and hence no certain proof that Dozier was still alive. Instead, it presented what was alleged to be Dozier's interrogation as part of his "proletarian trial."

Because portions of the Italian text were allegedly Dozier's own words, the intelligence community had been poring over the text for a week now in Verona, Rome, and Washington, trying to find some coded message from the general. Unfortunately, no one had been able to detect anything concrete. If Dozier had sent them a signal, the message had been lost in transmission.

Reed was sure that Dozier's original words had been rewritten for publication. For one thing, the general's use of Italian was rough-and-ready; he had always been able to make himself understood in the language, but he had never been capable of the facile, grammatically correct prose in this communiqué.

Some of the information in the communiqué could only have come from the general himself. His military assignments were a matter of public record, and the Red Brigades could have found a curriculum vitae somewhere in the Via Lungadige Catena apartment. But only Dozier could have produced the names of his various commanding officers and descriptions of his successive assignments.

Dozier had admitted no war crimes and revealed nothing classified, which meant that he was still managing to keep his interrogators at bay. But the tone of the communiqué suggested that the danger to his life was greater than ever. The Red Brigades had already decided he was guilty of genocide as a result of his assignment in Vietnam. Furthermore, they were clear that he had not "repented." Did this mean that the proletarian trial would conclude with a verdict of guilty and a sentence of death? How else could it end?

"Repentance" was very important to the Red Brigades. In the past, they had kidnapped a series of judges and factory managers whom they regarded as enemies of the proletariat. After their crimes had been explained to them, these antiproletarians had seen the error of their ways and apologized. The Red Brigades had then released them alive, under the formula that their death sentences had been suspended. They would probably allow Dozier to live if he were prepared to apologize publicly for his genocidal behavior in Vietnam. Somehow, it was difficult to imagine.

Bill Reed glared out of the window of his office, admitting that their early optimism was now fading. He had heard that the United States Military Academy at West Point had already begun rehearsing the memorial ceremony for their celebrated alumnus.

Although the CIA had a man trying to keep track of what the Interior Ministry was doing, there was still very little contact between the Americans and the Polizia di Stato; the DIGOS was sharing its secrets with no one.

Worse, the normally friendly Carabinieri were now furious at the Americans! The Air Force Office of Special Investigations had been coming up with detailed intelligence reports claiming that the general was being held in a rural farmhouse. The Air Force had refused to identify the source of this information but had demanded a long series of raids on farmhouses pinpointed on a detailed map of northeastern Italy.

In every case, the Carabinieri had found the houses either empty or occupied by legitimate farmers and finally demanded to know the source of this mysterious information.

Reluctantly, Air Force intelligence revealed that their source was a psychic from California who had worked with the Los Angeles Police Department in tracing lost children. It further developed that the Office of Special Investigations had been experimenting with clairvoyants and mystics for years as part of a supersecret program code-named Distant Viewing.

The affair had frayed everyone's nerves; to make matters worse, phone calls and letters kept pouring in, announcing that Dozier had been executed. Just after New Year's, someone had called Polizia di Stato headquarters in Rome with a convincing imitation of the standard terrorist telephone message.

"This is the Red Brigades," the caller had said. "We have done justice to the dirty American general. His body is in the Abruzzi mountains in a farmhouse between the towns of Popoli and Bussi, about thirty miles from Pescara." Convinced that the message was authentic, the authorities had pulled six hundred policemen and Carabinieri away from more useful duties to plough through the snow and ice. In the end, they had found nothing.

A few days later, another convincing announcement was made, this time claiming that Dozier's body had been dumped in a hydroelectric reservoir near the mountain town of L'Aquila. The police drained the reservoir, depriving several nearby villages of electricity and drinking water for a week. At a cost of millions of lire and thousands of man-hours, they found nothing but sludge at the bottom.

The search for Dozier was stalled and directionless. Reed slumped back in his chair, wondering what would happen next.

Clearly, there was going to be no deal. The American authorities always said they would never negotiate with terrorists and the Italians were hanging tough. Ninety-nine percent of the Italian public backed Prime Minister Spadolini's refusal to negotiate and even the opposition parties were not criticizing the government's performance. If Dozier were released unharmed or rescued, the prime minister would enjoy a triumph.

But the prime minister would even win if Dozier turned up dead, because the tragedy would generate even more support for Spadolini's antiterrorist campaign.

Faced with this situation, what would Savasta do? There was no way to extract any major publicity value from the Dozier operation now, except—except by executing Jim as a war criminal. This was clear to the police and it was clear to the politicians. How many more days would pass before it became clear to Savasta?

"Between the capitalist class and the proletariat," the communiqué said, "there can only be war. As the crisis of capitalism deepens, this war will become imperialist in character. And we must fight!"

You want a war, thought Reed with sudden anger, then you came to the right army, you bastards! We'll give you a war!

Then he calmed down and went back to work on the communiqué, this time going through the text line by line with a magnifying glass. There has to be something here, he was thinking. Something!

21

9:20 A.M., 15 JANUARY 1982
VIA LUNGADIGE CATENA, VERONA

Empty minds in empty apartments, she thought, looking back one last time to be sure that everything was the way it was when Jim left. There was no point in staying any longer.

There were a driver and bodyguards waiting for them, but Judy Dozier took her time and no one dared hurry her. For nearly a month she had lived here, working daily with the police, answering letters, posing for photographers, and receiving visits from Italian politicians and American military dignitaries, but now this phase had come to an end.

It was pointless to go on pretending that Jim was going to pop back in the front door as suddenly as he had disappeared. He would be back—she had to go on believing that—but it might not be tomorrow, or even next week.

Scott Dozier had reluctantly gone back to Florida to resume his classes at the community college. And it was time for her to leave too because there was nothing more to be accomplished here, enduring an infinity of empty hours, listening to the phone ring with inconsequential news, and reading day after day in the press that General Dozier's execution had been announced by yet another sinister group.

There had been wonderful support from everybody, right from the very beginning. The archbishop of Verona had brought her a personal message of warm comfort from Pope John Paul II, himself the target of a terrorist attack less than a year before. The State Department had been supportive as well. Secretary of State Alexander Haig had written an encouraging note, and Ambassador Rabb had visited her several times. President Reagan had called, and so had Italy's President Pertini and Prime Minister Spadolini.

But it was time to leave. Cheryl needed to get back to work and Judy had accepted an invitation from some old army friends, General Walt Ulmer and his wife, Marty, to stay with them in Frankfurt, where Walt was commanding the Third Armored Division. It was not an ideal solution, but then these were not ideal times.

"We'll be back soon, Mom," Cheryl said cheerfully. Judy summoned up a smile, but she realized that when she came back, everything would be different. Either Jim would be freed and they would come home hugging and kissing, or else one of these execution announcements would turn out to be true and she would be returning as a widow.

"Let's go then," she said. There was a huskiness in her voice as she closed the door firmly behind her.

22

"I don't know what's gone wrong," Savasta said. He had just returned from a two-day marathon session of the Comitato esecutivo at which the four surviving leaders of the Red Brigades tried to understand why disaster was stalking them. Accusations of incompetence had been exchanged. Lo Bianco had seemed terminally depressed. Novelli was stricken by the loss of Stefano Petrella, and Barbara Balzarani had been brutally critical.

The Rovigo Penitentiary breakout had been a minor success, but the attempted kidnapping of Cesare Romiti had been an unmitigated failure. The Executive Committee had slapped together a communiqué presenting the wounding of the commissioner as a major accomplishment, but public sympathy was going to the wounded policeman. And Senzani's group was virtually gone, thanks to Ennio Di Rocca's inability to keep his mouth shut!

"How was Massimiliano captured?" Emilia asked, and he heard the emotion in her voice. Massimiliano Corsi had been one of their oldest friends.

"According to Novelli, it was an incredible blunder," Savasta said. "Massimiliano wanted an authentic telegram to show to Simone, so he sent himself a telegram and then changed the name and the address. But he forgot to remove the original identification number. When the shooting was over, the police picked the telegram up off the floor and got Massimiliano's home address from Post Office records."

"Suppose he talks?" Emilia whispered.

"He's not going to talk!"

"They broke Ennio Di Rocca in a couple of days!"

"Even if he talked, Massimiliano couldn't tell them anything of importance about us," Savasta retorted. "Nobody has the address of this apartment except for the five of us. We can hold out forever."

"Is that what the Executive Committee wants us to do? Hold out forever?"

It was a good question. There was no point in trying now to open negotiations with the Italian government for a prisoner exchange. Spadolini would refuse. With the Winter of Fire campaign collapsing around them, the Red Brigades would look weak and desperate.

Had they extracted a genuine confession out of Dozier, an admission that Vietnam had been imperialist genocide or a statement that he was involved in the political-military subjugation of Italy, they could have declared his kidnapping a victory and let him go, releasing a tape recording of the general's repentance.

But Dozier was an unrepentant war criminal. Within the Red Brigades there was a strong feeling against the use of torture, and a confession extracted under duress would have no moral value. This left only execution as a viable option. But the Executive Committee had delayed making that decision.

Emilia sat next to him on the couch, putting her hand on his shoulder.

"I don't want us to have to kill him," she said.

Savasta shrugged. He was still experiencing psychological trauma from last year's termination of Giuseppe Taliercio, and he did not want to carry out another execution. But he knew he would shoot Dozier if the Esecutivo ordered him to do it.

"I don't either," he said. "But the Executive Committee will decide."

"When does the decision get made?"

"Soon," he told her.

23

4:25 P.M., 21 JANUARY 1982
VIA PINDEMONTE, PADUA

Is someone trying to tell me something?

Dozier was in the middle of George Orwell's *1984* and for the first time since college he was ruminating about Orwell's bleak vision of the future. No, surely, the choice of this particular book was accidental. They must have discovered the English original in a used-book shop somewhere.

WINTER OF FIRE

An accident, then, and yet something in the atmosphere had changed. The food was still arriving on time and in abundance, occasionally accompanied by a plastic cup of wine. Savasta and the others still came in for occasional political "interrogations" and even another photographic session in which his beard was again recorded for posterity. His captors no longer seemed to want to look him in the eye and seemed depressed and listless.

He tapped on the floor outside his section of the tent, his normal method of summoning the guard. It was the woman, and she called Savasta before opening his section of the tent.

"I would like to write a letter to my wife," Dozier announced. It would be good to say good-bye to the kids too, he thought: a kind of summing up . . .

"I'll have to think about it," Savasta said. "I'm not sure we can let you send letters."

"I don't need to send it. Just give me pen and paper so that I can compose a farewell letter to my wife. If anything should happen to me, then perhaps you could send it later."

"That won't be necessary!" Savasta told him. The woman looked away.

"I think it may be necessary."

"If it should become necessary, I'll let you know," Savasta promised and left.

The general sat back on his cot, but he left *1984* where he had dropped it. He began composing the letter in his head.

BOOK IV

THE
RESCUE

1

"I don't know where the general is," Massimiliano Corsi said. "I would tell you if I knew."

He listened for a response, but there was silence and the young man realized that he was alone in the room. They would be back in a few minutes, after they had drunk their coffee and smoked their cigarettes.

Corsi was seated on a wooden stool, his arms manacled behind his back. There was a heavy canvas bag over his head, secured with leather thongs that went around his neck and tied at the back. He was dressed in the same jeans and shirt that he had been wearing when a group of armed men barged into his room and taken him away, holding a gun to his head.

It had not been the kind of arrest he had always imagined he would someday face. There had been no lawyers, or fingerprints, or judges, or steel cells. In fact, there was something Argentinian about it all, more of a disappearance than a detention. At the very start, they had told him that he would be executed should Commissioner Nicola Simone die of his injuries.

At first, there had been an odd thrill about the experience, because the beatings they administered gave him a chance to measure his courage against their brutality. The Red Brigades had always seen the police as sadists, the blunt instruments of a dying regime. In contrast, the *brigatisti* saw themselves as soldiers who fought a clean fight and refrained from needless violence. Corsi knew that the Veneto column might execute their *generale* but they would never brutalize him. It was part of their code.

But the hurting had gone on too long, making it difficult for him to concentrate on codes of conduct and moral superiority. His head ached and his rib cage throbbed. He had begun to contemplate death and how it would mean an end to the pain.

* * *

167

"Hello, Massimiliano." An unfamiliar but sympathetic voice spoke.

"Who's there?"

"Look, I don't like this kind of police work." The man's accent was cultivated, the product of a university education; the men who hit him all spoke with vulgar regional accents. "You're a bright young fellow, and you must know what's happening. There's terrible pressure from the government to capture Savasta before he kills that general. If Dozier dies, these men will lose their jobs. So they feel authorized to play rough."

"I don't know where the general is!"

"I believe you. Look, I'm not asking you to betray anything or anyone, but if you could give me one name, just the name of someone who might lead us a step closer to Dozier, then I could get you out of here. Nobody would know it was you who had talked."

"Savasta never told anybody anything, even old friends. I don't know—"

"Somebody from Galati's old Verona brigade must be giving Savasta logistical support, no? Who?"

"Michele Galati has a young brother named Paolo." Corsi was trying to think of someone who would be guaranteed to know nothing. Michele's little brother was supposed to be half-crazy and maybe even a junkie. Nobody would trust Paolo with a secret. "He visits Michele every week in prison, brings him messages."

"We'll check it out," said the voice. There was the squeaking of hinges as the door opened and then closed, leaving him alone with his conscience.

Betrayal, he thought, weeping beneath the canvas mask as he realized that he had just taken the first step toward collaboration: *tradimento....*

2

The train from Novara stopped at track 1. As the passengers climbed down into the freezing rain, they were scrutinized by one of Commissioner Genova's men, standing in the shadows by the newspaper kiosk. The detective wore a broad-brimmed felt hat and what seemed to be a hearing aid in one ear.

The last passenger was a blond, baby-faced man in his early twenties, wearing jeans and a motorcyclist's leather jacket over a turtleneck sweater.

It was Paolo Galati and the detective recognized him immediately.

After a quick glance around the platform, Paolo Galati moved toward the terminal building, his shoulders hunched against the piercing wind. Commissioner Genova's man put a cigarette to his lips and then raised a gold cigarette lighter.

"He's wearing a leather jacket and he's alone!" he said into the lighter's microphone.

"We're ready." The response came through the hearing aid. The detective followed Galati through the passenger lounge, past the shuttered windows of the ticket booths, and through the revolving doors to the rain-swept street outside.

Paolo was trying to read the bus schedule in the flickering light from a streetlamp when Genova's team pulled up next to him in their unmarked car.

"Get in, Galati," one of the plainclothes men called. "Somebody downtown wants a word with you."

The back door of the sedan opened. Galati turned to flee, but Genova's man was standing behind him with a pistol.

"Come on, kid," he said, pushing Galati into the backseat. "This isn't going to hurt."

3

Be professional, Ruggiero Volinia told himself as he slogged through the torrential rain.

He made two careful passes up and down the Via Monte Ortigara and saw nothing suspicious. The parked cars were all empty, and even the corner bar was quiet. He paused on the curb opposite the Arcangeli apartment and wrestled with his conscience.

There was nothing that suggested danger. Before Christmas, the police had staged raid after raid, arresting half of the former student radicals in Verona, but Lisa and Alessandro had not been disturbed, which meant that their names were not on anybody's list.

So it was safe to see her, at least for a quick visit, he decided, crossing the Via Monte Ortigara. Savasta will never know.

He crept up the darkened stairwell toward the second story, his wet feet squishing across the tile floor. He listened at the apartment door before putting his key into the lock. Alessandro and Lisa were apparently already in their beds because there was no sound; he pushed open the door.

"Lisa!" he called. There was a muffled cry from the far end of the hallway and she stumbled out of her bedroom, putting on her wire-rimmed glasses. Then there was a flash of white nightgown as she darted toward him, barefooted. A moment later, she was in his arms, sobbing with joy.

"*Bimba!*" he cried, kissing her hair and feeling her warm body shivering in his arms.

"Oh, Ruggiero, I've missed you so much! Is it safe for you to be here?"

"For a little while." He followed her into the bedroom.

"Let's get your things dry." She pulled on his sleeves. Quickly, he shed his wet clothing and helped her arrange his trousers and shirt on the back of a chair facing an electric heater.

"Come to bed! You're so thin. You need to be back here where

I can feed you!" Beneath the covers, they made love once very fast, with a sense of urgency, and then a second time, more slowly. For a while, they lost track of time.

"I have to leave," Ruggiero told her, as they lay in one another's arms, her head tucked into his chest.

"Wait a while longer," she begged him. "It's been . . . how long?"

"Forty days," said Ruggiero. They fell silent, lying side by side, and he felt fatigue settling over him. It was cold outside. It was even cold in the bedroom. The only warm place in the world was under the covers next to her.

4

1:05 A.M., 27 JANUARY 1982
VERONA QUESTURA (STATE POLICE HEADQUARTERS)
VIA LUNGADIGE PORTA VITTORIA, VERONA

"If none of Michele's friends has broken the law," Commissioner Genova said, "you wouldn't be doing anything wrong in telling me their names."

Genova heard the fatigue in his voice as he spoke. For weeks now he had been questioning people who knew nothing or chose to say nothing of what they knew. Savasta's people had produced yet another communiqué, the fourth, filled with the same windy rhetoric. They had included a second photograph of Dozier sporting a beard. The pressure on DIGOS was becoming extreme and the investigation was stalled in its tracks.

"My brother liked to keep in contact with old friends." There was terror on Paolo Galati's face as he spoke. Michele Galati's little brother was apparently on the straight and narrow now, but there had been persistent stories about drugs and juvenile delinquency in his past. And Paolo was emotionally very volatile. Sometimes he giggled at Genova's jokes and sometimes—when Michele's name was mentioned—he burst into tears.

"Look, Paolo, I am going to talk to you frankly." Genova leaned forward and put a kindly hand on the young man's shoulder, deciding he would get some names out of him if it took all night. "You're in a little bit of trouble and it's trouble that could either get much worse or just go away, depending how much cooperation you show us."

"I don't know anything!" There was hysteria in the boy's voice.

"You know the names of the people you have been visiting on Michele's behalf!" Genova prompted him. "Look, you're carrying too much weight around on your shoulders. Liberate yourself from all these stupid secrets!"

"I don't have to tell you—"

"Yes, you do!" Genova's hand tightened on Galati's shoulder. "Otherwise I send you down the hall, where you get questioned by people with less patience than I have. Do you understand? There are some angry people in this building, and they want to talk to you."

There was a long silence. Genova watched Paolo's body trembling in terror.

"The names of the people Michele asked you to visit," Commissioner Genova commanded. "Start talking now!"

"Anna Paola Zonca, Roberto della Nave, and Andrea Carlassara," Paolo began slowly, his eyes brimming with tears. "Nazareno Mantovani and Alessandro Arcangeli. . . ."

"Who are they?" Genova was puzzled. None of these names had turned up on any of his lists.

"They're mostly all schoolteachers," said Paolo.

5

3:30 A.M., 27 JANUARY 1982
VIA MONTE ORTIGARA, VERONA

"Ruggiero!" she screamed.

They found me, he thought in sudden agony, sitting up naked in bed. He could see nothing but the glow from the electric heater, but beyond the sanctuary of their bedroom, there were crashing noises, as if doors were being knocked down.

They've been watching this apartment all along, he guessed. They must have known I was on active duty with the Red Brigades and figured I would eventually come back to see Lisa.

"*Bastardi!*" They heard Alessandro's angry scream from his room at the end of the hall. There was the sound of a fist striking flesh and then a grunt. Ruggiero stared wildly around the darkened room, trying to decide what to do. It was hard to be brave without trousers on. Lisa was screaming.

"There's somebody in here!" A harsh voice slapped at them from the door, and a flashlight seared across the room, searching them out.

"No!" Ruggiero shouted. The room filled up with people. The lights came on, and there were three pistols pointed at them. Lisa was absolutely shrieking now, letting out one piercing animal howl after another.

"Shut up!" One of the policemen snarled, jerking the blankets away and leaving them both naked on the mattress. "On your feet! Get your hands up!"

"Let us get our clothes on!" Ruggiero said, determined to defend his woman's honor. One of the men seized his foot and dragged him onto the floor. He cracked his head against a chest of drawers and felt a boot come crashing into his stomach.

"Oh God!" he gasped, falling to his hands and knees. Lisa had gone utterly silent. She was standing against the wall, her face white and her eyes wide with terror, her hands shielding her breasts. Somehow, she had managed to get her glasses on.

"Leave her alone, you bastards!" Ruggiero screamed. He tried to jump to his feet, but the policeman's foot caught him in the testicles and he collapsed again on the floor.

For a long time he was conscious of nothing but the pain in his body. When he recovered, Lisa was gone.

There was a man wearing jeans and a black leather jacket covering him nonchalantly with a pistol; Ruggiero could not decide whether it was the same man who kicked him or another.

"How did you find me?" he asked.

"What?" The policeman seemed amused. "Hey, get your clothes on! We got to get out of here."

Ruggiero climbed into his shirt and jeans. His hands trembled as he tied his shoes. Then the policeman put manacles around his wrists and led him away.

6

"Who the hell is he?" Commissioner Genova pointed to a tall young man who was handcuffed to a radiator at the end of the corridor.

The second floor of the Verona Questura resembled a scene from Dante's *Inferno*. On the basis of Paolo Galati's listing of his brother's contacts in Verona, they had set out to detain twelve people, but the arrest teams had come back with boyfriends and girlfriends and visiting relatives.

"I don't know," admitted the plainclothes man. "We found him in bed with the babe with those funny glasses."

"What babe with funny glasses?"

"Elisabetta . . . ah . . . wait a minute," said the detective, consulting a clipboard. "Her name is Elisabetta Arcangeli. She's an elementary school mistress and shares an apartment with her brother, Alessandro Arcangeli, who was on Paolo's list."

"Got it," said Genova, finding Alessandro's name in the sheaf of papers he held in his hand. "Has somebody talked to Arcangeli? What have we got out of him?"

"He admits to having sprayed 'Down with Nixon' on a wall in 1971. Should we let him and his sister go?"

"No! Somewhere in this mob, there has got to be someone who knows something. We keep asking questions until we get some answers!"

"Okay, *capo*. But how about lover boy down there? We don't even have a cell for him."

"Find out his name and run a records check on him," Genova said. "I'll talk to him after lunch, and then we can send him home. . . ."

7

1:45 P.M., 27 JANUARY 1982
VERONA QUESTURA (STATE POLICE HEADQUARTERS)
VIA LUNGADIGE PORTA VITTORIA, VERONA

I've got to get her out of here, Ruggiero thought. Even in the midst of an incredible din he could hear her sobbing voice in a distant room. Sometimes she made a yelping noise and his heart turned in his chest with the thought that they might be hurting her.

He tried to think of a strategy. Was it possible that the police knew that he was a member of the Red Brigades but did not know that he had participated in the Dozier kidnapping?

"Leave me alone!" he heard Lisa cry again. Were they beating her?

Ruggiero tugged at the handcuffs that held him to the radiator. The police had left him here nine hours ago and he was now suffering from a persistent cramp in his right leg. Because of the handcuffs, he could not stand up straight; because of the radiator's heat, he could not sit down.

"Okay, young fellow!" One of the officers who arrested him was unlocking his handcuffs. "Commissioner Genova wants to talk to you."

The detective guided him down a dusty corridor with a wooden floor and into a small, shabby office. Commissioner Genova turned out to be a very large man sitting behind a cluttered desk. "You can take the cuffs off him," he told the detective.

"Thank you."

"Well, we want you to be comfortable," Genova told him absently, studying a pink folder with RUGGIERO VOLINIA written on the cover. "Okay, why don't you tell me what you know?"

"I don't know anything."

Commissioner Genova gazed at him with an expression that seemed to waver somewhere between indifference and disappointment.

"I think we've passed the point where that kind of response is helpful. Our information is that you are a serving member of the Red Brigades, recruited by Michele Galati in 1978, since which time you have been active with the Verona brigade. Correct me if I'm wrong, but you are Ruggiero Volinia, are you not? Born in Porto Maggiore on 6 November 1957?"

"Yeah, but listen, I'm not . . . I've never been on active service with the Brigades." They know who I am, he thought. I'll have to give them that arms depot in Mestre. A lot of people know about the Mestre arsenal; they'll never trace the leak back to me.

"Really? Then perhaps you could define the exact nature of your relationship with the Brigate rosse."

"I used to know some people who maybe traveled with the Brigades. And not too long ago, I ran into this guy. . . ."

"His name?"

"I don't remember his name, but listen, we were driving through Mestre and this guy pointed out a garage and told me that the Red Brigades kept an arsenal of heavy weapons there, rocket launchers, mortars, stuff they got from the Palestinians."

"Where would we find this arsenal?" Commissioner Genova was writing, but he seemed only faintly interested.

"I don't remember the name of the street, but I could show you where it is." Volinia paused. "In return—you know that Elisabetta Arcangeli who was arrested with me?—I'd want you to let us both go, because she's never been involved in anything political, and I would have helped you all I could with this information about the arms deposit."

"We would think about it very seriously," Commissioner Genova told him. "If you were to give us a hand, we would want to do our best for you. Look, why don't we pop you in a car and send you along to Mestre, and if you will show the officers where this arsenal is, then we can think about making some kind of arrangement for you and Signorina Elisabetta Arcangeli." He glanced at Ruggiero. "You're sure she's not political?"

"Absolutely not!"

Commissioner Genova called his detective, who came in with the handcuffs.

They're going for it, Ruggiero exulted as they led him away. I'm going to take Lisa home with me. We'll go away, someplace like Australia, and start over.

8

6:30 P.M., 27 JANUARY 1982
VERONA QUESTURA (STATE POLICE HEADQUARTERS)
VIA LUNGADIGE PORTA VITTORIA, VERONA

The trend was clear. Exhausted, Genova looked up from the stack of interrogation notes and realized that Paolo Galati had led them to a half-dozen small fry from the moribund Verona brigade. And none of them knew where General Dozier was because Savasta had never trusted Michele Galati's people.

Damn! The commissioner put his head back against the wall, wondering whether he could snatch a few minutes' sleep. They had worked around the clock for too many days. The pressure from Prime Minister Spadolini's office was intense, and the Polizia di Stato high command had made the investigation into a race to find Dozier before the Carabinieri carried off the prize.

The phone rang. This is another high-ranking Interior Ministry bureaucrat wanting a progress report, he thought.

"Commissario?" One of his men was calling, excitement in his voice. "We're in Mestre. You know that kid we found in bed with the babe with the funny glasses? He was telling the truth! He just took us to this garage where we found enough heavy weapons for a small war. How did you know he was Red Brigades?"

"I didn't," Genova admitted. "I was doing my 'we-know-everything-so-you-might-as-well-confess' routine and he started telling me about this arsenal they got from the Palestinians."

"Do you suppose he knows where the general is?"

"Bring him back here on the double," Genova said, feeling his body fill up with new energy. "And we'll ask him."

9

12:35 A.M., 28 JANUARY 1982
VERONA QUESTURA (STATE POLICE HEADQUARTERS)
VIA LUNGADIGE PORTA VITTORIA, VERONA

"Come on, asshole!" one of the policeman shouted at him. "Who told you where those guns were?"

"I ... I can't ... I don't remember," Ruggiero said. He was finding it difficult to concentrate. Since his arrest twenty-two hours ago, he had had nothing to eat or drink and fragments of thought were butterflying across his mind. It was impossible to think with men screaming at him hour after hour.

He tried to focus upon one central, critical fact. The police could keep him awake until he went unconscious and they could send him to jail for a million years, but they could not kill him.

But Savasta could.

And would. In prison, Ruggiero would be exposed to the violence of men who were already serving life sentences and had nothing to lose from another homicide. They could murder him the way they had murdered other traitors.

It was humiliating to keep crying but the unhappiness kept pouring out of him. It seemed so unfair that they should treat him this way after he had led them to that enormous pile of military weapons!

"You're wasting our time! Goddamn it, get on your feet!" They hauled him out of the chair; Ruggiero felt the fear rushing through his system. His interrogators were working in teams, two at a time, and seemed prepared to keep it up forever. They were never rough with him when the commissioner was in the room, but Genova was gone at the moment, and these two mountainous cops seemed capable of any cruelty.

"Leave me alone!" he pleaded.

"Stand over there!" One of the policemen threw him across the tiny cell and his thin shoulders slammed against the concrete wall.

"Not here, jerk!" the other man screamed and he felt himself propelled to the other side of the cell. "Over there!"

His head cracked against the wall. He felt the room spin and sank to his knees.

"How did you know about those guns?"

"I don't remember!"

"You don't remember?" repeated the policeman. "How about your girlfriend, does she know?"

"She doesn't know anything."

"I think we need to ask her." The cop turned to his colleague. "Go downstairs and bring her up here."

"She might have a weapon concealed under her clothing," suggested the other policeman. "First, we'll give her a thorough body search."

"No, listen, don't do this! I want to talk to that commissioner." Ruggiero felt a sudden courage inside him. It doesn't matter about me, he thought. I've got to save Lisa.

"The commissioner is a busy man," the detective said. "He doesn't have time for a piece of shit like you."

"Get him! I'll tell him things he wants to know."

Suddenly, the two cops became businesslike. They eased Ruggiero into his chair and brushed his hair back from his forehead. The door to the cell was opened, and a rush of cool air swept in. He concentrated on what he wanted to say, knowing he had to get it right this time. There were footsteps and whispers in the corridor.

"I was told you wanted to see me." Genova's voice was cold. His massive body filled the doorway.

"I thought we had an arrangement," Ruggiero complained. "I showed you where that arsenal was, didn't I?"

"I am looking for an American named James Dozier," said the commissioner as if this conversation were not of great significance to him. "In return for some information about the general, we could make a real deal. Don't send for me again unless you have something significant to say!" He turned away.

"Wait!"

"What?" Over his shoulder, Genova gazed at him impassively, waiting.

"You can't cheat me again. This time I want an agreement ratified in the presence of a judge." Ruggiero's head felt clear, and he plunged ahead with a strange self-confidence. "I'll plead guilty for a suspended sentence, and I need new identity papers for myself and Signorina Arcangeli and one hundred million lire in cash."

"And what will you give us in return?" Ruggiero expected that Genova would tell him he was a fool, or bargain, or deny that there was that much money available, but instead he was making notes on a piece of paper.

"I'll give you Dozier," he told him.

"What did you say?" Commissioner Genova's voice was calm, but he stopped writing and looked up for the merest fraction of a second.

"Dozier," repeated Ruggiero Volinia. "Dozier!"

10

3:00 A.M., 28 JANUARY 1982
PADUA QUESTURA (STATE POLICE HEADQUARTERS)
PIAZZA RUZANTE, PADUA

"How long do we have?" asked Chief of Police Corrias. "How long do we need?"

Commissioner Genova glanced quickly around the table, watching the argument unfold. With his fellow DIGOS commissioners De Gregorio and Fioriolli, he was sitting in the conference room on the second floor of the Padua Questura with a group of local Polizia di Stato cops who had just been hauled out of bed with the cheerful news that they were going to war with Antonio Savasta.

"Four days," announced a staff officer, consulting his checklist. Most of the Padua cops wanted to delay the operation until there were enough senior Interior Ministry bureaucrats on the scene to take the rap for whatever went wrong. Assaulting a Red Brigades safe house was a disaster-prone operation; Savasta's track record suggested that he would be hard to surprise and reluctant to go down without a fight. "Maybe three if we hurry."

"Are you telling me I can't raid an apartment in my own jurisdiction in less than seventy-two hours?" Gianfranco Corrias objected. The Padua chief of police had a reputation for flexibility and imagination; some said he was the best cop in the northeast.

A lot had happened in the two and a half hours since Volinia's stunning announcement that he knew where Dozier was being held prisoner. To confirm their agreement, the DIGOS had pulled a Verona magistrate out of bed to offer Ruggiero a suspended sentence and to confirm the promise of a financial reward. One hundred million lire amounted to sixty thousand U.S. dollars and the money was to be drawn from a secret Polizia di Stato account.

After one quick call to DIGOS headquarters in Rome and another to Chief Corrias, Genova and his men had piled Volinia into an unmarked car and raced over to Padua for a quick reconnaissance of the Via Pindemonte. When they had fixed the location of Emanuela's apartment clearly in their minds, Genova and his men had descended upon the Padua Questura, where Corrias was already assembling his team. The staff planning conference had begun immediately.

"Has somebody called in the NOCS?" Corrias was asking.

"They're flying in from Sardinia," Genova told him. The Interior Ministry SWAT team was called the Nucleo operativo centrale di sicurezza, or NOCS for short. They had been trained to be the ultimate commando force, able to fly anywhere, drop out of the sky or pop out of the water, shoot any weapon, storm any airplane, blast their way through any obstacle, capture any terrorist, and then disappear afterward without a trace. "They'll be here by dawn."

"What do we know about the interior of the Frascella apartment?" the chief of police asked.

"We've got Volinia downstairs with my men, making a floor plan," Genova said. "So we'll know exactly where everything is when we attack."

"We're going to get that American killed if we try a frontal attack," objected one of the Padua staff officers. "We should surround the apartment and after we've got the residents out of the building, we open negotiations. We explain the situation to them and they come out with their hands up—"

"No, look, this is a Red Brigade operation," Genova said. "A diplomatic approach hands the initiative to Savasta. If he chooses to go down in a blaze of revolutionary glory, he can shoot it out with us and kill Dozier before we kill him. Or else he could simply execute the general and then surrender. We can't make his life sentence any longer and either way we lose!"

"The Americans would expect—"

"The Americans are potentially part of the problem," Genova said. "Suppose Savasta delays, waiting for the press and TV to show up. He then proposes that he and his friends be set free in exchange for the general's life. Mrs. Dozier goes on television and weeps. The Americans pressure the prime minister into a humanitarian solution and Savasta catches the next flight to Libya."

"You're right," Corrias intervened. "There will be no negotiations. So how soon can we be ready to move?"

"We should hit them hard in the middle of the night!" another officer proposed. "How about twenty-three hours from now? Is that enough time to get ready?"

"It's too long," said Genova. "If Savasta gets the merest hint that we are closing in on him, he will execute that general and vanish."

"So when?" asked Gianfranco Corrias. Genova looked at his watch.

"Right after breakfast," he said.

"After breakfast is good," said the chief of police. "Let's do it!"

11

7:45 A.M., 28 JANUARY 1982
VIA PINDEMONTE, PADUA

"What do you want?" asked the general, waking up quickly as he felt his space being invaded. Without his watch, he never knew what time it was anymore. It sometimes felt like the middle of the night when the lights went on and they came in to wake him up.

"It's your breakfast," responded Emilia Libera blankly as she set his food down on the porta-potty. The woman was wearing a dressing gown and the usual ski mask. "Buon appetito!"

He shook his head and woke up completely, facing breakfast and another day of captivity. More solitaire and more push-ups. Maybe another interrogation or more photographs. Dozier swung his legs off the cot and sat up to address his breakfast, wondering what life would be like when—and if—he was released.

Would his career be over? There was no rational reason why his career should suffer from this misfortune, because he had revealed no classified material and made no treasonous statements, but it suddenly occurred to him that he might escape with his life only to discover that they did not trust him anymore.

Who would know for sure that he had resisted their efforts to break him? Suppose the Red Brigades had been concocting the kinds of admissions about Vietnam and American imperialism that he had really been refusing to make? The army could by now think of him as a traitor. How would he prove that he had kept the faith? There would be no way. He could hardly get the Red Brigades to give him a testimonial.

For years now, the Department of Defense had been trusting him with its deepest secrets; without that security clearance, he wasn't ever going to get another good assignment or a promotion. He would have to quit.

Judy and I could go back to Florida and open a marina, he told himself as he munched his cornflakes, or we could do real estate. It had occurred to him that there would be a market for a specialized condominium for the elderly, in which hot meals, maybe even gourmet meals, would be delivered to each apartment three times a day, so that tenants who were infirm or handicapped could forget about cooking and relax. Assuming that you had a decent-size condominium, say one hundred twenty separate apartments, how would you organize a food delivery system that would produce upward of two hundred hot meals more or less simultaneously?

It would be a gigantic problem in logistics, but there was nothing he understood better than problems in transport and supply. In fact, there was nothing he liked better than a practical problem, the kind of thing you could get your brain around.

And he found he liked thinking about Florida. It would be good to go home again. Judy had been born and raised in Washington, D.C., but she had become a devoted convert to Florida life. And people were loyal in Florida! Did somebody have a yellow ribbon tied around an old oak tree somewhere near Arcadia? He might have been forgotten by everybody else, but down in Florida there would be people worrying about him.

We'll go back there, he told himself. If the army doesn't want me when this is all over, then Judy and I will head for home. Scott and I have got a lot of fishing to catch up on.

Libera came in for the tray.

"What's happening?" he said.

"Nothing's happening," she said, collecting the tray and leaving the tent.

A slow day in the people's penitentiary. Dozier flopped back on his cot to digest his breakfast and contemplate Florida. Assuming you had one hundred and twenty apartments on six floors, he began his calculations, you would need a minimum staff of twelve people. . . .

12

8:00 A.M., 28 JANUARY 1982
VIA PINDEMONTE, PADUA

Antonio was sleeping late but Emilia was hesitant to wake him. The troubles of the day would start soon enough and it had been a dreadful week.

Morale was rock-bottom: Cesare Di Lenardo was scowling at everyone and Emanuela kept bursting into tears. Giovanni Ciucci seemed to have given up talking altogether as he read and reread his books on Marx. Even Antonio had become withdrawn and silent. And the weather had been foul, with freezing rain and snow slashing down upon their little sanctuary.

Even Dozier seemed surly and depressed. Every time they tried to interrogate him, he insisted irritably that the time had come to make contact with the Italian authorities and start negotiating.

Nobody wanted to explain the facts of guerrilla warfare to the sullen, angry American. They had planned on negotiating for his release only after the successful abductions of Romiti and Simone and Senzani's victorious attack on the Christian Democratic Party Congress. A triumphant Red Brigades could have negotiated from a position of strength.

But the Winter of Fire campaign had been a disaster. The

Spadolini government would never negotiate now. The Dozier kidnapping had become an embarrassment.

The Americans had announced the availability of large sums of money for the general's release, but the Executive Committee believed that accepting a ransom would cheapen the whole operation, weakening its propaganda value.

And the police pressure was unbelievable. With the kidnap now beginning its forty-second day, there were still six thousand cops on the streets of northern Italy. There were even rumors that the prime minister was preparing to order Italian Army combat units into the crusade.

After five years of active revolutionary service, Emilia thought she could recognize the moment when an operation had run its course. The only plausible step at this point would be for the proletarian court to conclude its deliberations with the obvious verdict of guilty. And pronounce sentence.

This was precisely the problem. Although they respected the general's courage, nobody liked him very much. He approached every discussion with the unshakable confidence that America represented the cause of righteousness and that Marxism was silly and irredeemably wicked. He seemed to regard them with contempt, as if they were juvenile delinquents rather than revolutionaries.

But he was what he was; nobody wanted to shoot him. One dead general would not advance the revolution by much, and his execution might even create sympathy for the Americans. But it was hard to see what alternative they had.

Emilia shrugged and walked to the kitchen in her bare feet. It was cold in the hallway. Cesare was on guard in the tent room and he sent her a fierce, belligerent glance that frightened her a little.

In the living room, Emanuela was curled up in a sleeping bag on the couch. Giovanni Ciucci lay on his back on the floor, snoring gently, a book open on his belly.

In the kitchen there was light flooding in through the window, and the day was crisp and clear. I don't care what happens to the general, she thought as she made the coffee. Let's release him and go. Let's just walk out the front door and leave him here. I want to go home.

With two cups of cappuccino on a tray, she went back to the bedroom. For a long time, she sat and watched Antonio sleep. He had been the only man in her life; it was difficult to contemplate leaving him.

He stirred, and she stroked his face.

"You slept late," she murmured.

"What time is it?" His eyes flashed open with alarm.

"Just past eight. Cesare's on guard, and everybody else is asleep. I took the general his breakfast. And the sun is shining!"

"*Va bene.*" He hoisted himself up on one elbow and accepted his cup of cappuccino. "How are you? What is this, Thursday? Look, if the weather has broken, we need to get out for a little bit this weekend. I've got a meeting of the Esecutivo. You could come to Milan and shop while I—"

"We'll see," Emilia said, thinking that they could have had a cottage somewhere near Rome. He could have been her real husband, and she could have been his wife.

"If the others are sleeping, then you could come back to bed."

Soon we will have to say good-bye, she thought, as she slid beneath the covers. But not today.

13

11:05 A.M., 28 JANUARY 1982
PADUA QUESTURA (STATE POLICE HEADQUARTERS)
PIAZZA RUZANTE, PADUA

"The truck looks authentic," said the commander of the NOCS. He was a short, quiet man of unremarkable appearance, who looked like an accountant with muscles.

"It is authentic," Genova said. They had borrowed it from the Domenichelli Company, a wholesale firm that delivered food products several times a week to the Dea Supermarket on the Via Guizza.

In the courtyard behind the Questura, a thirteen-man NOCS assault team clustered around the tailgate of the truck. They were all dressed in civilian clothing, jeans, sneakers, and bulky sweatshirts covering specially designed bulletproof vests. They all carried Beretta machine pistols, and—like the terrorists they hunted—wore ski masks to prevent identification.

Two of the NOCS had already departed in a carpenter's mini-van for the Via Pindemonte, dressed as laborers and carrying a large quantity of rope. In his preparations, Chief Corrias had inspected architect's drawings for the apartment building and discovered a ventilation shaft running down from the roof past the bathroom of the Frascella flat. The two NOCS had been ordered to climb seven stories down into the shaft and dangle just above Emanuela's bathroom window. When their colleagues came in the front door, they would smash through the frosted glass and come through the bathroom window.

"We think that there are five people in the apartment, three men and two females." The NOCS commanding officer began a last-minute briefing for his team. "One of the women is a short, slender girl who is probably an untrained 'housekeeper,' but the others can be assumed to be Red Brigades professionals."

Genova was confident that this analysis was accurate. Ruggiero had testified that there had been five *brigatisti* in the flat. To be sure, a DIGOS sound crew had gone that morning to a house across the street from Emanuela's apartment and focused a laser beam against the windows of the Frascella flat. Whenever anyone within the safe house spoke, the air echoed against the glass, creating minute vibrations that could be detected and sometimes interpreted by the sensitive laser. After a morning of scanning the apartment, the sound team believed that there were five people talking in the apartment, although no useful intercepts had been made.

"We should be able to take them by surprise," the NOCS commander continued. "But watch out for the females. If anybody is going to shoot you in the back, it'll be a woman."

The SWAT team officer swung down off the tailgate of the Domenichelli van. "Boys, right now, nobody knows about this business but us, but if General Dozier turns out to be inside that flat, the world's attention will be on us within a few hours. And the honor of our nation is at stake! Today we show the world that the Italian police are the best on the planet!"

The NOCS accepted the notion that they were the best on the planet with quiet agreement and climbed into the back of the truck. Blondie was standing by with the Alfa and the commissioner was putting on his flak jacket when the NOCS commander approached for any last-minute instructions.

"You can leave in about five minutes," Genova told him. "I'll meet you at the street entrance after I've reviewed the situation on the Via Pindemonte. As your truck closes in on the target, the local cops will be setting up three concentric rings around the Via Pindemonte so that nobody gets in or out."

"Yeah, what are you doing with that flak jacket?"

"Thought I might need it," said Genova. "I'm coming in with you."

"You don't need to, y'know. You find 'em, we bust 'em. This part of the job is for professionals."

"Professionals? What do you think I am, an altar boy?"

"It's your ass, *Commissario*," said the commando chief, climbing up into the driver's seat of the Domenichelli van. "Don't get in our way, okay?"

14

11:21 A.M., 28 JANUARY 1982
VIA PINDEMONTE, PADUA

There was a lot of traffic in front of the Dea Supermarket. Blondie stopped at the light at the corner of the Via Guizza and the Via Pindemonte, giving Commissioner Genova thirty seconds to see whether his preparations were complete.

The parking lot was filling up with plainclothes policemen in unmarked cars, ready to clear pedestrians out of the way an instant before the operation began. In another moment, both ends of the Via Guizza would be sealed off to vehicular traffic to lessen the possibility of a civilian's being injured. In the event that the operation should degenerate into a protracted seige, a team of marksmen was standing by with tear gas and sniper's rifles.

Close in, just beneath Emanuela's window, a powerfully built young man was necking with a voluptuous blond woman. Genova watched the lovers, both Polizia di Stato undercover officers, and wondered how passionate you could get with a woman who wore a pistol suspended from her garter belt and a radio transmitter between her breasts.

Abruptly, there was a great rumbling noise in the air and the commissioner turned in time to see a giant bulldozer lumbering around the corner as workmen ran alongside shouting advice. The roar was appalling. The driver was a detective-inspector assigned to create some extra racket to cover any inadvertent noise caused by the attack team. The DIGOS's psychiatric advisers also believed that a high decibel level hampered the terrorists psychologically.

Let's hope it doesn't hamper us, thought Genova, and he raised the car microphone to his lips.

"Domenichelli Truck One to the Dea Supermarket on the Via Pindemonte," he said, delivering a coded clearance for the NOCS to enter the scene. This choreography had better work, he thought. Savasta could be looking at that bulldozer, wondering whether it is a legitimate work crew or cops creating a diversion. And he might have been watching our stand-up lovers out there, trying to decide how long that kind of vertical passion can endure. Savasta doesn't like coincidences, and he is not a guy who spends a lot of time in meditation before he gets out his gun.

"Go," he told Blondie, and the big Alfa swung around the corner just as the Domenichelli truck pulled into the parking lot and stopped up in front of the Dea Supermarket. Genova could see his men closing the doors of the store to prevent shoppers from wandering around what could soon become a battlefield. A moment later, Blondie parked the Alfa in front of the staircase that led to the Frascella flat.

"Here they come!" Blondie warned. In the rearview mirror, Genova saw the NOCS coming around the corner at a gallop keeping close to the side of the building. Genova waited until the last of the NOCS had passed and then raced up the flight of stairs behind them, noticing how quietly the commandos could move despite the equipment they carried. Everything metallic had been taped, and anything that was not strictly necessary had been left behind.

The NOCS commander stopped his attack party at the top of the steps, just short of the second floor. Carrying leather satchels, two NOCS slipped around the corner, approaching Signorina Frascella's door. Dropping silently to their knees, the two commandos attached a specialized explosive charge to the door handle. Designed to direct its blast in a specific direction with a minimum of fire and noise, the device had been preset, with a firing cap already inserted into the plastic explosive.

Genova crouched on the staircase, feeling clumsy in his flak jacket. The two munitions specialists were crawling backward, unrolling the wires that connected the charge on the door to the detonator.

This is it, Genova realized. He thought for an instant about Rina and then took out his pistol.

15

11:28 A.M., 28 JANUARY 1982
VIA PINDEMONTE, PADUA

"It's a robbery! Somebody is holding up the supermarket!" Cesare Di Lenardo shouted, looking out the kitchen window. Emanuela had been making lunch and she glanced anxiously at Savasta, who was standing in the corridor.

"What are you saying?" snapped Savasta.

"A guy with a ski mask just ran across the parking lot toward the store," Cesare explained. "He had a rifle—"

"I don't like that." Savasta darted into the tent room where Ciucci was guarding the general.

"What's wrong?"

"I don't know," Savasta told him, pulling the pistol from his belt and handing it to him. "There are men running around outside with rifles. Cesare thinks it's a robbery, but I—"

"What do we do?" Ciucci asked, taking the pistol and getting to his feet.

"Keep the general under control. Let me see what's happening!" Savasta spun out of the room.

"What's the matter?" Emilia asked as Savasta rushed into the bedroom, followed by Di Lenardo and Emanuela Frascella. Dropping to his knees, Savasta pulled two Sterlings and a couple of hand grenades out from under the bed while Di Lenardo rushed to the bedroom window and looked out.

"What do you see?"

"Nothing!" Di Lenardo grabbed a machine gun, slapping a magazine into its belly. "There's nobody out there!"

"The parking lot should be filled with people!" Savasta looked out and saw that there was no traffic in the street. The supermarket parking lot, normally overflowing people, was now still. The only activity was a team of workmen digging up the pavement on the opposite side of the Via Guizza, but as Savasta studied the crew, he realized that they were not actually doing anything beyond racing the bulldozer's motor.

Then he saw the sniper. The man was wearing a flak jacket and the same kind of woolen ski mask they themselves wore when they interrogated General Dozier. He was hidden behind a car in the supermarket parking lot, pointing a rifle with a telescopic sight at the bedroom window.

This is what the world looks like just before it comes to an end, Savasta thought. There was a raid coming, a blitz!

"The police," he said. No one answered.

"How long have we got?" Di Lenardo asked. Savasta shrugged, realizing that he had never planned for this eventuality.

What do we do? Can we escape? Savasta took a few steps toward the front door. Then he halted, hearing a slight bump as something moved in the corridor beyond their sanctuary.

They're out there! He pushed open the door to the bathroom, and through the frosted glass saw a thick rope and a man's legs. It was hopeless.

His mind was moving very slowly now, working only at an elemental level. He felt sad, although not very frightened. The others followed him into the living room. Emanuela had gone so white that he thought she would faint. Cesare was still holding the Sterling aggressively, his face flushed. Emilia was standing by the window, staring at the silent scene outside.

"We're boxed in," he told them, wondering whether the police had orders to kill them. There had been speculation within the Organizzazione that the police had embarked upon a take-no-prisoners policy.

Is this the end? he asked himself. We could try to trade the general's life for our freedom, but the police would never let us escape from here alive. Should we go down fighting and make it difficult for them? We could shoot the general and then die with our weapons in our hands. Would the legend be worth it? Would there be a legend? What kind of difference could we make?

"Antonio!" Emilia breathed his name. "What are we going to do?" Her voice was tiny and he realized that he could not bear the thought of her dying, no matter what happened to him. He pictured her lying on the floor, bullets in her beautiful body, dead, crumpled, now only a memory. He would be next to her, perhaps, a gun in his dead hand. Maybe the blood from his body would be mingling with hers, forming a common pool of crimson, but it would be no comfort to either of them.

"We surrender," he said, amazed that the decision was so obvious. He put the hand grenade and the machine gun on the couch.

"No!" Di Lenardo uttered a strangled cry, somewhere between a shout and a sob. Emanuela began to weep very softly as if she were frightened of interrupting their discussion.

"Do you want to see the revolution happen or not?" Savasta shouted at him. "History has stages, and this is the one where we go to prison. Someday we get out and carry on. You are no use to anyone dead!"

Di Lenardo laid the Sterling on the couch and stood in front of Emanuela, his big body screening her frailty. Savasta took Emilia's hand and squeezed it. She seemed calm although he could see the tears in her eyes.

"*Addio,*" she whispered and smiled.

He was smiling back when the world blew up. There was a roaring in the corridor, followed an instant later by a shock wave that nearly knocked them down. A great billow of smoke poured down the passageway toward them. Savasta looked to make sure that his friends all had their hands raised in a clear gesture of surrender. If they have orders to kill us then it won't make any difference, he realized. But I don't want us dying because they're overexcited!

There was glass breaking and the sound of men running through the smoke. Suddenly, he remembered leaving Ciucci guarding the general with a pistol, and he wondered what Giovanni would do. Then there were two men at the door, ski masks covering their faces, automatic weapons pointed in their direction.

Don't shoot! Don't kill us! He screamed in his mind.

Something hit him hard in his stomach, and he went down with a strangled groan, holding his belly with his hands. Men were pounding into the room, more men than they could ever have fought. There were cries from all around him, screams from Emilia and little Emanuela and a defiant shout from Cesare as bad things began to happen to each of them.

It was confusing. The police were shouting at them. Savasta lay facedown on the carpet, feeling his stomach with his fingers until he realized that he had been hit with a foot or a fist, not a bullet. Someone kicked him in the side of the head but he barely felt it.

There was chaos all around him. Someone was pulling down his trousers while a second man yanked his jogging suit jacket up over his head, leaving him naked between the ankles and the wrists. It was a fast way of immobilizing him and being sure that he was concealing no weapons.

"No, *ti prego!* Please!" He heard Emilia's voice, and he turned his head to find that she was lying next to him, her head pointed in his direction. There was a man's foot on her neck, pinning her to the floor while two other men yanked her jersey up over her head and pulled her slacks down around her heels.

"I'm sorry."

"It's okay," she answered.

This is the way the revolution ends, he thought. With our bare asses in the air. A policeman began kicking him in the ribs while someone else sat on his back, twisting his arms. There seemed to be nothing more to do. Antonio Savasta closed his eyes and surrendered himself to the vengeance of the law.

16

11:35 A.M., 28 JANUARY 1982
VIA PINDEMONTE, PADUA

There was a muffled roar, and Dozier sat up on his cot, pulling off his earphones. The walls of his tent were billowing in and out like a sail in light air.

In the outer chamber of the tent, Giovanni Ciucci was on his feet, a silenced automatic in his hand, and he was pointing the weapon in Dozier's direction.

Something's up, he thought. He got to his feet, arranging his chains behind him as well as possible, and stood at the foot of his cot. Ciucci waved the pistol at him, warning him to back off.

Is he going to kill me? Dozier asked himself. Should I charge?

Then there was a blur of arms and legs as a man kicked his way into the tent, knocking the revolver from Ciucci's hand. An instant later, a second man piled in and then a third, and Ciucci went facedown hard as one of the invaders cracked him across the back of the head with a Beretta machine pistol.

Who are these guys? Dozier wondered. One of the newcomers came spilling into Dozier's portion of the tent, his hands outstretched in what seemed to be an attack. He was dressed in the standard terrorist uniform: jeans, sneakers, and ski mask.

The intruder was shouting as he charged forward, putting his hands on Dozier's shoulders. Reacting instinctively, the general fought back, trying to thrust him away. As his hands gripped the man's shoulders, he felt a bulletproof vest beneath his sweatshirt.

This is a cop! The realization that he was being liberated suddenly came home to him. These are policemen! I'm being rescued!

"*Generale?*"

"Io sono Generale Dozier!" he roared back. Two other policemen stormed into the tent as well and people began hugging him. From down the hall, Dozier could hear screams and cries, and he wondered whether the fighting were still going on.

"It's the general! He's alive!"

"*Bellissimo!*" Dozier contributed to the merriment. "Molto bene! Wonderful! Okay, Polizia!"

"Let's get you out of here!" proposed one of the policemen, investigating the chains that held him to the cot.

"There ought to be a key!" Dozier said, pointing to the Yale locks. One of the policemen raced off, returning thirty seconds later with Savasta's key ring. There was more confusion as several hands tried to sort through the keys, but finally one of the NOCS found the right one and both locks popped open.

"I'm free!" Jim Dozier breathed. He rose unsteadily to his feet and hobbled out of the tent. Giovanni Ciucci was unconscious, and Dozier stepped over him. He wanted to observe the environment in which he had lived for so long, but after weeks of sensory deprivation, the sudden rush of images and sounds was almost too much for him and he felt a little faint.

There was an open cupboard in the hallway and one of its drawers was filled with American hand grenades. The apartment seemed messy, disorganized, pulsating with police. He could hear women crying and in the living room he saw four people stretched on the floor, facedown. He was surprised to see that there were two women there, Emilia Libera and a younger girl whose existence he had never suspected.

"I'm Commissioner Genova," said one of the policemen. "There could be a bomb in this apartment, and we want to take you out of here!"

He nodded and turned away, a little regretfully, because he would have liked to explore the apartment. With Commissioner Genova on one side of him and a blond policeman on the other, Dozier walked toward the door.

A moment later, he was on the street, still wearing the dark blue track suit with the white stripes. He realized that he was still without shoes, wearing only the socks provided to him by the Red Brigades. The sunlight was so bright that it hurt his eyes. There was a crowd of people on the sidewalk opposite them, cheering, chanting, "Po-li-zi-a! Po-li-zi-a!"

"These men will take you to the Questura," Commissioner Genova told him quietly, leading him to a white Alfa Romeo and opening the door. The large blond-haired man slipped behind the wheel, and a second policeman jumped into the backseat with a machine gun.

"Where am I?" Dozier asked. He wondered whether someone had thought to notify Judy and the kids. Where was everybody?

"Padua," one of the policemen told him. "It is a very beautiful city!"

"What day is it?" The Alfa pulled away from the curb, its siren howling.

"*Giovedi*," Blondie told him. "Thursday! 28 January!"

"Thursday," he repeated, still a little dazed. According to his calendar matchbox, it should have been Tuesday, 26 January. How had he managed to misplace two whole days?

I'll take tomorrow off, he thought, beginning to organize his schedule. My in-box must be sky-high. I'd better be back in the office by Monday.

17

"Bitch!" growled the man who was sitting on her back. He seemed to feel the need to say it every time he hit her, and he was hitting her a lot, slapping her across the side of the head, and sometimes pounding her shoulders with his closed fist. "Bitch!"

They're crazy with excitement, she thought. They came in expecting to kill or be killed. We surrendered and it made them crazy. In a few minutes, their senior officers will arrive and they will have to stop.

"Who are you?" The man was shouting in her ear. "Are you Libera?"

"I'm Libera," she said, wanting them to be able to notify her mother and father that she had been taken into custody alive. Her parents would be glad she was finally in jail, because it would mean an end to the waiting.

"What's your battle name?"

"I don't have one." He hit her hard in the side, just below her rib cage, making her cry out with pain.

"What's your battle name?"

"I don't have one," Emilia repeated and he hit her again, even harder. She could hear the sound of ripping cloth as someone tore a bedsheet into strips. With a rough, angry gesture, the policeman pulled her clothing back into place. He twisted her wrists behind her back and tied them together with a piece of sheet. With another piece, he blindfolded her, but not very well, because she could still see out of one eye.

"Antonio?" she called.

"Shut up!" Someone kicked her in the thigh, and they hauled her to her feet. She stumbled out of the apartment and down the marble stairs, wondering what would happen to the skirts and blouses she was leaving behind in her dresser.

Outside, there was sunlight, and she could feel cold air through her light jogging suit. Beneath the blindfold, she saw crowds of curious people and dozens of policemen, all staring at her.

The worst is over, she thought as they pushed her into the backseat of a car. Once we are at the Questura, there will be judges and lawyers and they will not be able to touch us again.

"What is your battle name?" the same voice demanded, but she shook her head.

I am going to tell them nothing, she decided. It would hurt no one to confess that I have been called "Martina" within the Organization, but once you start giving little things away, then it becomes difficult to stop when they begin asking the important questions. It's better not to start.

"You talk to me, bitch!" the man grabbed one of her breasts and squeezed it brutally.

"Don't do that to me!"

Suddenly, the siren stopped and the driver cut his speed, as if he no longer wished to draw attention to himself. At a moderate speed, the car made several turns; she saw that they were on the Via Acquapendente in south Padua, a long way from the State Police headquarters downtown. To their right was an eight-foot gray cement wall with concertina barbed wire on the top. Then they passed through a gate, guarded by policemen wearing flak jackets and carrying machine guns.

"What is your battle name, bitch?" the policeman said again.

She ignored him, peeking under her blindfold and seeing three massive interconnected four-story buildings. The walls were gray and the windows trimmed with a faded, melancholy blue. The words CASERMA PIETRO ILARDI appeared over the main entrance. The Ilardi Police Barracks? This was not a *questura* where she would find judges and lawyers. Why were they bringing her here?

The car stopped.

"Hey!" Her escort caught her peeking beneath the mask and punished her for it, hitting her in the abdomen.

"Oh, leave me alone!" she pleaded, suddenly frightened. "Where am I?"

"In a place where we make all the rules," he told her.

18

Their great adventure was winding down like a cheap watch.

Commissioner Genova stood on the sidewalk of the Via Pindemonte, watching the cars depart one after another as the prisoners were taken away. A triumph, he told himself, warding off the depression that always threatened after a blitz. After forty-two days of captivity, Dozier still looked as tough as a crate of old nails. Blondie had taken the general to the Questura in Piazza Ruzante while Genova himself stayed behind to oversee the safe transport of the prisoners. Upstairs, a forensics team was dissecting the Frascella apartment in their search for further clues.

The NOCS had been fiercely brilliant and there had only been one minor casualty among Savasta's group. Giovanni Ciucci had sustained a slight injury to the back of the head; he had been taken to the hospital for a checkup.

"Ready, *capo?*" Blondie called out as he returned with the Alfa Romeo.

"Yes, let's go to the Questura and say good-bye to our general. Then we get some rest. I've been told that we can talk to our prisoners at seven tomorrow morning."

"Seven tomorrow?" Blondie was perplexed. "Who gets to interrogate them in the meantime?"

"I don't know," said Genova. He slumped down in his seat and closed his eyes to discourage further questions. "Less charitable persons than ourselves."

19

12:15 P.M., 28 JANUARY 1982
PADUA QUESTURA (STATE POLICE HEADQUARTERS)
PIAZZA RUZANTE, PADUA

"Generale! Generale!" the photographer implored and Jim Dozier obediently grinned into the camera. He could hardly object to having his picture taken with men who had risked their lives to rescue him, but his real priorities were to talk to Judy, get a shave, and then take about three consecutive showers.

"Have you gotten through to her yet?" he asked a police sergeant who was hunched over a telephone in the corner of the police chief's office, trying to arrange a phone call to Frankfurt. Ambassador Max Rabb had just called to say that Judy was staying in Germany with Walt and Marty Ulmer.

"No, *Signore Generale.* The lines seemed to be jammed. . . ."

More reporters were pushing in at the door. The phones were ringing symphonically while a mob of junior officials crowded in to have their pictures taken with the famous American general. Dozier sipped a cappuccino, smiled with iron determination at the photographers, and waited for the ordeal to be over.

"Hello, I'm Salvatore Genova." Jim Dozier looked up, realizing that the speaker was the commissioner who had spoken to him in the apartment on the Via Pindemonte.

"You people do incredibly good work," Dozier told him. "How did you find me?"

"It was complicated!" Genova exploded with a sudden laugh, but before he could explain, there was a shout from the door, and Dozier looked up to see two welcome faces: SETAF's General George McFadden and Colonel Bill Reed. Commissioner Genova backed away as the two American officers fought their way through the crowd.

"Jim! We were wondering why we hadn't seen you in the Officer's Club!" McFadden said, throwing an arm around his shoulders.

"They had you listed as AWOL!" added Reed, looking haggard after forty-two consecutive sixteen-hour days.

"Hello, Bill," Dozier said. The two men shook hands. "How is your Judy?"

"My Judy is fine, sir," Reed told him. "And we can probably get a line through to yours if we go back to SETAF."

Dozier looked around, searching for Commissioner Genova, but the policeman had vanished.

"Let's go!" he decided. It was his second escape of the afternoon. Reed ran interference for the two American generals. They stumbled down the staircase, pursued by a half-dozen journalists, and climbed into McFadden's BMW.

In the backseat of the limousine was a representative of the Central Intelligence Agency. Reed, who knew every spy west of Zagreb, made the necessary introductions.

"I've been asked to conduct a preliminary debriefing," said the Agency man as the BMW picked up speed. "Is there anything you learned during your captivity that requires a quick response on our part?"

They were in open country now, and Dozier looked out the window at the green fields of northern Italy on either side of the road. I've missed greenness, he thought, feeling a certain reluctance to return so soon to active duty. I'll never take a green field for granted again. Then the general in him bounced back.

"They know where we are storing most of our nuclear weapons," he dictated as the CIA man scribbled notes. "We need to take immediate action to increase security at all field depots. . . ."

20

12:45 P.M., 28 JANUARY 1982
ILARDI STATE POLICE BARRACKS
VIA ACQUAPENDENTE, PADUA

"By tonight, you'll be pissing blood!" a man with a Calabrian accent told him. Savasta was sitting in the backseat of the police cruiser and there was a cop on either side of him. The hitting had begun again the moment they pulled away from the Via Pindemonte. It would have been easier to endure without the blindfold because he could have anticipated each blow, but the punches came without warning, hard and repetitive. They were not even asking him questions; this was pure punishment, a softening up for what was to come later.

I can take this, he told himself fiercely, although he began to realize that unless there were a revolution, he was going to spend the rest of his life in jail. Marx had written that capitalism would eventually crumble. But would it happen soon enough to do him any good?

"*Bastardo!*" swore the Calabrian, punching him in the testicles.

"*Cristo!*" Savasta doubled over in agony. "Don't—"

"Don't what? Are you going to start begging so soon?"

"*Va fa'n cullo!*" Using the classic Roman obscenity, Savasta was suggesting that his tormentor perform a biologically impossible act when the vehicle came to a halt.

"Okay, out you go!"

"Where are we?" They had not driven far enough to have arrived at the Questura in the Piazza Ruzante, but he followed as they pulled him out of the backseat. The pain in his genitals made it difficult to stand.

"Your tomb, Savasta. You'll never get out of here alive!"

He felt the coldness of a January day change to artificial heat as they entered a building. They walked along a corridor with a marble floor and then down two flights of stairs into a basement where the air was stale and old. He heard a metallic creak and the whine of rusted hinges as a door swung back. What kind of dungeon was this?

"In here!" They pushed him forward and made him sit on a hard stool. Angry hands replaced the torn sheet with a pair of handcuffs. When they substituted his blindfold with a canvas hood, he caught a glimpse of a small room with cement walls. The space was barely wide enough to hold them all.

"You are Antonio Savasta?" came a calm, authoritative voice, speaking with a cool Milanese accent. He hoped that this was a magistrate. The brutality would have to stop once he entered the judicial system because the police could not produce him in court with bruises. It struck him as ironic that he should have spent a decade trying to overthrow this legal system and was now reduced to hoping it would function the way it was supposed to.

"I am a member of the Red Brigades," he responded with the prescribed formula. "I am a political prisoner. I do not intend to respond to your questions."

"Who is the taller of the two women who were captured with you?"

"She is a serving member of the Brigate rosse and I don't know her real name."

"What is her battle name?"

"I will not answer that question."

"She was your girlfriend, wasn't she?"

"My woman is not in your custody and never will be," he shrugged.

"Where would we find Barbara Balzarani?"

"I don't know," he said, thinking that he needed to be silent for at least twenty-four hours. The blitz on the Via Pindemonte had been big and noisy and there would be news of the general's safe release on the evening news. The Esecutivo would move its headquarters to a new location unknown to him, and by this time tomorrow the Via Verga address would be worthless.

"Then you refuse to tell us anything?"

"I refuse."

"Kill him," the man from Milan ordered. There was the sound of shoes moving across the marble floor and the ritual squeak of the door's opening and then closing.

That's ridiculous, thought Savasta, feeling terror rising within him.

"You're an expert in these things," the policeman with the Calabrian accent told him and Savasta felt a cold, metallic, tubular object brushing across his cheek. "Recognize that? It's the silencer on a revolver and we've got carte blanche to do what we want with you."

"Go to hell!" Savasta said. As he spoke the Calabrian slipped the barrel of the revolver into his mouth.

"It's you who's going to hell!" the policeman said, pushing the barrel into Savasta's throat. "Good-bye, asshole!"

Savasta tried desperately to establish his self-control, telling himself that this was merely an interrogation technique, a crude threat. There was a distinct steel click, the sound of a hammer being drawn back as the revolver was cocked. Christ, no, don't!

The hammer fell and he could feel the weapon vibrate against the back of his throat.

But no bullet came.

"A malfunction," chuckled the Calabrian as he removed the pistol barrel from Savasta's mouth. In the background, he could hear another man laughing. "Let's have a cigarette and try again later."

Savasta found himself drenched with sweat and gasping for breath. There was a urine smell in the room and he realized with shame that he had wet himself. Then he heard matches striking sandpaper and sniffed tobacco smoke.

Out of long-disciplined habit, he tried to create a stratagem for himself, but the hopelessness of the situation had begun to overwhelm him. There was nothing to do. There were no decisions to make or tactics to invent. He was not in charge of anything anymore. His sole remaining task was to keep his mouth shut.

"Ahhhhhhhh!" he yelped with unexpected pain as the man standing behind him seared the back of his hand with the lighted end of the cigarette. He would have fallen off the chair had they not held him. "Let me out of here!"

"Why? This is a good place," the policeman told him. "You can scream all you want here. No one will ever hear you."

They burned the back of his hand again. Then the hitting began in earnest, and he screamed and screamed and screamed.

21

1:05 P.M., 28 JANUARY 1982
FRANKFURT, GERMANY

The ladies were chatting around the coffee table. An announcement had been made that luncheon would be served as soon as a tardy guest arrived. The hostess was Myra Withers, a chum and sorority sister from Judy's college days. Marty Ulmer was there, and Sherry Brown, and some other friends.

Everyone had been supportive in the weeks since her arrival in Germany as the house guest of Major General and Mrs. Ulmer. And the awful weather had broken. After weeks of cold days and gray, discouraging skies, today was warm and sunny.

If I were superstitious, Judy reflected, I would read some

meaning into the good weather. Maybe the winter is going to give us a break. Maybe we could just skip February and go straight into spring. Maybe Jim could come home today. . . .

A telephone rang in the den and Judy felt her body go tense. Every ringing phone for forty-two days had been a torture for her; at any moment the call could come saying that one of the announcements of General Dozier's execution had turned out to be true.

With a discreet smile, Myra Withers slipped out of the living room and disappeared into the den. The ringing stopped and a moment later, Myra called for Marty Ulmer to take the call. Marty smiled and disappeared, leaving a certain nervousness behind her. General Ulmer could be calling with some news from the Red Brigades. There had been five communiqués already; this could be the sixth.

Perhaps, perhaps, perhaps . . . Judy excused herself and walked into the back room. Maybe I can help with lunch, she thought. Maybe I can find out what's going on.

"Judy, it's Walt!" Marty Ulmer called out, holding the telephone out to her. "It's for you!"

A coldness came into Judy's body. Why would General Ulmer be calling her here? She was a guest in his home and any routine business could have waited until dinner. She put the phone to her ear, closing her eyes with dread.

"Judy? Are you standing up or sitting down?"

"Which should I be?"

"It doesn't matter!" Ulmer's voice rose in excitement. "The Italian police just rescued Jim. He's in good shape and they're taking him to Vicenza!"

"Oh, thank God!" she murmured. "Oh Walt. . . ."

"If you can get back to my house, we can get a line through to SETAF," Ulmer told her. "I'll meet you there."

The other luncheon guests crowded into the den.

"Jim's alive," Judy said. "We've got to go back to the Ulmers' and call him on the telephone. . . ."

There was a blur of activity as Judy was bundled into her coat and then out the door to a car. At the Ulmer residence, the general's aide was frantically trying to get a line opened to Italy. A moment later, Walt Ulmer himself appeared and shouted at telephone operators until he cleared a circuit.

It took a while. Judy sat numbly by his side, watching Walt's aide lay out cold cuts and cheese for an impromptu luncheon that everyone was too excited to eat. Suddenly, the uproar went silent. Walt handed her the phone.

"Jim?" she said, jumping to her feet with excitement.

"Hi, Hon, it's me! Let me tell you what happened." It was Jim. Judy sat down again quickly, her mind whirling with joy.

"Can you clear the line, please?" an operator interrupted.

"No!" exclaimed Dozier. "Listen, I . . ."

"There is a call from the White House for General James L. Dozier," said the operator. "It's President Reagan."

"Honey, you'd better talk to the president." Judy laughed, remembering when Mr. Reagan had been told that she was too busy to come to the phone. "I'll be down there just as fast as I can!"

"I love you!" Jim shouted, and the line went dead.

For a long time, Judy sat where she was, looking at the silent telephone. He's alive, she thought. He is still alive! Slowly, she became conscious of the outside world. Walt Ulmer was standing over her.

"I wonder how I'm going to keep all the promises I made to God," he said thoughtfully.

"Oh, Walt, he's alive!" Judy felt the tears welling up in her eyes.

"Come on, Judy," General Ulmer told her. "Let's take you home."

22

5:45 A.M., 29 JANUARY 1982
ILARDI STATE POLICE BARRACKS
VIA ACQUAPENDENTE, PADUA

No one is talking, Emilia told herself, as she sat on her chair, her arms pinned behind her and a canvas hood over her head. The police are getting desperate. Who gives in first? They're running out of time. We're running out of strength.

"They're coming for you soon, my beauty," someone said, but she tried to ignore the voice, to think of everything outside her canvas hood as unreal, irrelevant.

Earlier, a group of men had come into her cell, led by a man with a Calabrian accent. They had addressed her as Emilia Libera and told her that the others all had confessed and that things would go easier for her if she joined the group. This was a standard police stratagem; she decided that she would keep silent no matter what they did to her. Then they had beaten her; one man held her by the shoulders while a second stood between her knees and hit her in the abdomen, pausing occasionally to slap her across the side of her head. He particularly seemed to like hitting her breasts.

After a long time, they had left her with the promise that she would be visited by the *giustiziere della notte,* the night-avenger.

How long have we been here? It was hard to keep track of the passing hours. It might still be the middle of the night. It might already be well into the next day.

The police now seemed to be making their second sweep through the cells. She had heard Cesare Di Lenardo cursing horribly before the pain had moved to Giovanni Ciucci. Emilia had been relieved to hear Giovanni's voice, because he had been hurt during the raid and his presence here meant that the injury was not serious. Steadfastly, Giovanni had refused to tell the police anything; when they hit him, he grunted with the pain but never cried out.

Ciucci and Di Lenardo were both silent now, and Emanuela Frascella was howling, the shrieks of a privileged young woman who had never before been exposed to brutality. But she was saying nothing. Emilia would have thought that the millionaire's daughter would be talking by now. Even though Emanuela knew nothing of importance, she was guarding her treasure of little secrets with dogged desperation.

Emilia shivered, guessing that they would concentrate on her. By now, they must have understood that Frascella was merely a housekeeper for the Red Brigades. Ciucci and Di Lenardo were only foot soldiers and Antonio would never crack. This left her. . . .

"Where's Libera?" In the corridor, there was a man with an educated Milanese accent.

"In there!" responded the Calabrian.

"No!" Despite her vow of silence, a hoarse shout escaped from her lips as footsteps came in her direction. Emanuela had stopped screaming and had relapsed into a steady sobbing.

"On your knees before the night-avenger!" No one touched her. She shuffled off the chair and dropped to her knees on the cement floor.

"What is your name?" asked the Milanese.

She remained silent.

"Signorina, you must understand the situation," the voice explained. "We have Savasta and we want the other members of the Executive Committee. If you can tell us where we can find Barbara Balzarani, Giuseppe Lo Bianco, and Luigi Novelli, you will save yourself a lot of unpleasantness."

Emilia's knees were hurting. She did not know where Balzarani and Lo Bianco lived. The headquarters was someplace in Milan, but Antonio had always followed the rules about compartmentalization and he had never told her the address. Novelli would be in Rome somewhere, changing houses every night to avoid a trap.

"I'm waiting for your answer!"

Emilia remained silent, wondering how much more she could stand.

"Pull her pants down!" snapped the Milanese.

She shrieked as men seized her arms on either side, lifting her to her feet. She was still wearing the jogging suit in which she had been arrested. From behind, someone took hold of the bottoms and stripped her to the ankles.

"Don't do this, please," she begged as they stretched her out on the cement floor. "We never hurt the general! We never humiliated him like this!"

"We need to know where we can find Barbara Balzarani," the policeman repeated, kneeling between her legs. As he spoke, he ran his fingers through her pubic hair.

"Lo Bianco! Where is Giuseppe Lo Bianco?" The Milanese pulled out a few strands of pubic hair. She shouted with the pain.

"We can keep you here forever," he told her, pulling out more hair. "Nobody knows that you're here. We have a lot of time."

"Leave me alone! This is awful! We never tortured people!"

"Don't you understand?" he shouted, losing his temper and hitting her hard in the stomach. "We're accountable to no one!"

"No, no, please, stop him!" she appealed to the others. They can't do this to me, she thought as he pounded her again. Isn't there a law that says they can't torture us?

"Give me that stool!" screamed the man called the night-avenger. He now seemed demented with fury. "I'll shove it up you so far—"

"What—no, don't—control yourself!"

"Lo Bianco! I want Lo Bianco!" the policeman howled. Emilia felt the leg of the stool scraping up the inside of her thighs.

Suddenly, she sensed something in her surrendering and she let her body go slack.

"I'll tell you everything," she said quickly. "Get him away from me, and I'll tell you everything I know."

"I want Balzarani and Lo Bianco first," the night-avenger said, panting with exertion. "We can have the others later."

"Balzarani and Lo Bianco are living in an apartment in Milan."

"The address?"

"Only the members of the Esecutivo knew the address," she explained. "Antonio knows. . . ." She bit her lip, but the treason had escaped.

"Then you will have to ask him to tell us."

"I can ask him. . . ." She began to cry as she spoke. I will never be clean again, she thought, as they lifted her roughly to her feet and pulled up the trousers of her jogging suit. I am polluted.

23

6:30 A.M., 29 JANUARY 1982
ILARDI STATE POLICE BARRACKS
VIA ACQUAPENDENTE, PADUA

Someone called from the corridor. They stopped hitting him and walked out of the room.

Antonio Savasta swayed on the hard chair, half-conscious. Several times he had fallen off the chair, sometimes because he could not stop himself and twice because he thought he could rest a while on the floor. Then they had begun to kick him in the ribs whenever he lost his balance, and so he concentrated now on maintaining his position.

He was worried that they might have damaged his testicles, because there was a pain between his legs that did not seem to get any better, even when they were not hitting him there. His head ached and it was difficult to think. Vaguely, he remembered reading somewhere that there came a point in every torture session when you stopped caring, a plateau on which the pain moved away from you, assuming distance and irrelevance.

I don't want to be hurt anymore, he thought. I feel fragile, as if I could shatter like glass. He tried to take a deep breath to restore himself, but his battered rib cage hurt too much and the air in the room stank of urine and vomit and sweat, and so he took shallow breaths instead.

There were footsteps in the corridor and the low murmur of men talking. The door creaked open, and he waited for the sound of shoes scuffling against the cement floor. But there was nothing except the faint padding noise of bare feet.

"Antonio? Are you all right?"

Emilia! He was perplexed. Why would they interrupt a torture session to allow this bizarre visit?

"What are you doing here?"

"Antonio, they want to know where the Esecutivo meets."

"*Putana!*" he shrieked at her, realizing that she had begun to collaborate. "You whore! Get out! Get out!"

"Please!"

"Get out!" he shouted again. "Take her away!"

There was a murmured conversation in the corridor and, to his surprise, Emilia was removed. He could hear her crying in the hallway.

My love, he thought bitterly, wondering whether the Organizzazione would want to punish her, or whether they would pardon her for his sake. How much longer could he hold out? He realized that he was himself reaching the breaking point, that the moment was coming when he began to name names and list addresses. Once it started, it would be difficult to stop.

Unless he somehow managed to die. He was in a small room with cement walls. He might put his head down and fling himself as hard as he could against the wall. Would it be possible to commit suicide that way, dashing his brains out against the cement? Or would he weaken at the last instant, slackening, hanging back from death?

And if he died, would anything be achieved by his sacrifice? Emilia knew almost as much about the Organizzazione as he did and she had already begun to collaborate. With the information in her head alone, the police could cripple the Red Brigades and devastate the Rome column.

There was only one strategically important secret that he alone possessed: the address of the Executive Committee apartment in Milan. If the Esecutivo survived with its files intact, Barbara, Lo Bianco, and Novelli could rebuild. . . .

There were footsteps in the corridor, and he listened while the interrogation team reestablished its presence in his cell.

"Who's got a cigarette?" asked the man with the Calabrian accent and Savasta understood immediately that they were going to burn him again. With sudden clarity, he realized that he could take no more. It was time to start trading information for time, enough time for everyone to escape from the Via Verga.

It must be close to dawn. Balzarani and Lo Bianco should have heard about the raid on the Via Pindemonte and already fled. But there was a chance that the police had managed to censor the news; he had to give his colleagues a few more hours, at least until they had seen the morning papers.

"Bring me someone I can negotiate with," Savasta said.

"You can negotiate with me," responded the Calabrian.

"I want to talk to the organ grinder, not his monkey."

"Watch yourself, young man!"

"You only count as long as I keep silent," Savasta told him. "The moment I start to talk, I become important again and you go back to being insignificant. Now get me somebody in authority!"

He thought that they would hit him, but instead the men in the room walked away as if their task were finished. I'll talk to whoever comes to see me, he told himself. I need to kill a little time.

A long time passed before he heard footsteps in the corridor and felt the movement of air that signified that someone had entered his cell.

"I am Commissioner Salvatore Genova," a deep voice spoke. "You wanted to see me?"

"Yes . . . I thought it was time that we talked a little." So this is the famous Commissario Genova, he thought. We should have put more effort into killing him.

"Let's get you out of here," Genova said. One phase is coming to an end, Savasta thought, as men came forward to assist him to his feet. He could barely stand, and there was pain in his groin and chest, but they held his arms, helping him up two flights of stairs. They walked along a corridor with a wooden floor until they reached a room where the air smelled fresh. His handcuffs were removed and he was settled into a comfortable chair. When they took off the canvas hood, he was at first blinded by the light; he smelled the cappuccino before his eyes could focus upon it.

"Thought you might need some caffeine," the commissioner said. Genova appeared to be in his middle thirties. He was a big man with broad shoulders and his suit was handmade. He was clean-shaven and wore aviator glasses. His eyes were careful. His face gave very little away.

"I've been tortured," Savasta said, deciding to go over to the attack. "We never harmed a hair on the general's head! Your people used torture!"

"I'm sorry if someone treated you roughly," Commissioner Genova said with sincerity but without any sign of surprise. "Rough interrogation is not my style; if you decide to collaborate with me I will have you guarded by my own men and you won't be bothered again."

"Since when do the Italian police torture people?" Savasta persisted.

"Look, the war between us is almost over," Genova told him with sudden intensity. "Knowing that we were close to victory, that your people were about to be defeated, some of the local police may have become overenthusiastic. All this unhappiness can come to an end as soon as we negotiate a truce!"

"A truce? The war is not over! Marx wrote—"

"Marx wrote that capitalism would fall apart of its own internal contradictions and communism would emerge spontaneously," Genova interrupted. "Have you looked out a window recently? For better or worse, capitalism is not falling apart. It's evolving in strange and complicated ways, developing a flexibility and subtlety Marx never dreamed of. And Italy is getting more prosperous by the day. There may be a revolution someday, but it won't be soon; you chose the wrong moment in time to hustle history!"

Savasta sipped his coffee, astonished at the notion of a cop who read Marx. In the back of his mind, there was a voice saying that the commissioner was right, that their beautiful revolution was never going to happen.

"Look, this Winter of Fire nonsense has been a disaster," Genova told him. "At the end of every war, there comes a moment when the two opposing generals have to sit down and negotiate the terms of surrender, because anybody who gets killed now, one of your people or one of mine, is dying unnecessarily."

Savasta fell silent, stalling, trying to make up his mind. The faint light in the corridor told him that the sun was coming up. About eighteen hours must have passed since the raid. The Esecutivo would soon be taking evasive action and—he found himself thinking about Giovanna Esposito, the beautiful *vivandiere* who had always admired him. Would Giovanna understand that he could only hold out for so long to guard her safety?

"I can't take the responsibility for this alone." Savasta played for a little more time. "If we can convene a meeting of my group, I will ask the others to join me in making a unified decision."

"Are we playing games?" Genova gazed at him thoughtfully.

"No, but I need a meeting with my people," said Savasta.

"You got it," said the commissioner. "Meetings are always a good idea."

24

10:15 A.M., 29 JANUARY 1982
ILARDI STATE POLICE BARRACKS
VIA ACQUAPENDENTE, PADUA

The Ilardi State Police Barracks on the Via Acquapendente was a regional administrative headquarters for the Polizia di Stato as well as a residence for unmarried enlisted personnel. This lounge was the most cheerful environment Genova could locate within the general bleakness of the building. He wanted his prisoners to be relaxed while they reached their collective decision, but they needed to understand that the kind of creature comforts he had provided this morning, coffee and sandwiches, were privileges to be granted or withdrawn. The quality of their future life-style in custody depended on their willingness to cooperate.

The two women were led into the lounge first. Emilia Libera was still wearing the jogging suit in which she had been arrested, and Emanuela Frascella still had on her jeans and baggy sweater. The moment their handcuffs were removed, the two women collapsed into one another's arms, hugging and whispering to one another. Giovanni Ciucci appeared a moment later, a bandage on the back of his head and great livid bruises on his face. He looked puzzled and a little lost; the two women included him in the hug.

"Antonio should be here in a moment," Genova said.

"And Cesare?" Emanuela asked.

"He has declined our invitation," Genova explained. The dour Di Lenardo had guessed that they were going to be offered terms of surrender; he had refused to attend, and Genova had not insisted.

Savasta appeared at the door, his arms handcuffed in front of him. He looked tired and a little pale but fundamentally in control of himself.

There was a subtle tension in the air, but as soon as the guard had removed Savasta's handcuffs, he walked over to Emilia. "It's okay," he said, and took her in his arms. She placed her head on his shoulder, her arms hanging loosely by her sides. For a moment, no one moved or said anything.

Then Emanuela Frascella and Giovanni Ciucci joined the group for another round of hugs. Commissioner Genova watched from his corner, reminding himself that his guests were revolutionary terrorists who had been contemplating the murder of an American general. Yet they all seemed—in some strange and intense fashion—to love each other, the way soldiers do after a long campaign.

They separated and took seats around the table. Libera was dry-eyed and self-possessed but seemed distracted, as if she were not much concerned with what was said here. Savasta was beginning to radiate a certain bruised self-confidence, as if he were happy to be back in charge of his group, even if only temporarily. Ciucci and Frascella both looked shattered, perplexed, waiting for Savasta to tell them what to do. They will talk if he gives them permission, Genova speculated. And they will keep silent if that is his order.

"I want to leave you alone to talk and make your decisions," the commissioner said. "But I did want to explain your options. Parliament is passing a Penitence Law that allows judges to reduce sentences by as much as two-thirds to reward people who cooperate. We can offer you protection from your former colleagues as well as participation in our Witness Protection Program when you are released from prison. This means that the day could come when you can walk away from this and forget that it ever happened."

There was an exchange of glances around the table.

"All right? Then I will leave you to your deliberations." Commissioner Genova left the room, knowing that he would lose control of the case if his approach did not work. There were angry men in the Polizia di Stato who would prefer to beat the terrorists into submission. Savasta had killed a policeman; officers remembered that kind of thing.

He closed the door to give Savasta's group the illusion of privacy; naturally, the room had been wired to record their conversation. His own men were clustered in the corridor.

"I think we'll be going to Milan tonight," he told them.

"What for?"

"To arrest the Executive Committee!"

"How are we going to find them?"

"Savasta's going to tell us where they live," he promised. "Get ready to roll!"

25

2:15 P.M., 29 JANUARY 1982
HEADQUARTERS, SOUTHERN EUROPEAN TASK FORCE
CAMP EDERLE, VICENZA

"During the last six weeks I was on the receiving end of many prayers," General Dozier was saying as he moved the press conference toward a conclusion. He was embarrassed to be talking publicly about something as private as prayer but unwilling to leave out a thought that was important to him. Besides, they were holding this press conference in the SETAF chapel, and the environment made a difference.

He glanced over at Judy and Cheryl, who had flown down from Germany on the first available plane. They sent him quick smiles of encouragement, and he plunged back into his prepared text.

"When people are praying for you, you can feel it, and I want to express my thanks to the people at the praying end," he said. "The events of the past several weeks have reinforced in my mind that the enemies of freedom are many in this world of ours and that free men must constantly be prepared to contend with them."

There was a patter of applause as Dozier concluded his remarks, but he held his position on the speaker's platform, glancing over at his wife. An aide slipped a small box into his hand.

"By the way, Judy," he remarked casually, removing a slender jewelry box and opening it up for her. "I was unavoidably detained over Christmas, and I never did get to give this to you."

She stepped forward, a surprised smile on her face, to allow him to place the pendant around her neck. She hugged him and they kissed for the benefit of the photographers. Then he put his arm around her waist and led her out of the chapel to where a NATO staff car was waiting. It took a while. A lot of people were lining up to shake hands and say good-bye.

"By the way, what did the president say?" As their car pulled away, Judy suddenly remembered how yesterday's telephone conversation had been interrupted by Jim's commander-in-chief.

"Oh, breakfast!" Dozier slapped his forehead. "Forgot to tell you. He's invited us to have breakfast with him at the White House."

"I can see how that might have slipped your mind." Judy wondered what she should wear to breakfast with Ronald Reagan. "Whatever happened to those gray trousers you were wearing the night they kidnapped you?"

"I never got them back. I wonder. . . ."

"Hon, they wouldn't have been right for the White House," she told him, and they settled back for the ride home.

26

3:00 P.M., 29 JANUARY 1982
ILARDI STATE POLICE BARRACKS
VIA ACQUAPENDENTE, PADUA

"I think it's for the best," Genova told Savasta. "It must be emotionally difficult, but you should try and see your confession as a kind of self-liberation. Every secret you tell me is one less burden to carry around on your shoulders. Emilia seems relieved by the decision, don't you think?"

"Yes. I wonder if I'll ever feel the same way," Savasta said. For at least a year, he had been preparing himself for one of two destinies. He would either be killed in some apocalyptic shootout with the police or captured and sent to prison for life. Now he was trying to convince himself to accept the offer of a third destiny, that he help dismantle the Red Brigades, go to prison for a while, perhaps a long while, but emerge someday to create a new life for himself.

"We need to talk about some specifics," the commissioner said, glancing at his watch. "Where is the Executive Committee?"

This is going to be hard, Savasta thought, going over the arguments again in his mind. Emilia had already begun to confess, and her information would cripple the Organizzazione. There would be no point in spending the rest of his life in a maximum-security penitentiary to protect the few secrets that he knew and she did not! And if the Red Brigades were finished, it made sense to sweep the debris from the scene so that the proletariat could begin to make new plans for its future.

"There must have been a headquarters for your Executive Committee, somewhere you met and kept your records," Genova prompted him. "Am I right in supposing that Barbara Balzarani was a member of the Esecutivo?"

I don't want to sell out Barbara, he thought, suddenly remembering the halcyon days back in Rome when they had all worked together, he and Emilia, Barbara and Mario Moretti, Luigi and Martina Novelli, sure they could change Italy's future the way the Sandinistas had changed Nicaragua's. It was a hard dream to let go of.

"You must have realized that it would come to this," Genova pushed. "I will do my best to ensure that she is not hurt when we capture her, but it has to happen."

"She and Francesco Lo Bianco are living in an apartment in southwest Milan," said Savasta, telling himself that Barbara and Francesco and Giovanna would be long gone by now. Over twenty-eight hours had passed since the blitz. He had given them a running start. Giovanna Esposito must by now be over the border into Switzerland. They could not expect more. . . .

"Where exactly? And it has to be the right address the first time, Antonio," Genova warned him.

"It's the Via Andrea Verga. Number 22. On the second floor. Listen, I don't think you can take Francesco alive."

"It doesn't matter anymore," said Genova. The policeman exhaled and Savasta realized that he was also exhausted, nearing the end of his own tether. It had been a long war. Genova wrote "22 Via Andrea Verga" on a scrap of paper and left the office. For a long time, Savasta stared into his empty coffee cup.

Judas, he said to himself. Judas!

27

10:55 P.M., 29 JANUARY 1982
VIA VERGA, MILAN
REGION OF LOMBARDY

The story of Dozier's rescue had appeared in all the papers. The DIGOS had tried to keep crucial names out of print, but the Padua Questura leaked like a sieve and the identities of Savasta and Libera were now in the public domain.

As soon as Savasta had disclosed the address of the Via Andrea Verga safe house, the Milan DIGOS had mounted a discreet surveillance over number 22, establishing an observation post in an apartment across the street. As far as they could tell, the flat was still being used, because lights had gone on at sunset. No one had entered or left the residence since surveillance had begun at three-thirty that afternoon.

"We could be lucky," muttered one of Genova's men, crowded

into the backseat of the Alfa Romeo. They turned into the Via Verga. Behind them were two cars full of NOCS, the same commandos who had rescued the *generale americano* the previous day.

Genova nodded. With a minimal amount of good fortune, they would be able to make several dozen arrests over the next few weeks. If they could nail one or two members of the Esecutivo. . . . They were halfway down the length of the Via Verga when the radio sputtered an urgent communication from the Milanese Questura.

"Commissario!" came a distressed voice. "About five minutes ago on the evening news, a journalist said that Savasta was singing! Your target may have been alerted."

"Merda!" grunted someone in the backseat. Blondie hit the accelerator and the powerful Alfa roared down the Via Verga to number 22. Genova and his men hit the street fast and dashed to the top of the stairs.

He knocked hard and when there was no response, two of the NOCS hit the door with their shoulders. The door frame collapsed under the impact of their combined weight and the NOCS spread out with expert speed, swarming through the small apartment.

It was empty. In the living room, a color television was alive. On the dining room table were an open bottle of red Calabrian wine and several bowls of spaghetti *al ragù*.

The spaghetti was still warm.

In the back bedroom, there was an open window from which one could jump onto the top of a garage and thence into a maze of back alleys. A classic Lo Bianco escape, thought Genova bleakly. Anybody else would have finished his spaghetti.

"We'll get him, *capo!*" one of his men said. "He's running out of places to hide!"

Genova nodded, now tired and eager to be alone. The Executive Committee safe house was filled with ammunition and weapons, documentation and Red Brigades records, weeks of work for everybody.

But the people were gone. Clearly, they had fled after the late news. Had Savasta foreseen this, engineering this last piece of rebellion before his inevitable submission, his final service to the Red Brigades? Genova shrugged; he would never know for sure.

Genova wandered to the window and gazed into the shadows,

remembering something Savasta had said to him a few hours earlier. Antonio still believed that social injustice made revolution inevitable. Revolt and insurrection were the inevitable fruits of an economic system dedicated to keeping a few people rich while others remained desperately poor. As long as there were ghettos and slums, Savasta had predicted, there would always be revolutionaries.

"You remind me of Don Quixote," he had said. "Can't you see? I am only a windmill! The dragon is still out there!"

Genova stared out the open window, watching clouds drifting in over the city. Windmills and dragons, he was thinking. In the dark, they can be hard to tell apart.

EPILOGUE

On 28 January, as General Dozier was being rescued from the Red Brigades, President Ronald Reagan was hosting a lunch in celebration of the centennial of the birth of Franklin Delano Roosevelt. During the luncheon, Mr. Reagan was called out of the White House banquet room by an aide. When he returned to the table, he asked for the attention of the group and delivered the following remarks.

Earlier this morning, the Italian police rescued Brigadier General James Dozier. They rescued him from the terrorist hideaway in Padua where he had been held captive. His 42-day long ordeal has come to a happy ending, and the prayers of millions of Americans have been answered. I've spoken with the General by telephone and I'm happy to report that he's in fine shape. And I can tell you that just hearing him—I told Nancy he sounded as if he'd just gone down to the corner for a few minutes. [Laughter]

The same courage and resolve that James Dozier demonstrated on the battlefield in wartime have seen him through this new test with flying colors. His country and our allies can be very proud of this gallant man.

I've also talked with President Pertini of Italy, and expressed America's appreciation for the dedicated and effective work of the Italian authorities in tracking down General Dozier's kidnappers and saving his life. They too have acquitted themselves with honor.

His rescue is welcome news for all those who believe in the rule of law and the defense of our free institutions. We all share in the joy of his family at the return to freedom of a courageous soldier whose life has been dedicated to the defense of liberty.

And now, back to the regularly scheduled program. [Laughter]

The Doziers were President Reagan's guests at a prayer breakfast on 4 February. At the conclusion of the meal, President Reagan again spoke warmly of their courage.

General Dozier, I know you don't like being praised for what you only consider was doing your duty. Forgive me. I'm going to pull rank on you. [Laughter] We want to give thanks to God for answering our prayers. We want to salute the Italian authorities for their brilliant rescue, and Jim, we just want to thank you and Judith for your gallantry. Welcome home, soldier. Someone once said that a hero is no braver than any other man. He's just brave 5 minutes longer. Well, General, you were brave 42 days longer!

General and Mrs. Dozier returned briefly to their apartment on the Via Lungadige Catena and to NATO's LANDSOUTH Command in Verona. Intense publicity and a possible continuing threat to their security, however, made it unreasonable for them to remain in Verona, and the general was reassigned to Fort Knox in summer 1982. After a series of top-level assignments in Kentucky and Texas and subsequent promotion to the rank of major general, General Dozier retired from the army in 1985, returning with Judy to live in their beloved Florida.

The two American army officers who worried most and worked hardest during the Dozier kidnapping were Major General George McFadden and Colonel Bill Reed. General McFadden, the former commanding general of SETAF, has now retired from active duty and is living in Arlington, Virginia. Colonel William Reed has also retired from the army, moving on to become assistant vice president for administration and institutional advancement at Edinboro State College in Pennsylvania.

After contributing much to his country's victory over the Red Brigades, Carabiniere Major General Carlo Alberto Dalla

Chiesa was sent to Sicily to do battle with the Mafia. On 5 September 1982, the general and his young wife were ambushed and murdered by Mafia gunmen in a Palermo back street. His death constituted a tragic loss for the Italian Republic.

Coming slowly but sincerely to believe that the interests of the working class could not be advanced until the specter of terrorism had passed, Antonio Savasta put his encyclopedic memory at the service of the State Police DIGOS in the months following his arrest. As a result, Commissioner Salvatore Genova and his colleagues were able to arrest hundreds of Red Brigades operatives and break the back of Europe's largest terrorist organization. Italians were amazed to discover how many of the arrested *brigatisti* turned out to be normal, apparently apolitical people who had been neighbors, friends, schoolteachers, telephone operators, factory workers, and motor mechanics.

All of the *brigatisti* involved in the Dozier kidnapping were eventually taken into custody, directly or indirectly as a result of Savasta's testimony. Francesco Lo Bianco was captured on 21 April 1982, and Marcello Capuano followed him into prison a month later, after being badly wounded in a shoot-out with police. Luigi and Martina Novelli were seized in December of the same year while riding on a bus in downtown Rome. Running out of tricks, the elusive Pietro Vanzi stumbled into a police blockade in July 1983 and surrendered. Barbara Balzarani remained beyond the reach of the law, living tranquilly in the Rome suburb of Ostia until she was spotted in 1985 by a sharp-eyed Carabiniere and arrested.

Even the four women who escaped from the Rovigo prison were all eventually recaptured, together with their liberator, Sergio Segio. Sergio was eventually allowed to marry his beloved Susanna Ronconi, but the ceremony took place in prison.

The pivotal importance of the Dozier case has been confirmed by the rapid decline in the quality and quantity of terrorism in Italy since 1982. Although decimated by Antonio Savasta's revelations and stricken by internal feuds, the Red Brigades have not quite passed out of existence, but their operational capacity has been reduced to occasional assassinations at the rate of about one a year. Still in prison and likely to remain there for decades to come, Cesare Di Lenardo is one of the few prominent *brigatisti* who continue to advocate the use of political violence and terrorism. Nearly all other senior members of the Organizzazione have now publicly joined Savasta in calling for an end to armed violence.

"A government reduced to running electrical current into the testicles of its enemies is already strategically dead and buried," Cesare Di Lenardo shouted at the Dozier kidnap trial.

The public initially reacted to these charges with skepticism, believing that Di Lenardo was simply waging a propaganda war against the Italian police. Unexpectedly, the police medical consultant who had examined Di Lenardo produced photographs of some fifty electric burns on the young man's body, establishing that someone had systematically maltreated him.

A magistrate was persuaded to issue arrest warrants for those he deemed responsible. In summer 1982 while continuing with his intensive investigative work, a stunned Commissioner Salvatore Genova found himself indicted on torture charges together with four of the NOCS who had conducted the raid on the Via Pindemonte.

Insiders within the State Police establishment were incensed by what seemed to be a politically motivated attack on a brilliant police officer. Although there was reason to believe that someone had indeed mistreated Di Lenardo, no real evidence suggesting that Commissioner Genova was connected with the incident was ever presented.

Nineteen eighty-two was an election year in Italy. An angry public rendered its own judgment on the charges against Salvatore Genova by electing him to serve as a deputy to the Italian Parliament. Because of a provision in Italian law making parliamentarians immune from prosecution, this election removed Genova from the danger of facing criminal charges.

The four NOCS, however, were committed for trial. Antonio Savasta and his colleagues had nothing to gain by irritating the police at this stage in their own legal difficulties, but they appeared at the NOCS trial, testifying that they had been mistreated by unknown police officers. Again, there was no suggestion that Genova was involved, but the four NOCS were found guilty and sentenced to terms of imprisonment. Upon appeal, they were found innocent because of procedural problems in the earlier trial and released.

Becoming both a politician and a married man at the same time, Salvatore Genova took his new bride, Signora Rina Genova, to Rome in 1982, to begin his service as a deputy of the Italian Parliament. As a lawmaker, he became a nationally recognized spokesman for repentant terrorists serving prison sentences or enjoying "provisional liberty" under the Witness Protection Program. By the end of his term of office, he decided that a politician's life was less interesting than a detective's, and he declined to run for a second term. Since returning to his beloved city of Genoa and to active duty with the Polizia di Stato, he is now applying his investigative talents to the problem of organized crime.

The mercurial figure of the Marine Corps colonel Oliver North appears for the first time on the margin of the Dozier saga.

When General Dalla Chiesa suggested that money be secured in an effort to bribe Michele Galati, his request was passed to a State Department "Dozier Working Group" that met weekly in Washington throughout the kidnap crisis. Noel Koch represented the Pentagon, and Admiral John Poindexter advanced the views of the National Security Council, sending Oliver North, then only a major, as his substitute whenever he was unable to attend himself.

Because the use of government funds for this purpose was felt to be inappropriate, North volunteered to look into ways of raising the money privately. At North's request, H. Ross Perot sent the money to the American embassy in Rome. When Galati rejected Dalla Chiesa's offer, the Italians became concerned that the desperate Americans might try to give the money directly to the Red Brigades. Perot himself clearly believed that buying back the general was an option to be explored and referred to a "ransom attempt" several times in letters and published statements.

As far as the Savasta group was concerned, there never was any realistic chance of a ransom. Savasta disapproved vehemently of accepting money, and no channel of communications between the Veneto column and the American government had ever been established. Sources within the CIA have always been candid in admitting that they did not have a high-level contact within the Red Brigades. After General Dozier's release, Mr. Perot's money was reconverted into dollars and returned to him. Because the lira had declined sharply in value in the interim, Perot absorbed a financial loss as a result of his patriotism.

The search for James Dozier involved a few spies, the Mafia, and the Bulgarian secret service.

Italy's answer to the CIA is the Servizio per le Informazioni e la Sicurezza Militare (the Intelligence and Military Security Service) (SISMI). When Dozier disappeared, a SISMI secret agent in New York City managed to track down a renegade Italian lawyer named Dominico Lombino who had been hiding in the United States. A patriotic mafioso, Lombino agreed to return to Italy and help. When Italian intelligence attempted to get him out of the United States on a forged passport, however, he was spotted and nearly arrested by alert Immigration and Naturalization Service (INS) agents; an embarrassed CIA had to intervene to keep the mess out of the papers.

Once back in Italy, Lombino led the SISMI agents to an imprisoned Mafia drug dealer named Restelli. The crime lord had no idea where Dozier was being held, but he offered to find the missing general with his own men if the government would turn him loose. Deciding that life was complicated enough without bringing the Mafia into the case, the Italian police declined.

The most bizarre subplot in the Dozier affair, however, was the role played by Bulgarian intelligence.

During Mario Moretti's tenure as their leader, the Red Brigades maintained contacts with dissident anti-Arafat elements within the PLO. The load of heavy weapons brought back to Italy in 1979 by Moretti was one obvious fruit of this relationship. When Moretti went to prison, however, the connection was broken.

In 1981, the Executive Committee decided to try to reestablish contacts with the Palestinians and began looking for an intermediary. Loris Scricciolo, a loyal irregular with the Rome column, proposed that they work through his cousin, Luigi Scricciolo, whom he correctly believed to be an agent of Bulgarian intelligence; surely the Bulgarians could locate the dissidents within the PLO.

Luigi Scricciolo and his wife, Paola Elena, had both been recruited years before by Bulgarian intelligence and were being "run" by Colonel Ivan Tomov Dontchev, third secretary at the

Bulgarian embassy in Rome. Briefed by Paola Scricciolo and apparently fascinated by the prospect of interrogating a senior American military man, Colonel Dontchev sent back a message to the Red Brigades, offering money and guns in exchange for full participation in the kidnapping, including access to the prisoner.

Savasta opposed the Bulgarian connection on ideological grounds, not wishing to have the purity of the revolution contaminated by Stalinist Bulgarians, but the Esecutivo authorized Luigi Novelli to hold an exploratory meeting with Dontchev. With Luigi and Paola Elena Scricciolo acting as intermediaries, an appointment was made for 2 January 1982 at a cinema in Rome.

Luigi Novelli sent one of his colleagues to the meeting, but the Bulgarian representative was apparently concerned about the possibility of surveillance and did not appear. Before another meeting could be arranged, Dozier was rescued. Subsequently identified by Savasta, Luigi and Paola Elena Scricciolo were arrested while Colonel Ivan Dontchev returned precipitously to Bulgaria.

With the Via Pindemonte blitz an internationally acclaimed success, the Italian state moved quickly to mount a trial in Verona's Palazzo della Ragione. Within the courtroom, two steel cages were constructed. The first was for the two defiant prisoners, Cesare Di Lenardo and Alberta Biliato, the woman who had escorted the kidnap convoy to Padua. The second was for Savasta, Emilia Libera, and the others who had decided to take advantage of Italian legislation offering reduced sentences for repentance.

It was not a complicated trial. Savasta and the other *pentiti* ("repentant ones") pleaded guilty and Cesare Di Lenardo and Alberta Biliato refused to recognize the authority of the court and did not participate in their own defense. As a defiant Alberta Biliato told the panel of three judges, "In ten or fifteen years, we will see who has won and who has lost. The Red Brigades are still strong!"

After the Dozier trial and the subsequent appeals trial in December 1982 were both concluded, timely repentance was seen to have its advantages. For the crime of kidnapping General Dozier, Savasta received a nine-year term of imprisonment while Emilia Libera and Giovanni Ciucci were sentenced to seven years apiece (although they later received longer sentences for other crimes). The physician's daughter, Emanuela Frascella, was given four and a half years, and Ruggiero Volinia received a suspended sentence.

Cesare Di Lenardo was given twenty-six years in prison, close to the legal maximum under Italian law; Alberta Biliato was treated to an exemplary seventeen and a half years.

For Emilia Libera and Antonio Savasta, the end of the Dozier trial meant the beginning of a lengthy series of courtroom appearances in various parts of Italy, first as defendants in trials for their own previous crimes and later as prosecution witnesses in the trials of their former colleagues. This was painful for them, and their erstwhile allies shouted horrific abuse whenever they appeared in a courtroom. Maria Laura Braghetti, the *vivandiere* for the Moro kidnapping, murmured, "Bastard, you sold everybody but your mother!" to Savasta during one trial, and another former associate yelled, "We will feed your bodies to the pigs!" One serious attempt was made to kill Savasta; police arrested a group of young *brigatisti* preparing to shoot an antitank weapon at an armored car carrying him to a court appearance.

Thanks to his cooperation with the authorities, the studious Giovanni Ciucci was released from prison after a few years to find that his already fragile marriage had not survived the trauma of his arrest and conviction. Under the Italian government's Witness Protection Program, he lives on parole somewhere in central Italy.

Emanuela Frascella was also released after several years in prison but found that the experience had actually helped to solidify her family. Having forged a new relationship with a pair of warmly supportive parents, she is now living abroad and studying medicine.

Ruggiero Volinia was released almost immediately into the Witness Protection Program. Now married to the former Elisabetta (or Lisa) Arcangeli, he is the father of two children and lives with his family somewhere in northern Italy.

Senior Red Brigades personalities such as Barbara Balzarani, Marcello Capuano, Francesco Lo Bianco, Mario Moretti, Luigi Novelli, Giovanni Senzani, and Pietro Vanzi are all still serving long sentences, although suggestions have been made that an amnesty should be declared for all fully or even partially "repentant" *brigatisti*.

Of the other Red Brigades activists who participated in the Winter of Fire campaign, Massimiliano Corsi and Stefano Petrella are still in prison. Under interrogation by the police, Ennio Di Rocca revealed information leading to the arrest of Professor Giovanni Senzani. In July 1982, persons loyal to Senzani murdered Di Rocca in prison as a reprisal.

Despite Commissioner Genova's encouragement, Fulvia Miglietta never did inform on her former colleagues; becoming intensely religious, Fulvia eventually concluded that her life sentence was appropriate reward/punishment for her crimes.

Emilia Libera was incarcerated at the Paliano maximum-security prison in Frosinone (between Rome and Naples). Through arrangements made with the University of Rome, she resumed her university studies. In spring 1987, Libera informed Antonio Savasta that she regarded their engagement as terminated. At Christmas of that same year, she was given a brief "vacation" from Paliano to permit her to marry a fellow prisoner, Signore Sergio Calore. Libera has now been released and needs only a few more years of study to complete her doctorate in medicine.

Antonio Savasta is still at Paliano, where he was interviewed exhaustively for this book. Savasta is still charismatic and in good physical health. Several years of enforced healthy living and regular sessions in the gymnasium have filled out his once-slender frame. "Prison is like a refrigerator," he once said. "You should come out the same age you go in."

Savasta remains deeply interested in politics, but he no longer sees a role for himself in any ideological movement; in fact, he has been preparing for his own future by studying computer programming and plans to enter this field when he is released from prison.

His eventual release is now essentially a political decision for the Italian government. He could go free relatively soon or spend several more years in prison, depending on the political climate. Whenever the remaining fragments of the Red Brigades commit another crime, public opinion becomes more strongly opposed to clemency for repentant terrorists.

The only member of the Red Brigades in this story who has never been captured is the tall, olive-skinned Swiss-Italian beauty Giovanna Esposito, who served as the clandestine "housekeeper" for the Red Brigades Executive Committee. Minutes before Commissioner Genova launched his raid on the Via Verga in Milan, Giovanna followed Barbara Balzarani and Francesco Lo Bianco out the back window of her apartment and vanished.

If Savasta knows where she is or how she managed to escape, he has decided not to say.

A WHO'S WHO OF THE DOZIER KIDNAPPING

I. The Red Brigade Executive Committee: At the time of the Dozier abduction and the Winter of Fire campaign, the Executive Committee (or Esecutivo) consisted of the following four senior officials of the Brigate rosse.

BALZARANI, BARBARA, or "SARA" (chief of the Milan column): thirty-two years old in 1981 and the former companion of Mario Moretti, Balzarani had been one of the top leaders in the Red Brigades since the early 1970s.

LO BIANCO, FRANCESCO, or "GIUSEPPE" (chief of the Genoa column): thirty-one years of age in 1981 and a former steelworker from Calabria, Lo Bianco was fighting a desperate defensive action against the State Police in the port city of Genoa.

NOVELLI, LUIGI, or "ROMOLO" (chief of the Rome column): twenty-eight in 1981, Novelli was a quiet, cautious, experienced guerrilla leader, a longtime friend of Antonio Savasta.

SAVASTA, ANTONIO, or "EMILIO": born 1955, Red Brigades "irregular" with the Rome column 1975–78; "regular" with the Rome column 1978–80; Red Brigades "ambassador" to Sardinia 1979–80; chief, Veneto column 1980–82; member, Executive Committee of the Red Brigades, 1980–82.

II. Savasta's "Dozier" Team: The following people constituted the group assembled by Savasta to carry out the actual abduction of General Dozier.

BILIATO, ALBERTA, or "ANNA": born 1946, Red Brigades "irregular" with Veneto column, 1978–82.

231

CAPUANO, MARCELLO, or "ROLANDO" or "ALVARO": Red Brigades "regular" with the Rome column 1977–82.

CIUCCI, GIOVANNI, or "GIORGIO": born 1949, leader of Red Brigade cadre in Tuscany 1977–82; served as guard with the Via Pindemonte group; nicknamed "the soldier" by General Dozier.

DI LENARDO, CESARE, or "FABRIZIO": born 1960, Red Brigades "regular" with the Veneto column 1979–82; member of the Via Pindemonte group; nicknamed "the big guy" by General Dozier because of his height.

FRASCELLA, EMANUELA, or "DANIELA": born 1960, Red Brigades "irregular" with the Veneto column 1979–82; "housekeeper" for the Via Pindemonte group.

LIBERA, EMILIA, or "NADIA" or "MARTINA": born 1956, nicknamed "Milli," Red Brigades "irregular" with the Rome column 1976–78; "regular" with the Rome column 1978–81; "regular" with the Veneto column 1981–82.

VANZI, PIETRO, or "DANIELE": Red Brigades "irregular" with the Rome column 1976–78; "regular" with the Rome column 1978–84.

VOLINIA, RUGGIERO, or "FEDERICO": born 1957; a Red Brigades "irregular" with the Veneto column 1979–82; driver for the Dozier operation.

III. The Outer Circle: These *brigatisti* participated in other aspects of the Winter of Fire campaign.

ALIMONTI, GIOVANNI: Red Brigades "irregular" with the Rome column 1977–82; employed as a telephone operator at the switchboard of the Italian Parliament; alleged to have participated in the attack on Nicola Simone in 1982.

ARCANGELI, ALESSANDRO: born 1955; Red Brigades "irregular" with the Veneto column 1976–82 (Elisabetta's older brother).

ARCANGELI, ELISABETTA: born 1958; Red Brigades "irregular" with the Veneto column 1976–82; nicknamed "Lisa."

CORSI, MASSIMILIANO: Red Brigades "irregular" with the Rome

column; participated in the attack on Commissioner Nicola Simone in January 1982.

DI ROCCA, ENNIO: Red Brigades "irregular" with Rome column 1978–82; participated in attempted kidnapping of Cesare Romiti. Murdered in prison in 1982 for collaboration with the police.

ESPOSITO, GIOVANNA: born 1956; Swiss-born Italian from Ticino Canton; Red Brigades "irregular" with the Milan column 1980–82. "Housekeeper" for the Milan Executive Committee headquarters.

GALATI, MICHELE: Red Brigades "regular" member of Verona column 1976–80; chief of Veneto column 1978–80.

GALATI, PAOLO: born 1960; never formally a member of Red Brigades but performed courier services for his older brother, Michele.

LANZA, ARMANDO: Red Brigades "irregular" with the Veneto column 1979–82. Verona "housekeeper" for the Veneto column.

MIGLIETTA, FULVIA, or "NORA": Red Brigades "regular" 1971–81 with Genoa column.

MORETTI, MARIO: Red Brigades "regular" 1971–81; member of Red Brigades Executive Committee until his arrest in 1981.

PETRELLA, MARINA: Red Brigades "regular" with the Rome column 1977–82. Wife of Luigi Novelli.

PETRELLA, STEFANO: Red Brigades "regular" with the Rome column 1977–82; brother of Marina Petrella and brother-in-law of Luigi Novelli.

SCRICCIOLO, LORIS: Red Brigades "irregular" with the Rome column 1977–82.

SCRICCIOLO, LUIGI: chief of the foreign affairs office of the Italian Union of Laborers, later accused of being an agent of the Bulgarian intelligence services and collaborator with the Red Brigades.

SCRICCIOLO, PAOLA ELENA: co-worker and wife of Luigi Scricciolo.

SENZANI, GIOVANNI: probably in contact with senior Red Brigades leadership from the early 1970s as an "irregular" but not formally a "regular" member until 1980; arrested in 1982.

ZANCA, ROBERTO: born 1955; Red Brigades "irregular" with the Veneto column 1981–82; nurse and emergency medical attendant for the Dozier operation.

IV. The Italian Governmental Establishment: Italy is a multiparty parliamentary republic with a ceremonial president and an executive prime minister who reports to an elected bicameral parliament. The following Italian officials figured in the Dozier abduction.

DALLA CHIESA, CARLO ALBERTO: born 1920; first became famous during World War II as a commander of Italian partisans fighting against Mussolini's fascist forces; major general and vice-commandant of the Carabinieri in 1981–82 and leader of the Carabiniere antiterrorist effort; later murdered by the Mafia in Palermo on 3 September 1982.

GENOVA, SALVATORE: born 1948; nicknamed "Rino"; commissioner of the Italian State Police from 1977; deputy of the Italian Parliament 1983–87; State Police Organized Crime Bureau 1987– . Some confusion was created by the fact that Salvatore Genova's last name is identical to the Italian spelling of the city of "Genova," where Commissioner Genova has spent much of his career. In fact, both the Red Brigades and some members of the American intelligence community were mistakenly convinced that *Genova* was actually a cover name. In this book, we have skirted the problem by referring to the city of Genova by its Anglo-Saxon name, Genoa.

PERTINI, ALESSANDRO: president of the Italian Republic 1978–85.

SIMONE, NICOLA: commissioner of the Italian State Police, serving in the Rome DIGOS office in 1981–82.

SPADOLINI, GIOVANNI: prime minister of Italy from June 1981 to November 1982.

V. The American Establishment

DOZIER, JAMES LEE: born 1931; brigadier general (later major general), U.S. Army; deputy chief of staff for logistics and administration, Allied Land Forces Southern Europe, NATO, 1980–82.

DOZIER, JUDITH STIMPSON: General Dozier's wife.

KOCH, NOEL: deputy assistant secretary of defense for International Security Affairs (ISA) 1981–82.

MCFADDEN, GEORGE L.: major general, U.S. Army; commanding officer of the Southern European Task Force (SETAF) in Vicenza.

NORTH, OLIVER: major and later lieutenant colonel, U.S. Marine Corps; staff officer, National Security Council, the White House.

PEROT, H. ROSS: president, Control Data Corporation, 1981–82, and member, U.S. Intelligence Advisory Board.

RABB, MAXWELL: ambassador of the United States to the republic of Italy 1981–89.

REED, WILLIAM: lieutenant colonel, U.S. Army, 1981–82; commanding officer, Detachment E, Sixty-sixth Intelligence Group, Vicenza, Italy, and highest-ranking U.S. intelligence officer in northern Italy.

SOURCES AND
ACKNOWLEDGMENTS

The following books proved useful in researching the Dozier story:

BOCCA, GIORGIO. *Noi terroristi—12 anni di lotta armata ricostruiti e discussi con i protagonisti.* Milan: Garzanti, 1985.

DRAKE, RICHARD. *The Revolutionary Mystique and Terrorism in Contemporary Italy.* Bloomington and Indianapolis: Indiana University Press, 1989.

FENZI, ENRICO. *Armi e bagagli: un diario dalle Brigate rosse.* Genoa: Costa e Nolan, 1987.

FRANCESCHINI, ALBERTO. *Mara, Renato e io.* Milan: Mondadori, 1988.

GALLENI, MAURO, ed. *Rapporto sul terrorismo.* Milan: Rizzoli, 1981.

GALLI, GIORGIO. *Storia del partito armato 1968–1982.* Milan: Rizzoli, 1986.

GENOVA, SALVATORE. *Missione antiterrorismo.* Milan: Sugarco, 1985.

HERMAN, EDWARD, and BRODHEAD, FRANK. *The Rise and Fall of the Bulgarian Connection.* New York: Sheridan Square, 1986.

MORAN, SUE ELLEN, ed. *Court Depositions of Three Red Brigadists: A Rand Note.* Santa Monica, Calif.: Rand, 1986.

VALIANI, LEO. *I governi Spadolini e la lotta al terrorismo.* Rome: Edizioni della Voce, 1983.

A number of periodical sources were also important. For data on the unfolding of the Dozier case, we reviewed American newspapers such as *The New York Times* as well as the Italian dailies, *Il Corriere della sera* and *L'Arena* (Verona). Italy's two weekly

237

newsmagazines, *Panorama* and *L'Espresso,* were extremely useful. In the Verona Penal Chancellery, we reviewed the transcripts
of the various trials that followed the Dozier kidnapping.

Many of the interviews for this book were conducted with the
understanding that our gratitude would be discreet; a whispered
thanks, therefore, to those serving members of the American and
Italian intelligence, diplomatic, and law-enforcement commu-
nities who shared their experiences with us.

With the usual proviso that none of our informants is responsible for errors of fact or interpretation in this book, we should
like to acknowledge the generous help provided by the following
people:

> Dr. Nicola Amato, Italian Ministry of the Interior
> Mr. Edward Becker, National Security Archive
> Major General Carlo Casarico, Carabiniere National Police,
> retired
> Mr. Myron Creel, Horry County Police, South Carolina
> Attorney Maurizio Dipietropaolo
> Captain Cheryl Dozier, U.S. Air Force
> Major General James Lee Dozier, U.S. Army, retired
> Mrs. Judy Stimpson Dozier
> Mr. Scott Dozier
> Mr. Lawrence Eagleburger, deputy secretary of state
> Cavaliere John Favre, SETAF
> Dr. and Mrs. Marco Frascella
> Lieutenant Colonel Mario Gargiulo, U.S. Army
> Commissioner Salvatore Genova, Italian State Police
> Ambassador H. Allen Holmes, U.S. Department of State
> Mr. Noel Koch, former deputy under secretary of defense
> Dr. Michael Ledeen, former consultant, National Security
> Council
> Franca and Aldo Marulli
> Major General George McFadden, U.S. Army, retired
> Mr. H. Ross Perot
> The Honorable Maxwell Rabb, former American ambassador
> to Italy
> Colonel William A. Reed, Jr., U.S. Army, retired
> Signor Antonio Savasta
> Ambassador Robert Sayre, U.S. Department of State

Signor Pio Scudellari
Signor Antonio Siciliano, Cancelleria Penale, Verona
The Honorable Massimo Teodori, Italian Chamber of
   Deputies

An additional thanks to General Dozier and his family for
their help and encouragement throughout this long project.
The University of South Carolina Venture Fund helped pay
for a research trip to Italy during the writing of this book. Our
debt is also great to the librarians of USC—Coastal Carolina
College's Kimbel Library, especially Mary Bull, Sallie Clarkson,
Margaret Fain, and David Wilkie, who helped us find the complicated odds and ends we were looking for.

RICHARD OLIVER COLLIN
GORDON L. FREEDMAN